EVER
The Boston Celtics
GREEN

EVER
The Boston Celtics
GREEN

A History in the Words of Their
Players, Coaches, Fans, and Foes, from
1946 to the Present

Dan Shaughnessy

ST. MARTIN'S PRESS   NEW YORK

Design by Glen M. Edelstein

Library of Congress Cataloging-in-Publication Data

Shaughnessy, Dan.
    Ever green : the Boston Celtics / Dan Shaughnessy.
       p.   cm.
    ISBN 0-312-05083-6
    1. Boston Celtics (Basketball team)—History.   I. title.
GV885.52.B67S53   1990
796.323'64'0974461—dc20   90-37115
                                                                  CIP

First Edition: November 1990
10 9 8 7 6 5 4 3 2 1

To my brother, Bill, who taught me to love basketball, and to my mother, who gave us the strength to endure and the confidence to succeed.

Contents

Acknowledgments

I was born in Massachusetts in 1953 and was a worldly eighth-grader before I learned that the Celtics don't win the NBA championship every spring. "Great" is a word that is overused in our time, but I was forever spoiled by those truly great Boston Celtics championship teams.

My older brother Bill Shaughnessy was the best 6–1 pivot-man I ever saw and he gave me a special understanding and appreciation of the game. While watching TV or reading a newspaper downstairs, my father put up with a lot of "thump, thumping" and falling plaster, as Bill taught me to dribble upstairs.

Groton High School's John Fahey knows the game as well as anyone I've met. He is a great teacher and a true role model.

Bill Tanton, Dave Smith, Vince Doria, and Don Skwar had the confidence to hire me in Baltimore, Washington, and Boston; and Bob Ryan has been my basketball guru for almost twenty years. Thanks Bob, for your library, your knowledge, and your generosity. Thanks to everyone associated with the

Boston Neighborhood Basketball League. I cut my teeth writing about the city game. They are lessons well learned.

Peter May, Mike Fine, and Jackie MacMullan rank with the best basketball-beat writers and are good traveling companions. *Globe* systems whizzes Charlie Liftman and Sean Mullin made the technology less intimidating. My best friends, Kevin Dupont and Lesley Visser, are ever encouraging, and league publicists Brian McIntyre and Cheri White are the best at what they do. Thanks to Red Auerbach, Jan Volk, Todd Rosensweig, Jeff Twiss, and David Zaccaro in the Celtics front office. Thanks to proofreader Mary Kate Lane.

When you spend your professional life writing about sports, you learn that basketball people are among the most candid and cooperative. The Celtic family made this project enjoyable and relatively easy. True to his reputation, Bill Russell would not be interviewed, nor would he answer phone calls or letters. But he gave us his game, and that is more than enough.

There would be no book without the ideas and inspiration of Mark Levine. George Witte carried the ball when Mark left St. Martin's.

Thanks to my mother, Eileen Shaughnessy. She never minded driving us to all the games in the Wachusett League. Thanks to all the Shaughnessys and Wits in New Hampshire, Arizona, Colorado, Massachusetts, Michigan, Illinois, and Kentucky.

Thanks to Sarah, Kate, and Sam, who understood when Dad hibernated in his home office. Marilou gave me the love and encouragement I needed to keep the project going. She married me, and that's proof of the luck of the Irish.

Dan Shaughnessy
March 1990
Newton, Massachusetts

EVER
The Boston Celtics
GREEN

1

The Green Godfather

HISTORIC Boston. Stroll down the steps from City Hall Plaza, cross Congress Street, and there's Samuel Adams, standing in front of Faneuil Hall. Adams died in 1803 and in 1880 this statue was dedicated to the man who organized the American Revolution and signed the Declaration of Independence. Words carved in stone tell us that he was "a patriot . . . incorruptible and fearless." Today, there is even a local beer named after him.

Turn left, cross North Street, and there in Adams's shadow is a two-statue monument to James Michael Curley. A four-time congressman and four-term mayor of Boston, Curley, like Adams, was temperamental and successful. He was the consummate Boston-Irish pol, a man with great wit and wisdom who knew how to get things done. The plaque commemorating Curley does not reveal that while in office he served five months at a federal prison in Danbury, Connecticut. He forever will be known as the only Boston mayor to serve two terms simultaneously.

Walk through Faneuil Hall, where the fires of freedom were lit and where Boston was organized as a city in 1822, then wander down the arcade between the Quincy Market Building and the South Market and you come across yet another statue. This monument depicts a bald man sitting on a bench, holding a rolled-up program in his left hand and a cigar in his right. A tray is underneath the bench, and there's one basketball on the rack. The bench sits in front of a shoe boutique and an art gallery. The man is facing north—the direction of the Boston Garden. Well-dressed young men on their way to work walk by and, without breaking stride, rub his head for good luck. Young girls wearing high school varsity jackets drape their arms around him and pose for one another's photographs. Early in the morning, when the market is silent and still, pigeons walk on his feet and perch on his bald pate.

Centuries from now, when people explore this fabled place, they will perhaps wonder about the accomplishments of this odd figure. What prompted the city fathers to erect a statue in his honor? They probably won't know that this man was never a resident of Boston; never paid city property taxes; never claimed to be a patriot or incorruptible; and never held public office or even voted in a Massachusetts election. He organized no civic occasions, never played a minute for a Boston sports team, and received his mail in Washington, D.C., the entire time he worked in Boston.

The monument plaque reads, "Arnold 'Red' Auerbach. Inspirational leader of the Boston Celtics as an outstanding coach and general manager. He helped bring 15 World Championships to Boston. A member of the Hall of Fame, he has exceeded every record for consistent sports achievement. When measured against all standards of success, Red Auerbach stands alone for directing the Boston Celtics to more championships than any other team in sports. He has made the name of Boston synonymous with winning."

How will we explain Red Auerbach to future generations of Bostonians? It will not be sufficient to say that he was the godfather of Celtic Green, guardian of a fabled franchise. There is so much more.

Auerbach endures as the most revered, nonplaying sports figure in Hub history. In terms of longevity and success, there is no close runner-up.

Auerbach was lucky *and* good. He met presidents and kings. He took the message of the Boston Celtics around the world. He walked across the Boston Garden's parquet floorboards and challenged six-foot-eleven-inch, 250-pound Moses Malone to a fight. He pulled off more good trades than any person in the history of American sports. He broke color lines yet was accused of painting his team a whiter shade of pale. He has probably eaten more Chinese food and watched more "Hawaii Five-O" reruns than anyone in the Western World. He coached a professional sports team to eight consecutive world championships, something that is likely never to be duplicated. He has emptied several rooms with his cigar smoke and offended some people with his locker-room language and crusty manners. He baited officials and lodged protests after losing old-timers games. He dismissed reporters as nuisances and viewed all members of the fourth estate as either "for us or against us." There is no gray in Red.

Arnold Jacob Auerbach was born on September 20, 1917, son of Hyman and Marie Auerbach. His father left Minsk, Russia, when he was thirteen, settled in Brooklyn, and married Marie Thompson. Hyman and Marie lived in a third-floor apartment at 246 Lynch Street in the Williamsburg section of Brooklyn and had four children—three boys, then a girl. Arnold was the second born and the athletic member of the family. Hymie Auerbach ran a dry-cleaning and laundry establishment, and the kids helped round up the clothing from customers. The Auerbachs charged fifteen cents for pressing a suit. Red was good at it. This young man, who would later make a living by teaching the full-court press, got his start pressing pants for the upper-middle-class families of Brooklyn.

His brother Zang remembers that "Red was always a hustler. He always knew how to make money, and you always knew he was going to be successful. He had a way of making things work. When he was a little kid, we lived right up the street from a garage where taxicabs used to come to get gas. They would generally be waiting in a long line. Red would jump on the running board of a cab and start to wash the windows. He knew if he could get them clean before the cab pulled into the garage, the cabbie would probably give him a nickel. He knew how to make those nickels."

Years later, in a position to sign basketball players to multimillion-dollar pacts, agents would accuse Auerbach of throwing nickels around as if they were manhole covers. Indeed, Auerbach was much tighter with his owner's money than the owner. But he was always honest.

"In Brooklyn we had a club team composed of guys from different high schools," says Auerbach. "And there was no such thing as black, white, religion, anything. We had a Polish guy, a couple of Jewish guys, an Italian guy, and an Irish guy on our team. So there was none of this religious stuff. We had a team called the Pelicans, and we needed new uniforms, and it cost seventy-five dollars. This was 1934. How do you raise seventy-five dollars? So we ran three games and a dance. From Sunday noon to six o'clock we had the building to run three games and a dance for a quarter. We had a seven-piece band, and it was at the YMHA, and you got no seats, just a row of chairs around the court and the band up on the stage. We sell five hundred tickets. So we collect one hundred and twenty-five dollars. The building was twenty-five dollars. We got one hundred dollars left. The band was fourteen dollars. They got two dollars a man. They worked six hours for two dollars. So now, we got eleven left, plus the money for the uniforms. All of a sudden one guy says, 'Stiff the band.' I really wasn't brought up that way and I kind of didn't like it. I said, 'Come on, we got the goddamn money, pay 'em.' We had a vote and we lost the vote five–three. So we said to the band, 'You're lousy players, you're no damn good, so you don't get paid.'

The manager of the YMHA said if we didn't pay the band we couldn't come in anymore. We decided to pay the band, but a couple of the guys wanted to make them wait a couple of days. They finally paid the band. Do you know that the leader of the band was Alan King? He still remembers."

In the teeth of the Depression, Red (his hair really *was* red at this time) went to Eastern District High School and starred on the basketball court. He made All-Brooklyn, second team, when he was a senior, graduated in 1935, and enrolled at Seth Low Junior College. A five-foot-nine-inch guard, Auerbach played one season at Seth Low, but the school was shut down after his freshman year. He transferred to George Washington University, where he played under Bill Reinhart. This is where he learned the running game. An uncontested lay-up is the easiest two points in basketball, and the best way to create this situation is to beat the other team down the floor. Reinhart loved the fast break, and Auerbach was smart enough to see the advantage of the running game.

"Bill Reinhart was twenty-five years ahead of his time," says Auerbach. "Frank Keaney at Rhode Island got credit for the fast break, but he didn't know what he was doing to the extent that Bill Reinhart did. Bill Reinhart didn't have a helter-skelter rundown break. He had an organized break the way it's done today—outlet pass, go for the three-on-two, and so on."

Auerbach played three years at GW, captained the team in his senior season, and met Dorothy Lewis, who would be his lifelong bride. Auerbach was a junior and Dorothy a freshman when they met. Red got his bachelor's degree in physical education in 1940. With Reinhart's recommendation, Auerbach was able to land a position as basketball director at the prestigious St. Alban's Prep in Washington, D.C., in the fall of 1940. He was married in the spring of 1941, got his master's degree (he's since added six honorary degrees), and joined the faculty at Roosevelt High School, where he served as head basketball coach and gym teacher. At Roosevelt, he tried to recruit a muscular, six-foot-five-inch student who turned out to be too uncoordinated for the game. The student's name was Bowie Kuhn, and he went on to become commissioner of baseball. For spare change, Auerbach-the-teacher moonlighted as a part-time referee in D.C., an image that no doubt would bring smiles to the faces of zebras throughout the land. He enlisted in the navy in 1943, served at the Norfolk Naval Station, and was discharged in 1946. He saw a lot of basketball players during his years in the service, and he remembered all of their names.

While Auerbach was still in the service, Boston Bruins owner Walter Brown got other arena managers to start the Basketball Association of America, giving birth to both the Boston Celtics and, more important in Auerbach's case, the Washington Caps. Mike Uline owned Washington's Uline Arena and, therefore, owned the new Caps. Uline knew nothing about basketball, which would prove to be a common trait of many owners Auerbach later worked for. Uline wanted to hire Auerbach, but there was considerable risk involved in leaving Roosevelt for professional basketball. Red and Dorothy were starting a family, and he had security there. But he also had dreams and ambition. Auerbach decided the risk was worth taking. Due to his association with armed forces teams, Auerbach had a working file on where the prospective players were, and he sold himself to the owner by claiming that he could fill the roster with players from the service. Uline liked the idea, and Red Auerbach became a professional basketball coach. He was only twenty-nine, but he knew what he was doing. He spent five hundred dollars to get his team together, paid no one more than $8,500, stressed conditioning and defense, and went 49–11 in the 1946–47 season. He coached two more years in Washington before joining Tri-Cities for a year (Auerbach still has his Washington Caps jacket in his Celtics office). It was at Tri-Cities (Moline, Illinois; Rock Island, Illinois; and Davenport, Iowa) that Auerbach endured the only losing season of his career (28–29). He got into a dispute with club owner Ben Kerner and quit after Kerner made a trade against his wishes. (He would later get even with Kerner by trading two players to St. Louis for the rights to Bill Russell and by punching Kerner in the face during a play-off game.) Fortunately, Boston Celtics owner Walter Brown, swimming in a sea of debt, was looking for a head coach. Walter Brown was willing to give pro basketball one last shot in Boston. Brown's partner, Lou Pieri, wanted the young, fiesty, and successful Auerbach. Pieri was the money man in the organization, and Brown followed his wishes.

In 1950, Auerbach, at thirty-two, became the third coach in the history of the Boston Celtics, succeeding Honey Russell and Doggie Julian. The Redhead got off to a rocky start by insulting local college great Bob Cousy. Cousy was a ball-handling wizard, the magic man of Mount St. James, where he played for Holy Cross's 1947 NCAA champions, and led the Crusaders to two other tournament appearances. There was tremendous pressure to bring Cousy to Boston, but Auerbach didn't want the kid and said, "I'm not interested in drafting someone just because he happens to be a local yokel." Due to trades, folding of other teams, and names that were picked out of a hat, the Celtics wound up getting Cousy despite Auerbach's doubts. It would prove to be the first instance in which good fortune augmented Red's coaching skills.

The Celtics went from 22–46 to 39–30 in Auerbach's first year on the job. They made the play-offs that year and in each of the next five years of Auerbach's tenure, but the team gained the reputation as a bridesmaid. They were good, but they didn't have the big man to put them over the top.

The big man arrived in the autumn of 1956. It's possible that Boston sports historians would treat Auerbach no better than former Red Sox Manager Joe Cronin or former Patriots' coach Mike Holovak if not for the arrival of William Felton Russell. Knowing that the Rochester Royals planned to take guard Sihugo Green with the number-one pick in the nation, Auerbach traded forwards Ed Macauley and Cliff Hagen to St.

Louis for the Hawks' number-two pick. Russell was Boston's pick.

Auerbach coached ten NBA seasons after the 1956 draft and won nine championships, including eight straight—another example of his good luck. Russell was highly touted, but *no one* could have predicted this kind of success. From 1956 to 1966 the Boston Celtics became the New York Yankees of basketball, and Auerbach was Jake Ruppert, Ed Barrow, Miller Huggins, Joe McCarthy, and Casey Stengel rolled into one. The Celtics revolutionized the pro running game. They spread the scoring around. They stayed in good shape and put forth the same effort every night. They ran the same seven plays over and over. They evolved into the best pressure team in the history of sports. They became synonymous with their sport. They went to the White House to meet President Kennedy. Then the Boston Celtics became global, like Mickey Mouse; they went to Yugoslavia, Rumania, United Arab Republic, Poland. "Celtic pride" and "Celtic mystique" were entered into the dictionary of sports. Hockey had the Montreal Canadiens and baseball had the New York Yankees, but Boston's pro basketball team was the ultimate sports institution. Capping each win, the man at the front end of the bench would unwrap a huge cigar and light it up. Name a better sports tradition than *that*.

Auerbach: "When I got out of college I smoked a pipe for a while, then I smoked a pipe and an occasional cigar, and then I went to predominantly cigars. I still own a lot of good pipes. When the game was decided, in my mind, a good coach starts to scheme for the next game. If we got a twenty-point lead with seven minutes to go, I didn't want to take a chance on an injury to a Russell or Cousy. So [I'd] put these other guys in, and to give 'em this confidence, I'd sit and relax. I used to get mad, and I still do, when I watch a college team leading 100–62 with eight minutes to go, and the coach is up there coaching. I say, sit down, enjoy it, and think about the next game. What can I try that can be applicable to my next game?

I wanted to show my players that this game, for all intents and purposes, is over. And everything we do now should help us in the next game. One time we were leading Philly by forty-five points in the third period. I took all the regulars out, and the subs went in, and I lit the cigar. And they were kind of fooling around, and we wind up winning by about fifteen. That's perfect for me. I went into that dressing room, and I laid them out. I said, 'People are paying their money to see you play basketball, and you were like nothing out there.' Why? I wanted them mad enough for the next game. . . . There was one time I nearly lost a game after lighting the cigar. [Tom] Heinsohn fouled a guy. We were three points ahead with about five seconds left, and instead of letting a guy go in and shoot, he fouled him and the guy made a three-point play and we had to win in overtime."

He has never smoked a cigarette. Not one. Auerbach retired from the bench in 1966, and the Boston Garden outlawed smoking a year later. Go figure.

The victory cigar bothered Cousy. "It made all of us uncomfortable," says the Cooz. "It was more offensive to us and everyone else on the road. When he did this, it got everyone's attention. And hell, we had enough hostility focused on us as it was. This was another trigger point. The fans were already pissed off because then it looked like they'd lose the game. And they did. This was an irritant. He sat benignly and comfortably on the bench, smoking away, with a guard behind him. Meanwhile, we were out on the floor taking all this abuse. The feeling among the players was, 'Why get their attention any more? Why piss 'em off?' The fans would get more belligerent and hostile toward us, and we had to bust our tails to keep the lead because once he went for the cigar, the other team's intensity went up one hundred percent. I hated that thing. Paul Seymour [Syracuse, 1949–60] told me that his ambition in life was not to win an NBA championship as much as it was to have Arnold light up prematurely, lose in a game they were involved in so he could go down and just stuff that cigar in his face. That's all [Seymour] wanted to do in sports. It created this kind of reaction from opponents. As players, who needs it?"

Dolph Schayes, an Auerbach foe for fifteen seasons, says, "To be truthful, in those days most of us would love to have shoved that cigar right down his throat. He was very arrogant. He took no quarter, gave none."

Auerbach inspired additional contempt from officials and rival teams. Just as he is the best-known nonplayer in NBA history, he is the most despised. The Celtics are famous for their smugness and institutional arrogance, and it starts at the top.

Ask Red if he believes he was hated, and he answers, "No. Really not. I think there were some that were jealous. I think there were some who were afraid. I don't think [longtime Laker coach] Freddy Schaus liked me, but at the same time, they had a retirement party for him a couple of months ago and I was invited to go, so there was no real animosity. It was just a frustration on his part because he never beat me."

Auerbach's detractors claimed that the Redhead was lucky, but Russell, a man not easily impressed, said, "Red Auerbach was the best coach in the history of professional sports."

Cousy says, "He was expedient. He wasted as little time and effort as was necessary to accomplish his goals. I think his strength was once the game began he dealt with adjustments that had to be made about as well as anyone that's coached. On a professional level, coaching has a more minimal impact than on a college level. I can see why Auerbach was so successful. He knew talent. He knew how to attract it. He got to where he was going in the most direct way. He let the talent do their thing—play an aggressive defense, try to keep the opponent from doing what he prefers to do, control the defensive board, and then run like hell. I think you have a tendency in basketball, more than the other sports, to over-coach. I think if the coach introduces his ego he's got problems. Strangely enough, Arnold was never a shrinking violet in terms of ego, and yet he was always smart enough to temper it and let the players do their thing without interfering. We had those seven damn plays, but we would feel we had had a successful offensive outing if we never had to call a play. His basic approach in training camp every year was just to get us in shape. We spent very little time with technicalities, half-court stuff. There was no individual instruction to speak of at all."

Tom Sanders says, "He changed the face of basketball because he was the first person to draft people who could play at the defensive end of the court."

Tom Heinsohn played nine years for Auerbach and later coached the Celtics for nine more years. Heinsohn says, "He put the style of play in, but Red's great ability was to get everybody's head involved and to use ideas that the players would come up with. In the last two minutes of a ball game, in the Celtics huddle—everybody thought Red was a tyrant—the first words out of his mouth would be 'Anybody got anything?' What that meant was that he trusted everybody that was playing for him to act like a coach and spot little things. We had five coaches on the floor. So you'd come in and say "I can do this or that," and he would listen to all that input and make a decision. And when you had stepped up and made a statement, that made it pride of authorship. You would try and make the goddamn thing work. He was great like that. He wasn't the dictator everybody thought he was. The style of play was up-tempo. Every year, as successful as we were, we'd start out with the basics of basketball—rebounding, dribbling, passing, running. And the practices were really the training camp. Many guys that came from other teams in the latter stages of their careers couldn't believe our training camp. Willie Naulls fainted the first time he practiced with us. Carl Braun said, 'You guys have been doing this? All the years I played with the Knicks, the first two weeks we spent getting acquainted. You guys are serious here.' "

K. C. Jones: "He treated each player differently. And you

can't treat everybody the same. The only person he didn't intimidate was Russell and maybe Cousy. Of course, you couldn't intimidate Heinie 'cause he was too busy shooting the ball and thinking 'my shot, my shot, my shot.' "

Auerbach's responsibilities grew with his fame. Walter Brown died in 1964, and by 1966 Auerbach was coach, general manager, and scouting director; he also handled TV and radio rights and the club's lease with the Boston Garden. With Brown gone, Auerbach controlled the purse strings. When Brown was alive, players always attempted to negotiate with him because he was considered a soft touch. When the owner died, everybody had to go through frugal Red. Auerbach was the original tightwad when it came to negotiating, and it took him a long time to get used to player agents. There was one plus—Auerbach never let statistics get in the way of negotiations. Your dollar worth was set when you answered the question "How much did you help us win?" Russell, Sanders, and Jones were not penalized simply because their contributions didn't show up in the scoring column.

Meanwhile, plenty of Red's own cash was going down the tubes. He continued to blister the officials, and his fine fees were higher than his state taxes.

"Red always wanted the edge," says Earl Strom, an NBA official who worked four decades before retiring in 1990. "For years he had that classic feud with Mendy Rudolph, but I think they really respected one another, deep down."

"The officials have a hard job, I know that," says Auerbach. "I just want consistency. It's the same now as it was then. You don't want guys to get intimidated by the fans or by the other coach. So you do things. I was always thinking about how I could get the next call. A good coach has to get the official's attention every now and then. If you don't do that, you're not doing your job."

While Red was coaching, Dorothy Auerbach was raising two young girls in Washington, D.C., and Red was living in a downtown Boston hotel, rushing home for an occasional day off. "I considered it a dual citizenship," he says. "One of my daughters had asthma, and she couldn't take this climate. That was one of the reasons why I didn't move. And after a while, you're there a certain number of years. . . . Also, there was another factor that might not make sense but I felt that since this situation existed I might as well make the most of it: A guy coaching on his own that didn't have to come back home at night in various moods could be better prepared for adversity. This way, when I would go home, I didn't have to make all these silly appearances. I could just say, 'I'm sorry, I'm going home.'

"The whole secret of coaching, in my opinion, was the ability to unwind and go to sleep, win or lose. I remember Cousy for years used to laugh at me because I didn't go out. I'd just get some Chinese food or a sandwich and go to my room, take a bath, and watch TV. When he was coaching, he found out he did the same thing."

Dave Cowens didn't play for Auerbach, but he saw the method at work and dealt with Red for more than a decade. "Red was a real player's coach," says Cowens. "He kept everything relatively simple, easy to comprehend. Everybody was aware of what they were supposed to be doing. When you have people working for you, if they know what they're supposed to be doing it makes it easier for 'em. Then it's just a matter of their desire and how far they want to take it themselves. Red, I think, always kept a pretty good handle on how to deal with people."

Auerbach: "You must have the ability to communicate. That is your key. It's not what you say, it's what did they absorb. I wouldn't do that much talking. We never even sat down for time-outs. We'd stand there and psych out the other team that we could run all day. . . . I'm proudest of the fact that the people I coached all turned out to be great people, reputable citizens and so on. I was able to maintain the dignity of the Celtics and live up to everything that Walter Brown stood for because I really liked the man."

Would the Red Way work in 1990? Maybe. He thinks he could deal with today's athlete, and Auerbach is far more flexible than most people think he is.

"In college, if you got caught smoking, you got thrown off the training table for a week," he says. "Coaches were very, very strict. I have a theory: I never put anything as etched in gold. I always keep a person guessing what I would do, and this is important. For example, if I say that if I catch a kid smoking he's thrown off the team, that's an awful, awful tough penalty. Even in those days. You got to have a little compassion. So I would tell 'em, 'Look, if you get caught smoking the penalty is going to be tremendous,' but they don't know what the penalty would be. See what I mean? You don't etch it in stone. You box yourself in. That's what a lot of colleges do. If a kid is late for practice, through no fault of his own—he might have overslept or whatever it is—but they got a rule. You don't come to practice, you miss the next game. And they're going to the fuckin' NCAAs and they've got to bench a kid like they did J. R. Reid last year or somebody like that. It's ridiculous. Don't box yourself in.

"I think it [his style] would work just as good today. No question in my mind whatsoever. People are people. I know the money is different, and you have agents to contend with. But the difference today with the ball players of a few years ago is that today there are more of them, but they're no better. Nobody's gonna tell me that Bill Russell and [Wilt] Chamberlain and [Bob] Pettit and [Elgin] Baylor and [Jerry] West and [Oscar] Robertson and [Bob] Cousy and [Bill] Sharman and all those guys would not be stars today. They'd all be in the two-million-dollar class. There are just more of 'em today. And they train earlier today because of the remuneration of a pro."

Auerbach announced he was retiring from the bench *before* the start of the 1965–66 season. He put the pressure on himself and dared the rest of the league to knock him off in his final season. "You've got one more shot at Auerbach," he announced. Nobody could do it. The Philadelphia 76ers won more regular-season games than the Celtics, but the Celtics won the play-offs. During the 1966 finals against the Los Angeles Lakers, Auerbach announced that Russell would take over as coach. The Celts won the next three games and took the series in seven, winning the finale, 95–93, at the Boston Garden. It was the Redhead's eighth straight title. His career-winning percentage was .662. He coached 938 wins and 479 losses and went 99–69 in the play-offs. His favorite expression was, "The Celtics aren't a team; they're a way of life."

At the War Memorial Auditorium, Boston mayor John Collins presented Auerbach with the Medal for Distinguished Achievement, "the most prestigious civic honor bestowed by the city," said Collins. Part of the citation read, "In the field of competitive sports he stands alone. In the major sport to which he has given most of his life he has made the name Boston synonymous with success."

It has been a quarter century since Auerbach left the bench, but he's remained a great presence on Causeway Street and across the nation. He made more good trades, blundered into several dubious draft picks, wrote books, did videos, and settled into his rightful place as the game's guru.

Auerbach was already established as a great judge of talent and shrewd dealer when he moved into the role of full-time general manager in 1967. In the 1950s he'd acquired Bill Sharman and Bob Brannum for the rights to Charlie Shea. He'd swung the trade to get the rights to Russell. He'd signed Willie Naulls, Larry Siegfried, and Don Nelson as free agents. One of his first deals after leaving the bench was to trade Mel Counts for a supposedly washed-up forward named Bailey Howell. When Cousy, in his forties, wanted to come out of retirement for a few games with the Royals (Cousy was coaching Cincinnati at the time), Auerbach demanded and got a player—Bill Dinwiddie. Red drafted Don Chaney, Jo Jo White, and Dave Cowens, setting the table for a pair of championships in the 1970s. He drafted Charlie Scott, who had already signed with the ABA, then later traded Scott's rights for Paul Silas.

There were some dark days in the late 1970s, and Auerbach was not involved in the 1979 trade that delivered Bob McAdoo from the Knicks for three first-round draft picks. Celtics owner John Y. Brown made the McAdoo deal, and almost drove Auerbach out of town. In the fifteen years after Walter Brown's death, the Celtics had eleven owners, but Walter Brown was the one who came closest to losing the franchise's top asset; Red had an offer to join the Knicks and came very close to leaving the Celtics. It would have been a bad time to leave. Auerbach had pulled one of his greatest moves, drafting junior eligible Larry Bird with the sixth pick of 1978. The Celtics had to sign Bird before the 1979 draft in order to bring him to Boston, and Auerbach was needed to talk the Hoosier hick into joining. Red was on a roll after that. He swapped McAdoo to Detroit for a pair of number-one picks in the 1980 draft (thank you, Dick Vitale) and used them to make a deal that effectively swapped Joe Barry Carroll in exchange for Robert Parish and Kevin McHale. He drafted Danny Ainge and got the kid to leave the Toronto Blue Jays. He traded Rick Robey for Dennis Johnson. He got Quinn Buckner for the rights to retiree-in-waiting Cowens. He got Scott Wedman for Darren Tillis. It seemed that he could always find the right player to suit his needs. He swapped Gerald Henderson for Seattle's 1986 first-round draft pick and wound up getting the number-two pick in the nation, Len Bias (this one had a tragic end when Bias died of cocaine intoxication).

With Red, loyalty was always as important as winning. If you were loyal to him, he was loyal to you. Cross him and you had an enemy for life. It certainly can't be an accident that more than thirty of Auerbach's former players became coaches. Russell was coach when the Celtics won championships in 1968 and 1969, and former Celtic Tom Heinsohn was coach when the Celts won in 1974 and 1976. K. C. Jones, another starter from the golden days, was head coach for the 1984 and 1986 flag-raisings. Of the 1963–64 starting five (Russell, Heinsohn,

K. C. Jones, Sam Jones, and Sanders), Sam Jones was the only member who did not eventually coach the team.

"Loyalty is something that's got to be both ways," Auerbach explains. "To expect loyalty, you've got to give it. That doesn't mean you can't trade a player or you can't let a player go. Loyalty simply means good chemistry, a camaraderie, and it means that a guy gives you everything he's got to the best of his ability. That's loyalty. And when he's through playing, *my* loyalty comes in. That's where I help out if I can. I don't have to tell you how many people I've helped in different things, but it's because I wanted to. It don't make any difference what it is. It doesn't have to do with basketball. I'm interested in what they are doing in life."

The only nonfamily member who brought a title to Boston was Bill Fitch, hired to start the Larry Bird era in 1979. Fitch was a devout basketball man, an indefatigable student and teacher of the game. Unlike the other Celtic coaches, the "family" guys, Fitch was never comfortable with Auerbach's huge shadow. Example: The Celtics were eating in a coffee shop on the road during one of Fitch's seasons in the early 1980s. Auerbach spotted muscular rookie Charles Bradley and gave the kid a couple of friendly tips in free-throw shooting. Fitch later confided to his general manager, "I wish you wouldn't do that." Auerbach steered clear after the incident and was not much of a presence at practices or on the road during the final years of Fitch's tenure. When Fitch resigned after the 1982–83 season, K. C. Jones was hired and Auerbach was back. Jones's philosophy was, "I have the finest research book in the world available to me. That's Red. He's an encyclopedia of basketball. I listen to him and take advantage of his knowledge. . . . He had more than seventy-five percent to do with this league surviving by what he did with the Celtics. The man has such knowledge and sense of this game, hey, why would I shut that out? You can have ego and be dumb or you can have ego and be smart."

Family member Jones was in charge. The planets were back in order. All was right with the Celtics universe.

Fitch should have talked to Heinsohn. Heinsohn coached the Celtics for nine years and won two championships, but he admitted, "If you're going to be coach of the Boston Celtics, the first thing you've got to realize is that it is Red Auerbach's team. He may not make you feel that way personally, but the press and the public do."

Paul Silas was a Celtic player on championship teams and later coached in the NBA. He admitted he was skeptical about the alleged Celtic mystique. Today he says, "I know now he started something that I don't think will ever exist again—a family type of atmosphere that you probably can't have now because of the economics of sports and so forth. He could afford to get players and keep them. He could mold players who came from the outside into that tradition. That's very tough to do. Only he could do it. The mystique lives on."

Auerbach can be a lovable teddy bear, and he can be gruff. The embraceable Red surfaced in 1982 when he drafted Indiana's Landon Turner in the tenth round. Turner, a star front-courtman for the Hoosiers, had been paralyzed in a car accident. He will never walk, but he can always say he was drafted by the Celtics. Stone Age Red surfaced in 1984 when he barred *Boston Globe* female reporter Lesley Visser from the Celtics locker room after a loss (ever competitive, he is always in a bad mood after losses) in Madison Square Garden. The incident took place just a year after Auerbach attended Visser's wedding at the Ritz in Boston. At the 1984 NBA meetings in Salt Lake City, a young Boston sportswriter brought his wife and their one-month-old baby daughter to the league gathering. During one of the hospitality events, the couple stood in a lobby, showing off their newborn child. Auerbach, father of two, was an interested onlooker. He greeted the writer with his usual suspicion, pinched the child's cheek, and told the wife, "Lady, you got a lot of balls bringing that baby out here. Yes sir, a lot of balls." Then he walked away, shaking his head, smoking his cigar, and chuckling to himself. The young woman did not know whether she'd been complimented or insulted.

Boston Mayor Ray Flynn has his own Red Auerbach story. Flynn was drafted by Syracuse in the fouth round in 1963, but he entered the service instead of the NBA. In the fall of 1964, the 76ers traded him to Boston for a second-round draft choice. He joined the Celtics during the preseason and competed with Larry Siegfried for the final roster spot. Ray Flynn ran up and down the court with Bill Russell, John Havlicek, Sam Jones, and Tom Heinsohn, but he wasn't quite good enough to make the cut. "Our last exhibition was against the St. Louis Hawks," remembers Flynn. "It was the night before the opening game. We were still one over on the roster. After the game, Red Auerbach called me into his room. We were staying at the Holiday Inn. He said, 'Ray, I've got something to tell you. Sit down. This is probably one of the hardest things I've ever done. I don't know anybody who's worked harder to make this team and to make professional basketball than you have. I remember seeing you in the Boston Garden as a kid when Joe Casey, the electrician, used to let you sneak in. Walter Brown used to chase you, and then he got sick of chasing you out of the place. I've seen you as a young kid. You deserve to make it, but my job is to put the best basketball players on the court, and there's nothing more that I'd like to do than see you out there and make the team. But I'd be going against what I personally believe in if I did that as a favor rather than as something that was deserved.'

"It's almost incomprehensible for me to explain that to people. It's almost like a made-up story. In all the years since, meeting presidents and world leaders, there's not a message that I have more respect for than that which Red Auerbach said to me that night. I went back to Southie to the corner. My friends wanted to console me, but I was okay. His message has never left me. I'm probably Red Auerbach's greatest admirer. I wasn't good enough. I didn't deserve to make the team, and that's good enough for me."

"The hardest thing is to let players go," says Auerbach. "No question about that. It's a hard thing. I hate to feel that I am an important cog in a person's life, and I hate to feel that I'm the one that would hinder it, and it's tough. There were some funny ones though. Jimmy Smith was a big guy with no neck, and somebody told him that if I called him over during practice it meant I was going to let him go. So one day in practice I said, 'Jimmy, I got to talk to you,' and he started running the other way, screaming, 'Not me, not me.' I also had one guy I had to let go, and the day before I let him go I saw a gun in his bag. I was shit-scared, believe me."

Only Auerbach's players and his friends knew what a bad driver he could be. Frank Ramsey remembers, "Walter Brown tried to sell basketball up there, and we would play fourteen straight days during exhibition season. We would get in cars and drive all the way up to Holton, Maine. We played in every little gym. Red would go on the Maine Turnpike. He'd hit Portland circle and start on the Maine Turnpike at night. He was in the fog and following the white lines, and he drove into a Howard Johnson's doing about eighty miles an hour. [Gene] Conley was sitting right next to him, and he swallowed his chewing tobacco."

Auerbach whizzed through the Howard Johnson's parking lot, then back onto the highway without slowing down for a second.

Cousy says, "He was cuckoo. I haven't ridden with him since 1951. That was my first year. The penalty for being a rookie was that you rode with Auerbach on exhibitions. We used to play nineteen games, and we drove all over New England. He's wrecked more cars than Evel Kneivel. I remember once a little town in Vermont. We were driving through it around eighty miles an hour, and the damn thing just exploded. We sort of guided it to the side. When the other guys came along, we picked up our stuff and left. For all I know, the damn thing is still there. We'd go to Bangor, and he'd literally start out two hours after us. Then, he'd boast about beating us there. We'd get to the hotel, and he'd be sitting there puffing on his cigar. More cars died under him. They would just expire. He was fearless and reckless. His driving was terrible. It's amazing that the man stayed alive this long."

"I get in very few accidents," says Auerbach, knocking on wood as he speaks. "But it was funny when Walter Brown got a call from the captain of the state police in Maine saying, 'If you don't tell that goddamn Auerbach to slow down, I'm going to lock his ass up.' "

It was in the summer of 1984 that Auerbach officially retired as general manager of the Celtics. He was committed to spending more time at his Washington condominium on Massachusetts Avenue and at the Woodmont Country Club in Rockville, Maryland. Vice President-legal counsel-contract specialist Jan Volk was promoted to general manager (akin to Dan Rather replacing Walter Cronkite), but Red always insisted, "I'll only be a phone call away." Typically, the Celtics won the NBA crown in 1984. The Green have always been generous with farewell gifts.

But he'll never say good-bye to the Celtics. Throughout the 1980s, he kept his huge corner office on the eighth floor of 150 Causeway Street and was as much a presence as ever. Platters of food would be delivered on game days, and guests would be entertained before games and at halftimes. During the games, Red would sit with the owners in his usual seat— midcourt, loge one, row seven, seat one. Easily spotted in one of his many plaid sportcoats, he could yell at the refs from the stands, without fear of adding to his NBA-record fine total.

Auerbach has presence even when not in the Boston Garden. It has nothing to do with his no. 2 hanging from the rafters (Walter Brown got no. 1). Four decades of winning creates an indelible image. Auerbach's image is one of a man who'll win at all costs. He is always looking for an edge and his rivals know this. He's been accused of using Gordon Liddy–dirty tricks, and there were probably times when he adjusted the temperature of his building to suit his team. Four decades later, NBA opponents are hopelessly spooked by the ghost of Red. If the visitor's tiny locker room at the Garden is too hot or too cold (it's never comfortable), it's assumed that Red did it. If the visiting team doesn't get its luggage at Logan Airport, Red gets the credit/blame. Food poisoning, traffic jams, power outages, fire alarms, groupies, reckless cabbies—rival coaches and general managers suspect that Red might be behind any and all of it. Like a pitcher accused of throwing spitters, Red doesn't have to do anything special anymore; half of the opponents are beaten before they step into the box. Red doesn't mind perpetuating the image. "I gave a speech the other day on how to gain the competitive edge," he told a crowd at a basketball dinner in 1989. "I told them, 'You're paying me for nothing. I can give the whole speech in one word. Cheat!' Then I said, 'Here's how you do it. In hockey, got a slow team? Have soft ice. In football, got a slow team? Let the grass grow. In baseball? Fool around with the height of the mound. In basketball? Loosen the rims. Hell, lower the rims if you have to.' "

"They think he does those things, and he's never done anything to change their opinion," says Heinsohn. "He loves that mystique. They could never figure Red out. He would antagonize the shit out of them. He had the cigar. He had a great team. They would try to denigrate him by saying anybody could win with that team. They'd never really give him his due. It was just that he let the guys play. They were always just trying to rationalize why they couldn't beat him."

Auerbach: "When we played here and it was one hundred degrees on the court, the half of the court we shot on was seventy degrees and theirs was one hundred. What the hell do they think we got any different? If we had anything any better, then I'd buy that. But people didn't know that in those days; I not only had no control in the Garden, I was relegated to practically humiliation by some of the people involved in the Garden. You know how much control I had? People would come to the box office and ask for Celtics tickets, and the guy behind the window would say, 'What the hell do you want to watch basketball for?' What really caused other teams to have a defeatist attitude in our building was the fact that we were good."

Auerbach left his cherished Garden loge seat during a game only once, and that was when Larry Bird got into a fight with Philadelphia hatchet man Marc Iavaroni. Bird and Iavaroni were both tossed out of the game. It's an old Auerbach trick—you're always willing to lose your goon if he can take their star with him. He could not stand to see one of his own stunts pulled in his own building. NBA officials were on strike, and scab refs were trying to keep order. Auerbach crossed the floor, got in Moses Malone's face, and challenged the behemoth to fight. No one takes over Auerbach's building when Red is sitting right there on his loge throne. Sixer coach Billy Cunningham came out of the melee with a torn sportcoat. Auerbach came out with his legend enhanced.

"That showed me he was a true Celtic," Bird said. "He makes sure everyone is treated fairly and brings out the best in everybody. He knows where his heart is, what he's made of. He'll be a part of the Celtics till he dies."

Rick Carlisle played three years with the Celts, all after Red "retired." Carlisle remembers, "Red was one of the nonvisual things that kind of surfaced. He was very discreet about what he did or when he talked to the team or to individual guys. He always did it in a constructive way, and you always felt he was on your side. If you were on that team, you knew that you had his okay at some point, and he wanted to make sure that you did your best. When you have a good game, he'll come in and just give you a nod or a gesture. That'll give you a great feeling. If you played a horseshit game he'll come in and dump ashes at your feet and keep walking."

The Celtics retired Auerbach's number on the first weekend in January 1985. Bill Russell came out of hiding and highlighted the festivities when he gave Auerbach a bear hug in the middle of the presentation. At that time a Red Auerbach foundation was established by Permanent Charities of Boston. The money is raised in Red's name and distributed to charities involved in youth development. His statue was dedicated on September 20, 1985. After retiring from the Celtics, Red taught a course in sports law for two years at Harvard. He remains very busy on the lecture circuit today. Corporations hire him to talk to their employees about motivation and success. He's in greater demand than Tip O'Neill and Gordon Liddy.

Red Auerbach loves *stuff*. All of his apartments and offices are shrines, featuring dizzying arrays of collectibles and memorabilia. Inventory in these places would take weeks. The Smithsonian should get a load of Red's attic. There seems to be at least one of everything. His old Washington Caps jacket hangs next to a photo of Red with John F. Kennedy. The wall is plastered with framed remembrances of Red with the rich and famous, Red with presidents, Red with his players, Red with his fans. Souvenir mugs from Miller Lite sit on shelves next to trophies and plaques. Laminated newspaper articles recount the glory days, and cartoons of Red portray a cigar-smoking hothead—always yelling at the refs. There are boxes of cigars and engraved cigarette lighters and plastic facsimilies of Red on Roundball. There's a giant cardboard cutout of Auerbach, larger than life, just like the man himself. He has souvenirs from around the world and photographs and scraps of championships past and present. He has bought artifacts on six continents ("Never made it to Antarctica"), haggling over every penny each time. Red is particularly proud of his collection of letter openers. "I have one of the largest collections of letter openers in the country," he says. "I'm a collector. I started collecting boxes, but they were too big. They took up too much room in my travel suitcase. I never liked to use fingers opening mail. The first letter opener I bought was in Turkey. It's legitimate ivory."

Red liked to give his draft picks little gifts—mugs, pictures, ashtrays with Celtic logos. As John Havlicek noted, "Draft choices walk out of Red's office with so much stuff it looks like they had a big day at the boardwalk somewhere."

Now in his seventies, after struggling to regain his good health for a few years, Auerbach still has a way of looking at the most complex situations and solving them simply. He plays raquetball and tennis regularly, beating younger legs with guts and guile. This is a man who wastes no motion. There is a reason for everything he does. He knows what he wants. He wants to win; he wins. He knows when others are letting him win, and he doesn't like it.

Auerbach never dabbled in hype and promotion. Today's NBA is a triumph of Madison Avenue marketing, and the Celtics are a vital part of the selling of the league, but Auerbach won't have any part of it. He believes people want good, winning basketball and will eventually buy the product if the product is good. He doesn't encourage mega-marketing and never cared much about public relations. If people in the media don't see things his way, they are know-nothings. Only his close friends are allowed to disagree with him.

Red says he doesn't spend much time looking at his statue: "I think I've been over there to see the statue maybe three or four times. People have sent me pictures that they take with the statue. But it kind of scares me. How many statues do you know of people who're still living?"

It's fun to make a trip to Auerbach's chambers on the afternoon of a Celtics play-off game in the Garden. Vice presidents of finance, marketing, communications, and sales scurry about. The ticket-sales director is knee-deep in memos, and a team of public-relations people photocopy notes, answer phones, and assemble media lists. General Manager Jan Volk takes calls from television executives, player agents, and reporters. Secretaries tackle the mail. The place is a beehive. And in the corner office at the end of the hall, the office that overlooks miles of snarled traffic on the Southeast Expressway, Red Auerbach sits, smokes cigars, and watches "The People's

Court." His longtime secretary, Mary Faherty, sees that he is not interrupted until Judge Wapner makes his ruling. In the old days, Auerbach did all the jobs now carried out by this fourteen-person (plus a raft of interns) front office. Today he can sit back, make a few organizational decisions (turkey or roast beef for tonight's party spread?), and enjoy the event. Ex-players start wandering in anytime after six o'clock. There's a bar and buffet in the boardroom adjoining Red's office. Bob Brannum, a husky forward who served as team enforcer in the early 1950s, still tells the story of how he instinctively tried to hide a drink from Auerbach during one of these parties. You never get old enough to swear in front of your mother, and you never get old enough to drink in front of your coach—especially if your coach was Red Auerbach.

Auerbach's wisdom is tapped when it's time to make a trade or dive into the draft pool, but Red is no longer involved in the day-to-day operation of the Boston Celtics. He remains a presence. When Auerbach officially "retired' in 1985, Cousy noted, "I think from time to time when everyone tries to think about what the Celtic mystique is, we should just point to Arnold [Cooz always calls Red by his real name]. He personifies what Celtic mystique means. When he steps down and ceases to play any part in the organization, I think the unit will be more susceptible to what happens to other teams. Arnold's presence has somewhat neutralized all that.

"He was there at the beginning, and he's still there sitting in his chair being adored. He's the glue that holds it all together, even though he's not there that much. I think when [he] is no longer there, there will be, in bad times, a deterioration. I think the thing could fall apart quicker. I think now the fact that players know that he's up there, that he's involved, creates some sort of attitude."

Auerbach is the lion in winter, sharp as ever, still Red after all these years.

2
The Green Garden

WATCHING the Celtics win championships at the Boston Garden is something America's sports fans have been doing since Milton Berle was the biggest star on television. In each of the last four decades, the Celtics have won no less than two World Championships. From 1957 to 1969, they won the NBA crown eleven times in thirteen years, establishing themselves as the greatest dynasty in the history of professional sports. A Celtic appearance in the play-offs is a seasonal Boston event, no less than the L Street Brownies swimming in Dorchester Bay on January 1, marathoners gathering in Hopkinton on Patriots' Day, and the Pops playing the Esplanade for the Fourth of July.

Each April, May, and sometimes June, America tunes in to the NBA and sees the Boston Garden's beautiful, gleaming parquet floor. This is tradition. The Celtics wear black, high-top sneakers, and always there's a round man with a rolled-up program yelling at the refs. Banners flutter from the hardwood heavens above. Lucky Celtics ticket holders appear to be hanging over the perimeter of the court, and the sights and sounds are crisp, colorful, and comfortable. Sitting in your living room in Dubuque, Iowa, you'd figure the Boston Garden is the most splendid sports palace in the land.

That's the image. But this is about the *real* Boston Garden experience. This is what it is like to watch the Boston Celtics in person from the second floor of North Station:

Getting there is not fun. Your best bet is the Massachusetts Bay Transit Authority's Green Line with trolley cars originating at Boston College, Cleveland Circle, and Riverside in Newton. The final stop is North Station. Hop off the train, push through the one-way metal turnstile door, and gaze out at Causeway Street—an arcade of awakening desires. Fast-food joints line the south side of the street, and outdoor vendors offer chicken teriyaki, hot pretzels, and grilled sausages. The horizon is sheer grime; rusty cars adorned with fluorescent-orange parking tickets, vacant stores with plywood-boarded windows, souvenir shops with faded posters of Dave Cowens, and kids hanging around selling tickets—or just hanging around. Nobody pays attention to the WALK and DON'T WALK signs at the corners on Causeway. If there are no cars, or if you can intimidate a car to stop, you dart into the street; if a crazed cabbie is blowing his horn and ripping out his rearview mirror, you don't walk.

There are other rail routes to the North Station. You can ride the train in from Ipswich or Lincoln, points north and west. When you get off the train, you don't have to cross Causeway Street. You are there. You can tell by the giant billboard of Larry Bird smiling at a candy bar. The waiting area stinks of urine, and in the hallway there's usually a line of pinball wizards and video magicians who feed a steady stream of quarters into electronic babysitters. Half the people seem to be just hanging out, while the other half are coming and going—using the train station for what it was designed for. The trains don't run to Montreal and Portland anymore;

you can only get to the suburbs. Just look for the giant letters—RAILROAD TICKETS—over the ticket windows. There are plenty of pay phones, a bank machine, flower shop, fruit stand, and yuppie chow from Au Bon Pain. New York newspapers can be purchased a few feet from the ticket windows, and the Bruins Pro Sport Shop reminds you who really owns the Boston Garden. The Sports Café rests between the ground-level entrances, and this is where some gather to toast the Celtics before, during, and after games. It used to be called "The Horse." It has never been as popular as it should be. On those rare nights when you have to wait for a table, you can look at a lot of old pictures and stand on a piece of the original Garden floor. Norm and Cliff of "Cheers" would like this place.

Getting to the Garden via automobile is painful and slow. Storrow Drive jams just after the big curve near the Massachusetts Eye and Ear Infirmary. From Medford and Everett you can try the McGrath & O'Brien Highway and get bottlenecked after you pass the Museum of Science. Riding the Expressway north is hopeless, even after the Callahan Tunnel cutoff. It's frustrating because as you creep closer, you can see the simple blue and yellow letters atop the giant, windowless yellow-brick facade; you can see NORTH STATION BOSTON GARDEN, but you can't seem to get there. It's best just to tune in Boston sports radio talk-show host Eddie Andelman and enjoy the gridlock. Does it make you feel any better to know that Red Auerbach can watch you stalled in traffic from his fifth-floor corner office on 151 Merrimack Street?

Folks in the financial district can walk to the game—through Quincy Market or Government Center, down Canal Street or Merrimack Street, under the El tracks, and into the steamy train station. It's easy to picture the old days here—men in big hats, women in sensible shoes, kids selling newspapers. Leigh Montville in *Sports Illustrated* said this was a neighborhood where "Jimmy Cagney very easily could have tipped his hat to George Raft." Cigar smoke, past, present, and future, makes the air eternally stale and gray. You want to send your clothes to the cleaners if you spend more than twenty minutes in the drafty barn.

Larry Bird on his first look at the Garden: "I'd never seen any arenas so I really didn't know. I thought it was pretty neat that the railroad station was below and the gym was up above. In high school there was a place we played we had to walk these stairs, and I thought that was so neat. We had to walk up these little-bitty staircases and . . . duck going up there, and they filled it up with about three thousand people, and I thought that was unbelievable. So I liked that about the Garden. And you can see good in there. I can tell right away when I walk in a gym if the lighting is pretty good."

In 1928, New York's Madison Square Garden boxing promoter, Tex Rickard, plotted to mass-produce the fabled Gotham arena. Rickard envisioned six Garden copies in major metropolitan cities and decided to start in Boston on top of the North Station, Hub home of the Boston and Maine Railroad. It took less than a year to build the Boston Garden. It was an ambitious undertaking—a hotel on one side and an office building on the other. The Boston Madison Square Garden was christened in 1928 when Honeyboy Finnegan won a ten-round decision against Andre Routis on November 17. The Bruins moved in immediately. Soon after, Rickard died, and his interest in the building was passed on to a pair of New Yorkers who sold the stock to Boston millionaire Henry Lapham and George V. Brown. The *Boston Evening American* held a rename-the-building contest, and Dorchester's Ruth Fasano came up with the catchy, clever "Boston Garden."

George V. Brown's son, Walter, assumed the duties of Boston Garden manager, and later, owner. He booked a unique professional ice show that came to be known as the Ice Follies. He later used this show to help his basketball team procure the services of Bill Russell. The Ringling Brothers and Barnum & Bailey Circus made their Garden debut in April 1929. In the 1930s Brown also booked a six-day bicycle race, a hunting and fishing show, a Notre Dame football game, midget auto races, a winter ski exhibition, amateur hockey, the Sonja Henjie Ice Revue, and rodeos. In the 1940s, Brown tried women's softball, book shows, the Shriners Ball, and big bands. Calvin Coolidge spoke here. In 1940 a rally for presidential candidate Franklin Delano Roosevelt was held, and Bob Hope did an army-navy relief show. During World War II the Garden was used for War Bond Shows featuring Judy Garland, Gene Kelly, and Greer Garson. On May 2, 1953, Bishop John J. Writer celebrated a night Mass for eleven thousand people. Liberace played the Garden and signed autographs until four o'clock in the morning. John F. Kennedy held his final presidential campaign rally at the Garden in 1960. Elvis played the Garden. The Beatles stormed the premises in 1964 ("They didn't sing a word, it was all taped," insists forty-year Garden employee Bill McNamara), and, in 1972, the same night Boston Mayor Kevin White bailed them out of a Rhode Island jail, the Stones performed a famous midnight rambler show. High school kids dream of playing in the Garden. They believed the building president, Eddie Powers, when he called it the "House of Magic." Walpole's Joe Morgan and Norwood's Richie Hebner longed to play hockey in the Garden before they went on to baseball fame. The Needham High Rockets filled the place seven times when Robbie Ftorek skated center ice in the 1960s. Matignon's Warriors were not allowed to shave their heads until they advanced far enough to skate on the Garden ice. The Tech Tourney was *the* event of the high school basketball season until Somerville's Billy Endicott was beat up after a game and the tourney was phased out. The Beanpot College Hockey tournament features Harvard, Northeastern, Boston University, and Boston College. Their fans were stranded here when the blizzard of 1978 disrupted the event. College basketball was a premier attraction when Bob Cousy and Company won a national championship for Holy Cross in the 1950s. There were doubleheaders with big-name schools. In the 1980s, the Big East brought college hoops back to the house

that Cooz rocked. The Garden arena was built for the sweet
science (hence the vertical slant to the seating), and the roll
call of boxers who fought in Boston includes Joe Louis, Sugar
Ray Robinson, Jake LaMotta, Gene Tunney, Rocky Marciano,
Muhammad Ali, and Marvin Hagler.

In 1990, the biggest fight is the battle to find a parking space
within a mile of the joint. The Brinks robbery took place near
the Boston Garden, and area parking-lot owners operate in
the spirit of that event. In 1989 the friendly Sardine Brothers
were getting fifteen dollars per car for a Celtics game. You're
better off taking your chances with one of those glowing orange
parking tickets. Fifteen dollars is the same price you'd pay for
an expired parking meter, and Mayor Flynn needs the money
more than the Sardine Brothers do.

Streets around the building are narrow and littered with
loading zones, construction sites, or residents-only parking.
The area is always busy. Benjie D. scalps tickets in front of
Richie Boyajian's barbershop. A son of Greek immigrants,
Benjie's been scalping for more years than he spent in school.
He still lives with his parents in a two-family house in Brighton.
He used to be a busboy at Anthony's Pier 4, but the money
on the street is better—especially on nights when the Celtics
are playing an attractive opponent. Out-of-towners patronize
the scalpers. Desperate folks in business who need to impress
clients turn to scalpers when they can't get tickets anywhere
else.

Garden-neighborhood regulars walk past the scalpers and
buy cigars from tobacco shops or make pick-ups at the shoe
repair shop. Cardboard pizza joints dot the street corners, and
there's cheap jewelry being sold everywhere. Drunks line the
cold brick walls, and dark saloons do business throughout the
day. Sullivan's Tap fits the era, and the Fours is a popular
spot across the Garden on Canal Street. The 99 is another
popular pre- and postgame watering hole.

Inside and out, the Garden is always crowded and noisy.
Huge television trucks park in front of 150 Causeway, steel

wheels screech from the elevated tracks, and fat pigeons wad-
dle on the dirty sidewalk below. Meteorologists would dispute
this claim, but it seems to rain more in this spot than in any
other place in New England. Shangri-la it ain't.

When it gets near game time, you turn in your ticket in a
first-floor hallway, then start walking up the old cement ramps.
No use waiting around for the escalators or elevators; there
are none. The arena lobbies are big and bright. Smoking is
allowed and the air is always stale and usually cold. If it's
November, you can smell dung left over from the circus.

The Garden is easily the oldest NBA Arena. Chicago Stadium is six years younger, and the rest of the league theaters
are infants by comparison. How strange then to discover that
there are people who work at the Boston Garden who are
actually older than the building and who remember when the
place was built. "I was there before the roof went on," Eddie
Lee said in 1989. Lee was the original timekeeper and was
working in the purchasing department in 1989. Head usher
Mo Harrington had fifty-one years of experience and remembered a succession of uniform jackets that went from blue,
brown, red, mustard, back to red again. Winnie Walsh started
operating the switchboard in 1928. These are the Garden folk,
and to them the place is home. You won't want to miss Rudolph
Edwards, aka "Spider," who pushes a mop across the parquet
after each period of every game. Spider wears a green satin
Celtics jacket and one of his many hats. His face is as stoic
and expressionless as Robert Parish's. Tony Nota ran the clock
for four decades before he died while working the Boston Marathon. Walter Randell was an original Garden employee and
was still working as a Celtics equipment man when he died in
1985. Walter's wife still attends every Celtics home game. John
Kiley played the organ from 1941 until he got into a spat with
ownership in 1984. Too bad. Kiley was the answer to the oft-
repeated, juvenile trivia question: Who's the only man to play
for the Red Sox, Celtics, Bruins, and Patriots? Howie McHugh
was the much-loved Celtics publicist from 1946 until his death

in 1983. How may PR men have been tossed out of games by Jake O'Donnell? Some of these men and women were stuck in the Garden for five days during the blizzard of 1978.

The crew behind the scenes can transform the Garden from basketball arena to hockey arena in an hour and a half. It takes them a little longer to go from pucks to hoops; the parquet comes off faster than it goes down. These folks call themselves the "bull gang," and they are as efficient and professional as any of the teams that play in the arena.

Bill McNamara was born in Natick, Massachusetts, in 1912, the same year the Copley Plaza Hotel opened. He went to Boston College High and Holy Cross before going into the service. He started working at the Garden as an usher in 1945, a year before the Celtics were born. He was in a crew of twenty-eight Garden ushers who would go to the Arena to work basketball games when the Celtics played on the other side of town. Now he works in the press room. Press hospitality was never high on Red Auerbach's list, and McNamara remembers, "Red was very bitter against the press in a way."

Game Day.

Two hours before the opening tap, McNamara puts out the salt-and-pepper shakers in the empty press room while Larry Bird walks through his daily solo shooting session. Bird likes to get to the gym early. He calls every arena a gym. Bird might be the only person in America who thinks of the eighty-thousand-seat Pontiac Silverdome as a gym. For his private Garden shootaround, Bird is accompanied by the assistant equipment handler, Joe Quatato, aka "Joe Q." Joe Q. is one of the "little people" Bird embraces. The Celtic superstar likes unpretentious people who don't want anything from him. Bird also likes hard workers. Joe Q. works hard and asks nothing of Bird; he just wants to be his friend. He is the man Bird trusts to catch the basketball when it crashes through the net and to toss it back to him. The routine lasts about twenty minutes. Bird has been known to sink fifty or sixty consecutive medium-range set shots during this warm-up set. It is his private moment on the Garden floor. Television technicians, sportswriters, and club officials are the only people around, and they go about their business without giving Bird more than a glance. Bird can work in peace, without distraction from autograph hounds and yahoos who want to flash a camera in his face. Bird has a photo of Joe Q. in his locker; it is a picture of Joe Q. during his high school football days, when he had more hair than he has today. When Larry Bird was married in the fall of 1989, Joe Q. was one of a handful of people who attended the wedding.

Bird is the only veteran who shows up early. Locker room protocol dictates that rookies get taped first, so the young guys have to show up early to get any attention from trainer Ed Lacerte. Kevin McHale, Robert Parish, and Dennis Johnson ("DJ") will be the last to arrive. Assistant coach Chris Ford slips a video of tonight's opponent in the clubhouse VCR, and it serves as background Muzak while the Celtics get dressed for warm-ups. Only the coaches watch the tape. Occasionally, the announcer's voice will rise, and Parish might glance at the screen for a moment. There is mail on each player's chair, and a couple of basketballs rest on the wooden table in the middle of the room. The balls need to be signed and will be auctioned off for charity. The message board next to the TV tells players to be at Logan Airport tomorrow morning at 9:15 for a Northwest flight to Detroit.

Back in the arena, you find your way to your seats and notice that the chairs are small and hard and there is no leg room. A recent paint job gave the dank theater a citrus-orange and yellow look, but there's only so much you can do to improve the ambience. The ceiling appears to be layers of unfinished, colorless insulation. It smells like a beer was spilled under your seat. Yesterday. The incline is particularly steep upstairs (the place was built for boxing, remember?), and it's a miracle that no upper-deck drunk has toppled over the rail and into the loge during an event. There used to be a second balcony, and this is where the loyal, leather-lunged Gallery Gods hung out during Bruins games. The second balcony was often empty during Celtics games. Kids populated this uppermost region, and the bigots from Southie and Charlestown dubbed it "Nigger Heaven." Today, this area is where the high rollers sit in luxury boxes, drinking champagne, trading stock tips, and watching the game on television monitors.

The Garden is particularly famous for its obstructed-view seats. The building was not designed for basketball, and only 20 percent of the seating is in the desirable sideline (unobstructed) area. Capacity for basketball is 14,890, almost a thousand more than the announced 13,909 of the golden days. Overhangs are the biggest impediments and there are seats where fans can see only one basket and no scoreboards. Everything is yellow or orange, everything except the parquet and the flags. The Celtics have stitched sixteen championship banners. The Bruins counter with 25 flags, but that includes division titles and the Celtics scoff at such transparent tactics. The Bruins have won five Stanley Cups and should have only five banners. The Boston Celtics would be embarrassed to brag about anything less than a World Championship. That's what makes them the Celtics.

The Celtic flags are sacred relics—royal emblems signifying strength, stability, and supremacy. The banners have transformed an archaic entertainment palace into the Sistine Chapel of sport. The Bruins already had flags when the Celtics won their first championship in 1957, and Red Auerbach and Walter Brown contracted New England Flag and Banner Company of Watertown to stitch the first championship banner. It was made of cotton bunting and measured eight feet by twelve feet. Little did they know it would turn out to be a standing order, like red roses and a new dress for every anniversary. New England Flag made eleven banners in thirteen years, and the Garden ceiling started to look like a clothesline outside a three-decker in Brighton. The flags come down for a washing every now and then. (Equipment manager Walter Randell always uses Tide.) Joe Studley took over New England Flag in 1970, and when the Celtics won in 1974, Studley discovered that the banner blueprint (greenprint?) was lost. The plans were eventually found and four more flags have been made. The new ones are made of nylon and cost $475 each. Replacements have also been made when high-wire thieves made off with some of the originals.

"That's a terrible feeling," says General Manager Jan Volk. "When you look up and say, 'Oh my God, 1957 is missing.'"

Auerbach says, "The charisma of those banners is unbelievable. Every ballplayer you talk to first talks about two things— those banners and our parquet floor."

M. L. Carr admits, "When you're a player for another team and you first come into the Boston Garden, you can't wait to put your bags down and take a look at those banners. You don't have to be a genius to know that to have that many championships, this team knows how to win. Other teams' veterans always tell the kids how these flags don't win games, but that just shows you that they're thinking about it."

K. C. Jones had a hand in putting eleven of the banners in place (eight playing, three coaching). When he coached with Washington and Seattle, he was careful not to make a big deal of the flags. "There's enough to think about without putting that into their heads," says Jones.

Next to the championship banners, there are two white banners, each divided into eight panels, like windowpanes through which we view the past. The sixteen squares contain fifteen retired numbers and one retired nickname ("Loscy," for Jim Loscutoff, was retired after the number was given to Dave Cowens). The Celts are running out of available two-digit numbers. Except for no. 20, everything from 14 (Cousy) to 25 (K. C. Jones) is gone for good. Ed Macauley's no. 22 is retired, and that makes him the only prechampionship player to have his number in the rafters. Macauley was traded for the draft rights to Bill Russell, which should be reason enough to retire any man's number. The retired numbers spark a lot of arguments. Why Jo Jo and not Chaney? What'll happen to DJ and

Danny Ainge? In January 1990, Boston sports radio's Eddie Andelman spent two hours on the air fielding calls on the pros and cons of retiring Ainge's number.

Top and bottom. That's what the Celtics are famous for. The flags are the top; the parquet is the bottom. It is the same floor that Russell played on. The floor is almost forty-five years old. "It is constantly maintained and being reworked," says Volk. "It's like the old farmer with the craftsman's ax that he's had for thirty years. He's so proud of it. He says, 'You know, I've replaced two heads and I've put three new handles on it, but it's still the same ax.' Well, it's the same floor, but it regenerates."

Inspecting the floor in 1987, Cleveland guard Ron Harper said, "Man, my driveway is better than this."

Magic Johnson says, "Some courts are fast and some are slow. This one here is a little softer. Here you have to dribble that much harder just to make the ball come up."

The floor was built for $10,000 by a Brookline man named DiNatale in 1946. Due to the war effort, hardwood was in short supply, but DiNatale had some oak scraps cut from a forest in Tennessee. The boards were an inch-and-a-half thick and exceptionally strong because they were cut against the grain. Panels measuring five feet by five feet were cut and arranged in an alternating pattern to form the famous parquet effect. The 264 heavy panels don't fit snugly anymore, and you can place four quarters in some of the gaps between boards. The extra thickness of the boards has allowed workers to refinish the floor three times.

Ainge says, "A lot of times you're dribbling the ball upcourt, the ball won't come back to you. So the guys who do a lot of fancy dribbling, they never know. They go behind their back and they come up empty."

Volk says if the Celtics relocate, the floor will accompany them. This is a comfort for Celtic fans across the land: "There's been considerable discussion about it, and some people don't want to bring it, but we're planning on taking the floor with us."

There is no air-conditioning in the Boston Garden. Someday, you might ask former Laker coach Pat Riley what he thinks of North Station's climate control. For thirty years, the Boston Garden has been a Laker graveyard (Scott Ostler, formerly of the *Los Angeles Times*, calls the Garden a trash compactor for Laker basketball teams). Celtics fans remember Boston's pivotal Game 5 victory against the Lakers in the 1984 finals. It was close to one hundred degrees inside the Garden, and it's hard to forget the picture of Kareem Abdul-Jabbar inhaling oxygen from a mask late in the game. During the winter, there is heat in the Garden, but never quite enough if you're sitting near the floor. Plywood covers the Bruins' ice, and the big chill creeps through your sole.

The only sounds you hear before games, are old-timey organ music and a low-level crowd buzz. Suddenly, tall men in white and green warm-ups come up from a portal in the center of the arena, and PA man Andy Jick announces, "Ladies and Gentlemen, the Boston Celtics." In the old days, the PA man was Weldon Haire, and Jick sounds almost exactly like him. There is little shtick to Jick. When the Celts come out for warm-ups, he does not ask the crowd to welcome "your" Boston Celtics.

There is no rock and roll blaring from the speakers, no flash-dancing cheerleaders, and no oversize feathered creatures trying to sell the sport. Red Auerbach has a particular disdain for gimmickry. The game makes it on its own, or not at all.

John Kiley is seventy-seven years old and started playing the organ for the Celtics when they were formed in 1946. He resigned in the mid-1980s when he got into a spat with Paul Mooney, who was then in charge of the Garden. He introduced Victor Herbert's "It's a Great Day Tonight for the Irish," as the official Celtics theme song. "Attendance in the early days was weak," says Kiley. "I saw a complete change when Cousy came in. They started getting more college kids. I was never very close to Red. Walter Brown was the one that hired me. They left me on their own. Most of them didn't like me to do that pep music—you know, playing in between plays and stuff. They thought it was just distracting. People don't like it."

At the end of the Celtics bench, you can't miss Francis O'Bryant. He's five-foot-five, black, round as a basketball, and solid as a truck. A handsome man with a trimmed beard, O'Bryant has been sitting on the Celtics bench for twenty years. He started as a ballboy when he was eleven and now hands out stats between quarters and serves in a variety of other formal and informal capacities. By day, he is a court officer at the Middlesex County Courthouse in Cambridge. By night, he is a Garden person, a fixture. He has missed only one Celtics home game in twenty years. The players used to call him "Bubbles," because he looks like a bubble. Now everybody calls him Francis.

"I used to be a fan and buy balcony seats," says O'Bryant. "Before the game I'd get everybody's autograph. I would go to my seat, then run down before halftime to see the players file into the locker room. I got very friendly with Howie McHugh, the publicity director, and Walter Randell, the equipment manager. I would wait around after the game, and they always saw me. I was a nice guy, quiet, and never got into any trouble or anything. And one day they decided to ask me if I wanted to be a ballboy."

He has been there ever since, handing out towels, wiping the floor, and doling out stats. He has been on national television more than any player in the National Hockey League. He has gone into the stands to retrieve Tom Heinsohn's shoe when the coach kicked it into the crowd. He has tackled fans who tried to make off with basketballs. He took off the ballboy uniform in 1976 when he started growing sideburns, but he continues to serve. He does not do it for the money. He has been a part of five World Championships. Not bad for a five-foot-five-inch guy nicknamed "Bubbles."

Across the floor, General Manager Jan Volk sits to the right of Red. Volk is the man who assumed the general manager's duties when Auerbach "retired" in 1984. Insiders will tell you that Volk was doing most of the technical work years before Red officially anointed him his successor. As long as Red is alive, Volk will get credit for nothing, only blame. When good things happen, everybody assumes Red is behind the strategy. When things fall apart, it's because of that lawyer Volk, the man who has never worn sneakers or worked up a sweat. Volk took a lot of heat when the Knicks bounced Boston from the play-offs in the spring of 1990.

"How can I ever resent Red Auerbach?" Volk asks. "If it weren't for Red, my being here wouldn't be half as meaningful as it is now. Red has only helped me in what I do; he not only gave me the opportunity and taught me, has guided me and given me support when I needed it, but also made the legend that the Boston Celtics *are* into something so meaningful that my just being here is important. If my background was as a player or a coach, I might be more inclined to expect whatever I do to be reported, and I might therefore feel concerned about not getting credit, but that's not my background. And most lawyers, most businessmen, most people in most professions work for the satisfaction that they gain from doing a good job."

Jan Volk looks and acts nothing like Red, but he was his logical successor. Volk's family was living in Newton when Auerbach took over the Celtics in 1950. Ten years later, Jerry Volk, Jan's father, approached Auerbach about using his camp for rookie camp. Auerbach went for it. Camp Milbrook came cheap, and the Celts didn't have any money. Jan was thirteen when the Celtics invaded his dad's camp in August 1960. "He was a kid," remembers Red. "He used to chase us around. He was a little sharper than most kids, maybe, but just a kid."

Jan Volk got coffee for the Celtics people. His brother, Mark, was assistant trainer of the team. When Jan was old enough to drive, he would be dispatched to the airport to pick up the new talent. Willie Naulls joined the Celtics in 1963, and the first person he met was sixteen-year-old Jan; the kid had just got his driver's license and picked up Naulls at Logan Airport in his father's Oldsmobile convertible.

Volk went to Columbia Law School, passed the bar in 1971, and joined the Celtics that autumn. The stencil man spent a lot of time changing titles on Volk's door. Volk progressed from director of ticket sales to equipment purchaser to business manager to vice president–house counsel, and finally to general manager. He was twenty-four years old before he stopped calling his boss "Mr. Auerbach" and started calling him "Red."

"He corrected me quickly, and in a way that I didn't misunderstand," remembers Volk.

The second general manager of the Celtics has never worked for anyone else. He is family. Each game night, at about half past five, he sees the caterer delivering the evening's buffet to the conference room next to Red's office. Ex-players wander in unannounced. There is little ceremony if you are a family member. No one stops at the receptionist's desk.

Auerbach says, "I don't have as much control over it as I used to, but my guys know that they have an open invitation."

Says Volk, "For the most part, they're treated very rudely . . . which tells them that they're still loved."

While the high rollers and alumni gather with Auerbach, Volk, and the owners, the crew at the scorer's table arrive for work. Stan Muir is the official scorer and Miriam Strauss-Yorks types the play-by-play. Dave Gately is the crew chief, and Bob Myerson (24-second clock), George Hect (minutes), Steve Nazzaro (steals, blocks, turnovers), Rich Steckloff (fouls), George Yorks (assistant scoreboard), Royal Doughty (assistant scorer), and Kirk Stepanian (rebounds, shots) catalog the action. Bruce Dove runs the clock. Tony Nota was the clock operator until 1972, when Auerbach fired him one last time. Nota believed in following the letter of the law. Red believed in home-court advantage. When Nota failed to let the clock run out against the Knicks in 1972, he was gone.

Fans Rita Kissane, thirty-five, and Joanne Borcakian, twenty-eight, sit in the first row directly behind the west-end basket support. Kissane has attended almost every game since 1970. Borcakian has missed only ten games since 1974. Kissane works in the investment department of the treasurer's office at the state house and walks down Beacon Hill to the Garden every game night. "My father used to take me when I was in grammar school," she says. "When I was in high school, he told me to take my friends. I got my first season ticket in 1970. I was thirteen years old, and I paid for it with babysitting money. I'd pay all year. All year long I'd come with my ten dollars to the Celtics offices. The first year was Cowens's rookie year, and you could lie down in the front row. It was wonderful. It was four dollars a ticket."

Rita and Joanne used to hang homemade banners from the upper-deck facades. By 1981, they were hanging as many as forty signs per night. Al McGuire did a nationally televised feature on Rita and Joanne, the "Sign Girls."

"People associated those banners with the Celtics, and we loved it," she says. "I still know people in the balcony that wave to us now. Not everyone gets their number retired, but we felt that every player deserves a banner. The Celtics were always fun to watch, they always gave it their best. The thing about mystique and pride—you like to be associated with it. I love green."

Rita gets a lot of television air time, and her family still remembers the year that her uncle Andrew, watching a tape of the NBA finals in a pub in Deptford, England, spotted Rita and rushed to the phone to call the relatives back in Massachusetts.

Rita's signs are ancient history—like 13,909 capacity and ten-thousand-dollar player salaries, homemade signs are not allowed anymore. In 1989, billboards cost thirty thousand dollars per year. The age of innocence has turned into the age of dollars and cents. There is precious little blank space left. Beer and whiskey signs wallpaper the Garden facades, and you wonder how long it will be before JIM-BOB'S PORK SAUSAGE will hang next to the 1957 championship banner. Kissane doesn't bring her banners anymore, but she's still got her vocal chords, and she's in the officials' faces at least twice a game.

At the other end of the court, the east end, sits John Mahoney, a redheaded maniac. His carrot top seems fitting. Dave Cowens and Bill Walton are two redheads who helped bring championships to Boston, and, of course, Arnold "Red" Auerbach is the greatest redheaded Celtic of them all. In that tradition, Mahoney lets the refs have it for the full forty-eight minutes. Naturally, he gets plenty of support from the regulars who surround him. Mahoney is a purchasing manager for Digital, lives in Lowell, and has been a ticket holder for ten years. He says what's special to him is "the concept of team spirit, and the perception that you have to win. It's no good unless you win. The flags hanging up there mean a lot."

Mahoney often engages in a running dialogue with referee Earl Strom. "Earl and I have a way of getting on each other's nerves," he says. "But I know the limits. The first thing you've got to do is not be vulgar. You can't swear. That's just being stupid. So you just tell them basic things about officiating. They've got to realize that sooner or later they've lost it and it's time to hang 'em up. You've got to be consistent. If you're going to call it for one side, call it for the other side. I like to do it. You get up and yell at the officials a little bit, and you work off your frustrations. You don't yell at home, and you don't yell at work. If you yell in the middle of the road, they'll put you away. You've got to do something. Here it's supposed to be sanctioned. It's okay to do it."

The *Boston Globe*'s Bob Ryan sits at the press table, about eight seats in from the Celtics bench. Colleagues cheerfully address Ryan as the "Commissioner," and anyone arriving four hours before game time would not be surprised to find Ryan measuring the baskets to make sure everything is up to code. This is an exaggeration, of course, but sportswriters do remember the night that referee Hue Hollins came over to the press table to explain a call during a time-out. It was as if Hollins felt compelled to explain it to a league representative before filing an official report. The definitive NBA source, Ryan has covered the Celtics since 1969 and is perceived as keeper of the flame. An opinionated, animated sort, he's been known to get involved in the games. When Rick Mahorn broke in with the Bullets, Ryan wrote a column about Mahorn's dirty play under the basket. Washington played at Boston Garden a few days later, and after Mahorn was called for a foul, Bullets coach Gene Shue whipped around, pointed a finger in Ryan's face, and said, "That's your fault, Bob Ryan, your fault!" Dennis Johnson sometimes gets annoyed when Ryan becomes loud at courtside. He once dribbled past the press table and said, "Hey, Bob, keep it down. We got a game goin' on out here." Ryan is part of a long line of scribes who stayed with the Celtics over the years. The *Globe*'s Jack Barry was a loyal supporter of both Walter Brown and professional basketball in the early years, and Sam Brogna and Sammy Cohen were also there at the start. Auerbach felt he had to educate the region about basketball, and the press played an important role. "Dave Eagan and Sammy Cohen of the *Record* did as much for us as anybody," says Auerbach. "Most of the writers didn't know anything about basketball. Bill Cunningham was a big columnist in the early days, and he never came over. When I asked him why, he said, 'Tell me something funny about it.' I told him to get lost."

Sports radio legend Eddie Andelman says, "If it wasn't for the old *Boston Record-American*, definitely the Celtics would have left town."

High above courtside sits Johnny Most, in the same perch he's been in since 1952. Most is as much a Boston landmark as the Bunker Hill Monument and Kenmore Square's Citgo sign. A native New Yorker, Most played football and basketball for Brooklyn College. He began his career broadcasting Knicks games under the tutelage of Marty Glickman. Auerbach brought him on board in 1952 (Curt Gowdy was Most's predecessor), and he's never left. Gravel-throated (he bragged that he gargles with Dran-O), the ultimate homer, Celtic fans identify with Most as much as with any player. He is not just the voice of the Celtics, he *is* the Celtics. Fans call out to him wherever he goes. Taverns hold Johnny Most sound-alike contests. Most shills for products on the radio and television. Generations of Boston hoop fans were raised to turn down their television sound and turn up Johnny when the Celtics play on the tube. In the 1960s, Most's record, *Havlicek Stole the Ball*, got more Boston airplay than *Sgt. Pepper's Lonely Hearts Club Band*. Addicted to cigarettes and coffee, Most was in poor health for the latter part of the 1980s and temporarily had to give up traveling with the team. It was not the same without him. Bird loved to kid Most about smoking on the bus. Bill Fitch and Heinsohn had fun with his hearing aid. Most hates to wear the device, and Heinsohn could be heard screaming, "Johnny, put your hearing aid in. I'm sick of fucking yelling at you." Never adept with mechanical devices, Most caused a lot of double-talk when he used a tape recorder to do a pregame show with the Celtics coach. Invariably, Most would do an interview, then learn that he forgot to push "record." When K. C. Jones coached the Celtics, he and Most did more encores than Bruce Springsteen.

Most sees only one color: green. All rival players are the enemy. His best nicknames were for Jeff Ruland and Rick Mahorn: "McFilthy" and "McNasty." "That was never phony," says Most. "But it was never long-lasting. I didn't hate Isiah forever. I didn't hate Laimbeer forever. I didn't hate even Mahorn forever. But when they were in the act of doing something that was injurious to my friends, I was angry and I always will be. That's my nature." His voice rises during games, and at particularly frenetic moments, Most goes into what has been called his "dog-whistle" voice—only true fans can understand him when Johnny reaches this plateau. He got into an argument with broadcast partner Glenn Ordway and concluded the spat by yelling, "I'm the show." The players loved it and said, "I'm the show" whenever they saw Most weeks after the outburst. Bird told him. "Forget it, Johnny, *I'm* the show."

After triple-bypass surgery in September 1989, Most sat out the first twenty-eight games of the 1989–90 season. He returned on the night of January 3, 1990, and it kindled memories of Elvis Presley's 1969 comeback concert at the International Hotel in Las Vegas. Most was introduced to the Garden sellout and received a standing ovation. He was interviewed by four television stations and was the subject of columns in both Boston newspapers' sports sections. He expressed concern about his voice: "I think some of the gravel is out . . . because I don't smoke anymore." Asked how long he planned to stay behind the mike, Most answered, "Till they kick dirt in my face, babe, till they kick dirt in my face."

Most's poor health put him back on the shelf in the spring of 1990.

How do you retire an announcer's number? Do you hang his microphone from the rafters, or simply leave his chair empty for eternity?

The Garden crowd has changed a lot in recent years. There hasn't been an empty seat at a game since December 19, 1980, when the Celtics and Houston Rockets drew only 14,570 people. A decade of sellouts followed, but as the Celtics became more attractive, they became less accessible. There are few gym rats at the games. Ticket prices peaked at thirty-two dollars in 1989, and only the elite have both the money and clout to gain admittance. It's a white wine and designer eyeglasses crowd; a crowd studied in the nuances of the game. Celtics fans can spot an illegal defense faster than Jake O'Donnell can. When they hear "zipper," they know that Bird is coming off a low pick to take a pass and attempt a fall-away jumper from out top. They know that "hawk" means a clearout for Bird. They know who the Celtics should foul if they're trying to come back in the late stages of a close game. They know when the Celts are in the penalty situation and how many time-outs Jimmy Rodgers has left. You can always tell when an unthreatening opponent is in town; tickets for the less desirable games are usually the ones given as gifts. Ushers always have to work harder when the Los Angeles Clippers are in Boston, for example. When the Lakers come to the Garden, it's all the regulars, and they know where their seats are.

Almost everybody in the stands is white and has disposable income. Few fans flinch when paying three dollars for a Steve's Ice Cream Bar. That's more than Celtics tickets used to cost—but then again, Bob Cousy signed for $10,000 in 1950 and Larry Bird signed for $650,000 when he got out of college.

Robert Nobtzel, a Boston Garden vendor who sells yuppie ice cream bars, says, "For me, the Celtics are better than the Bruins. I make more money. It's more of an upper crowd. They're more well dressed. Bruins fans give me more of a hard time about the price, and if they see somebody buying, they'll yell, 'You're crazy paying three dollars.' . . . Another thing I noticed is that at a Celtics game, during the national anthem, it's quiet until the last line. At Bruins games, they roar halfway through the song."

"Fans meant more to the old Celtics," says superfan Kissane. "The older guys know what it was like to play in this building when it was half full. And they knew us fans then. They still remember us. Don Nelson, when he comes in with Golden State, or the Duck [Don Chaney], with Houston—they'll always acknowledge us. It's a different thing now. The thing is so out of proportion. The whole perspective of things has grown so big. It's a business and that's how you have to treat things, as a business. It can't be the way it always used to be, but it definitely was more fun. In those days, anyone who came to a game knew basketball. They came to enjoy basketball, win or lose. Now people come to their one game, and they'll tell us to sit down or that we're too loud."

The game is usually the same. A sellout crowd of 14,890 fills the Garden, cheers for the home team, and goes home happy.

The 1985–86 Celtics went 40–1 at home. You can always hear the bettors in the closing minutes. The Celtics might be ahead by eleven with one minute to play, but if the spread is more than eleven, there are still people cursing and pounding their fists every time they miss.

Rita Kissane is among the last to leave. She meets friends after the game, crosses Causeway, takes the Green Line to Lechmere, then hops on the number 88 or 87 bus to Arlington. She gets off on the Arlington-Somerville line and walks home. Kissane bought a house after the 1988–89 season; the Celtics lasted only three games in the play-offs, and she had extra cash because she didn't have to fly to Los Angeles for the finals.

Auerbach and the owners entertain friends and former players after the game. Red isn't much of a drinker and usually leaves quickly to grab a little Chinese food before going to bed.

This from David Halberstam's book *The Breaks of the Game* concerning veteran coach Jack Ramsay: "Ramsay was sensitive about Boston, and he did not, above all else, want a bad performance there. A game in Boston was part of history and in some way more important because it was against Auerbach. In a relatively new and uncertain league, Boston was the only team with any real tradition and past. Even the sheer ugliness and crumminess of the Boston Garden seemed to reflect that."

Cousy admits, "There was always the suspicion that the Celtics would do something illegal to get an edge."

This suspicion never goes away. Cousy tells a story about coaching the Legends Game at the 1988 NBA All Star weekend. Cowens won the old-timer's "unclassic," pushing somebody out of the way and scoring on an offensive rebound. In the convivial atmosphere of the postgame locker room, Dolph Schayes, then sixty years old, said to Cousy, "Nothing ever changes in this goddamned league. The Celtics are going to find a way to cheat or do something to win."

Decades of success bred a national following that is more

colorful and vocal than ever. Every night the Celtics play, there are people from coast-to-coast cheering for the green.

Cousy: "I think that's a phenomenon that doesn't exist anyplace [else]. Even if you're anti-Celtics, you can't minimize what the Celtics did. Go into other sports. The Yankees and Montreal won more championships I guess, but no one has dominated so completely in that short a time span. In the early years of television, Celtics was all you heard. They focused on their best product. What was on TV was all Celtics. The basketball people that were out there were inundated with and suffocated by the Celtics."

3
Green Origins

JUNE 6, 1946, was a fair, warm day in the northeast corner of the United States. It was the second anniversary of the Allies landing on Normandy beaches, and it was two days after Juan Peron was installed as president of Argentina. The AFL Seafarers' International Union threatened a work stoppage that would idle sixty-two thousand men. Chicago was smoldering from a fire that killed fifty-eight people in the LaSalle Hotel. President Truman appointed Treasury Secretary Fred M. Vinson as chief justice of the Supreme Court, and General Dwight D. Eisenhower was awarded an honorary degree at the 295th commencement at Harvard University. At Fenway Park, Ted Williams homered to beat the St. Louis Browns and boost the Red Sox record to 36–9. It looked like a World Series championship was finally coming to Boston.

While all this was going on, the Boston Celtics were born in New York City at the Commodore Hotel on East Forty-second Street next to Grand Central Station. Boston's Walter Brown, Cleveland's Al Sutphin, and New York's Ned Irish

met with nine or ten other prominent American arena oper-
ators and formed the eleven-member Basketball Association
of America (BAA). All but one (Washington) of the franchise
members had ties to professional hockey clubs. The ten teams
with hockey connections were in New York, Philadelphia,
Providence, Toronto, Chicago, Cleveland, Detroit, Pittsburgh,
St. Louis, and, of course, Boston.

There was logic behind the formation of the BAA. Arena
owners were concerned about too many dark nights during
the winter. Hockey teams played only a couple of games per
week, and you could book only so many boxing matches, track
meets, ice shows, rodeos, and circus events. There were no
tractor pulls, no Wrestlemania, no Bruce Springsteen concerts
in 1946. But there were a lot of free, happy Americans with
dollars to spend, looking for entertainment. The war was over.
It was a time of peace and prosperity. Pro basketball hadn't
fared well in the past, but the timing seemed right. The country
had been stripped of its best athletes during World War II,
but the hearty soldiers were finally home, and it was time to
get on with life.

The Boston BAA team didn't have a name when Walter
Brown left New York with a franchise in his pocket. It didn't
come until later in the year when Brown kicked around some
ideas with his promotions man, Howie McHugh, a former
standout goalie at Dartmouth. The names "Whirlwinds," "Un-
icorns," and "Olympics" were suggested and, luckily, rejected.
(Imagine, years later, trying to promote "Whirlwind pride" or
"Unicorn mystique.") Brown suddenly hit on "Celtics." The
name had a great basketball tradition from the old Original
Celtics in New York. And Boston was full of Irishmen. They'd
put the team in green uniforms and call them the Boston Celtics. McHugh was dubious. He explained to Brown that no team
with an Irish name had ever done well in Boston. The football
Shamrocks failed. But Brown was in love with his idea, and
the Celtics had their name.

There had been Celtics basketball teams before Walter

Brown used the name—two of them were from New York. In 1914 Frank McCormack organized a team to represent a settlement house on Manhattan's West Side. The New York Celtics had star players named Pete Barry and Johnny Witte. They were disbanded when America entered World War I. After the war, New York promoters Jim and Tom Furey reorganized the Celtics. McCormack was unwilling to give up the name, so the Fureys called their team the Original Celtics. Barry and Witte came over from the New York Celtics, and the Original Celtics became the dominant team in the New York region. They were the first team with individual contracts and are credited with the establishment of zone defense and the center position. The Original Celtics were the most famous barnstorming team of their time, and they joined the American Basketball League (ABL) in 1926. They dominated the ABL until they were dissolved in 1928–29. The Cleveland Rosenblums became the next team to use "Celtics," but the name was up for grabs when the BAA was formed in 1946.

John Davis "Honey" Russell was the first coach of the Boston Celtics. Russell was Seton Hall's basketball coach and was managing a baseball team in Rutland (Northern League) when he agreed to coach the Celts. Brown allowed him to finish the baseball season before reporting to training camp in October. This hurt the Celtics; while Honey Russell was making out lineup cards in Rutland, Boston's BAA rivals were signing the best players. The Celtics started out in a big hole.

The Celts practiced at the Boston Arena Annex, and Russell slept in a cot in his office. He welcomed twenty tryouts to the first practice. The postwar housing shortage added to the primitive conditions. The players worked out on a second-floor gym and slept on cots downstairs at night. Boston didn't care at all about the Celtics at this time. The Red Sox were battling through their first World Series in twenty-eight years, and pro basketball generated the enthusiasm box lacrosse or indoor soccer gets today. Boston was a baseball-hockey town. It was as if the Celtics did not exist.

Russell put together a ragtag team that included Harold
Kottman, Tony Kappen, Art Spector, Warren Fenley, former
Harvard forward Wyndol Gray, Red Wallace, Virgil Vaugn,
Al Brightman, brothers Connie and Johnny Simmons, five-
foot-six-inch guard Mel Hirsch, and a former Seton Hall star
named Kevin "Chuck" Connors.

Needham insurance broker Harold Furash was at the first
Celtics practice. "I had just come home from the service," says
Furash. "I got out in May 1945 and was involved with the
Young Mens Hebrew Association. I was oriented to basketball
as a youngster. In the winter of 1945–46 there was a basketball
league formed through New England, and the Boston team
was operated by Ralph Wheeler: the Goodwins. Vic Segal was
on the team. He came from Davenport, Iowa, and played on
Sundays for the Goodwins. When the Celtics were formed,
Walter Brown signed Vic Segal to play. I had gotten to know
Vic, so I went to the first practice to see how he stacked up
with the other guys. Well, it turned out that all the guys Walter
Brown had brought in from out of town signed for more money,
so Vic said, 'Forget it.' He wasn't even there. There was a
little bit in the paper about it. The practice was held at the
old BU [Boston University] gym on St. Botolph Street. It's
now torn down. Nobody knew about it. Jock Semple was there.
Walter figured that Jock, a marathon runner, would know how
to get these guys in shape. I remember Jock took them on a
five-mile run, and boy, there was great consternation about
that. That didn't last. These were basketball players. It was
a very unstructured situation. Outside of people from the West
End House and people from the Roxbury YMHA [Young Mens
Hebrew Association], nobody knew anything about basketball."

On Saturday, November 2, the Celtics traveled south to the
Rhode Island Auditorium in Providence to play their first
game. A crowd of 4,406 watched the Providence Steamrollers
beat Boston, 59–53.

The *Boston Sunday Globe* carried this account of the first

game in the history of the Boston Celtics: "With Earl Shannon and Dino Martin leading in scoring, the Providence Steam-rollers of the Basket Ball Association of America tonight defeated the Boston Celtics, 59 to 53, in the opening game of the season. Martin made 18 points and Shannon 15."

That's it. The story was wedged between a schedule for Boston Park football and Watertown's 32–7 high school football victory over Framingham. It was better than coverage in the *Boston Post*. The now-defunct *Post* refused to give the upstart Celtics any coverage for the first two seasons.

"The papers wouldn't put box scores in because they didn't know how to type them up," Red Auerbach says.

The home opener was played three days later, and again, the Celtics didn't get much attention. Tuesday, November 5, was election day, and it is fairly certain that no one walked around Boston muttering, "I wonder if Wyndol Gray can go baseline against the Chicago Stags tonight."

This was a day when a twenty-nine-year-old Brookline-born war hero named John F. Kennedy was first elected to Congress. While the Celtics were warming up at the Boston Arena, Kennedy was awaiting returns from the eleventh congressional district. Henry Cabot Lodge, Jr., was going to the Senate, JFK was going to Congress, and the Celtics were going to battle with the 1–0 Stags at the Arena. The Stags were fresh off a sixteen-point opening-night win against the New York Knickerbockers. Did anybody care?

Seven of the Celtics' thirty home games were scheduled for the Arena because of Boston Garden commitments. Gene Autry's rodeo was in town the night the Celts played their first game in Boston. Tickets ranged from $1.25 to $2.75, and a tidy crowd of 4,329 turned out for the opener.

Two Knights of Columbus teams served as the warm-up act; the North Cambridge Council K. of C. battled the Pere Marquettes while the Arena started to fill up. The Celtics and Stags were scheduled to tap off at 8:45, but there was a delay that had nothing to do with a K. of C. overtime.

The Arena had an eleven-thousand-dollar parquet floor, which had been cut from scraps because of wartime shortages and stacked in storage while hockey games were played. The glass backboards and floorboards were installed hours before the game was to begin. Glass boards were state-of-the-art in 1946, and there was some fascination with the see-through backboards when the green-clad Celtics came out for warm-ups. John Kiley was at the organ.

Connors, later famous as the star of the television show "The Rifleman," was showboating during warm-ups and shattered the west-end glass backboard during lay-ups.

"It went all milky and fell out in a thousand pieces," remembered Honey Russell.

Years later, Baltimore's Gus Johnson became famous for breaking glass boards, and, of course, Philadelphia 76er man-child Darrell Dawkins made his name shattering a pair of boards in the late 1970s. Dawkins's feats inspired poetry and the invention of collapsible rims, but on the night of November 5, 1946, Connors's stunt was not funny. While the opening-night crowd waited impatiently, Brown sent a truck to the Boston Garden, where a replacement board was discovered behind the Brahma bull pens. Cattle had to be moved to get to the backboard, and publicist Howie McHugh bribed a couple of drunk cowboys to carry the new board to the truck. If not for the work of McHugh, there is a possibility the Celtics and Stags would have played a five-on-five *half-court* game. Many fans had left by the time the Celtics and Stags got started, and few were around at the finish when the Stags won, 57–55. Johnny Simmons led the Celtics with thirteen points while the unlucky Connors scored eight.

Eddie Andelman was a young boy living in Brookline when the Celtics played that game. "The constituency at that time was comprised basically of people who had played basketball at the high school and college level. And I would say it was a large Jewish population. Hockey was a game that wasn't played much by Jewish kids. Basketball was much more of an inner-city game. The game was popular with Jewish people on the streets of New York, and if you look back to CCNY [City College of New York] and a lot of the schools that had night school, a lot of the Jews played basketball. I went to every Celtic game I could. I was one of the few people there opening night. The availability of tickets and the price of tickets was definitely a big factor. Second of all, I was one of those overweight people, and there was no way I could possibly stand on skates with my ankles. Who the hell played hockey? Basketball was something everybody played. In gym, everybody shot baskets. I lived next door to a sportswriter named Murray Kramer. He was a basketball aficionado. He was very close to Red, and through Murray we got some occasional free tickets. Ordinarily tickets were sixty cents, and we'd sit in the Garden gallery. We called it 'nosebleed heaven.' One year I remember sneaking out of the house with friends of mine. The Celtics were playing a midnight game after the ice show. It was the only time they could get court time."

The Celtics finally got to play in the Garden on November 16, and they beat the Toronto Huskies, 53–49. You might say this established the greatest home-court advantage in sports history, but there were dark days ahead. It turns out that the shattered backboard on opening night was a harbinger. The 1946–47 Celtics were a disaster. They finished in last place with a 22–38 record, twenty-seven games behind Red Auerbach's Washington Caps. They averaged 3,608 people per game and never managed to fill half of the Boston Garden. Their top crowd was 6,327, and this was at a time when Holy Cross had no trouble drawing 13,909 for a Garden visit.

Four BAA teams folded before the start of the second season: Detroit, Toronto, Cleveland, and Pittsburgh. League officials also trimmed the schedule from sixty to forty-eight games. Ed Sadowski and Dutch Garfinkel were the stars of Honey Russell's second Celtics edition, but the team didn't improve much and finished 20–28. Sadowski had been a player-coach at Toronto the year before, and Russell thought the high scorer was out to get his job. Despite the poor record, this was Boston's first play-off team. The 1947–48 Celtics finished in third place and played Chicago in a best-of-three series. The entire series was played at the Boston Arena because Chicago Stadium and Boston Garden were booked. The Celts and Stags split the first two games, but Chicago won the series with an 81–74 victory in Game 3 on April 2. A few hours after the play-off loss, Walter Brown gently dismissed Honey Russell, agreeing to pay Russell for the remaining year of his three-year contract.

There were rumors that Sadowski might take over for Russell, but Brown wanted to tap some of that Holy Cross magic and opted for Alvin "Doggie" Julian. Holy Cross is a small (2,400 students) Jesuit liberal-arts college in Worcester, forty miles due west of Boston. The school is located on Mount St. James, and is the midpoint between Boston and Springfield, the town where James Naismith, a phys ed teacher, invented basketball. Despite the fact that the game was invented in Massachusetts, basketball still hadn't caught on in New England. Boston was and always will be a baseball town, and in the winter there's a hard-core hockey interest that goes back to the turn of the century. Basketball wasn't even a distant third. The Boston city school system had dropped the sport in 1925, and there was little local interest in the pro game. The college hoop game was the only basketball that generated any interest and that was due to the strength of the Holy Cross program in the 1940s. In 1947 the Holy Cross Crusaders became the first (and still the only) New England team to win the NCAA basketball championship. Bob Cousy was a freshman on that team, and Julian was the coach. They practiced in an airplane hanger on the campus hill and played their home games in the Worcester Auditorium or the Boston Garden. They won eighteen in a row the year after winning the NCAA and were eliminated by eventual-winner Kentucky in the Eastern finals. Their games routinely filled the Boston Garden, and Brown, who headed the Boston Garden Arena Corporation, wanted his Celtics to do what the college kids were doing: attract crowds. Julian was hired.

Crusader stars George Kaftan and Dermie O'Connell graduated in January 1949 and joined Julian and Brown's team. The Celtics drew 10,691 people the night the Crusader stars made their NBA debut, and home attendance was up 30 percent by the end of the season. But there wasn't enough "Purple Magic" to put the Celtics in the play-offs or in the black. The third Celtics edition finished 25–35—out of the play-offs and $100,000 in the red. The start-up venture had lost $350,000 in three years, and stockholders were urging Brown to cut losses and fold the franchise. Brown asked for another year.

The 1948–49 season was the final year of the BAA. The league absorbed six survivors of the rival National Basketball League (NBL) and formed the National Basketball Association (NBA) on August 3, 1949. These were days when sideshows were welcome, and the Celtics had one of the best in Tony Lavelli. A former Yale captain, Lavelli had a dazzling long-range hook shot and could entertain the crowd by playing the accordian at halftime. The night of December 22, 1949, was memorable. Lavelli came off the bench to score twenty-six, twenty-three of them after he'd played "Lady of Spain" and other selections at the half. The Celtics outscored the World Champion Minneapolis Lakers, 53–32, in the second half, and beat George Mikan and Company, 87–69. Unfortunately, there weren't many other victories, and there were plenty of embarrassing nights—like the evening the Celts and Warriors drew 216 fans for a game in Providence. The Celtics finished 22–46, the worst year in franchise history. It was clear that Julian had been unable to bring any Holy Cross magic to pro basketball, and he resigned at the end of the season.

If not for Brown, that might have been it for the Celtics. Four seasons had yielded an aggregate record of 89–147 and almost a half-million dollars of debt. After the 1949–50 season, another $100,000 loss, disgruntled stockholders sold the team to Brown. The Celtic owner had to sell his home (he had just paid off his house when he started the franchise in 1946) and other private investments to stay afloat. Money man Lou Pieri was brought in from Providence, and Brown was prepared to give it another year or two. They went looking for a coach.

It would be impossible to guess what might have happend to the NBA if Brown hadn't decided to hang on for one more season, but it can be safely stated that the 1950–51 Boston Celtics forever changed the face of professional basketball. This team went 39–30, a vast improvement for a team that had never played .500 ball, but still a modest record. It was not yet time for championship flags. The Celtics were wiped out by the New York Knicks in a two-game play-off.

There are three important new faces in the 1950–51 Boston Celtics team photograph: Red Auerbach, Bob Cousy, and Chuck Cooper. Auerbach was Brown's new coach in 1950, and he has been with the Celtics every year since. Cousy was a rookie that year and is credited as the little big man who revolutionized the pro game, adding a new dimension of passing and fast break skills. Cooper, a forward from Duquesne, Pennsylvania, was Boston's second-round draft selection in 1950 and the first black man drafted by an NBA team.

Julian's resignation in the spring of 1950 was unexpected but couldn't have come at a better time. The Celtics needed a coach, and the best pro coach in the land was available. Auerbach had resigned from Tri-Cities because owner Ben Kerner had traded John Mahnken to the Celtics for Gene Englund. Kerner made the deal against Auerbach's wishes, and Auerbach quit after the Blackhawks were blown out of the play-offs. Lou Pieri, Brown's new Celtic partner, was a big Auerbach fan, and there was pressure from the media to hire the native New Yorker. The thirty-two-year-old Auerbach was summoned to Boston and signed a one-year deal worth ten thousand dollars. The job was simple: turn the Celtics into winners or watch them fall into the Atlantic ocean.

Auerbach not only was a good coach, he was also Jewish, and that held some appeal for the few hard-core Celtic fans in existence. The Celtics in their early years were largely supported by the Jewish community of greater Boston, specifically Brookline. To this day, the Celts remain indebted to the Jewish community, and each year the team's kickoff dinner is hosted by the B'nai B'rith Sports Lodge.

Although he was a hit with Pieri and with the Jewish community, Auerbach was a little too fresh for some Bostonians. When Brown introduced him at a basketball luncheon at the Hotel Lenox, Auerbach managed to offend most of the college coaches on the dais—first by recommending fake injuries to stop the clock and then by insulting Colby Coach Lee Williams, who had bragged about not complaining to the officials for an entire season. Red said that any coach who didn't get on the officials wasn't doing his job.

The Redhead was even less popular when he bypassed college legend Bob "the Cooz" Cousy on draft day. The last-place, financially strapped Celtics had the number-one pick in the entire draft, and Auerbach selected six-eleven Bowling Green center Charlie Share. The local outrage should have been smothered some when Philadelphia, Baltimore, Washington, Chicago, Minneapolis, Indianapolis, and Syracuse also bypassed the Cooz, but there was no soothing the wounded natives. Cousy had filled the Garden for four years and played on three NCAA teams and one NCAA championship team; he was the little wizard who made the game so much fun to watch. Tri-Cities' Ben Kerner, Auerbach's former employer, drafted Cousy with the ninth pick.

A few days after the draft, Auerbach met the press and the first question was about Cousy. "I don't give a damn for sentiment or names," said Auerbach. "That goes for Cousy and everybody else. The only thing that counts with me is ability, and Cousy still hasn't proven to me that he's got that ability. I'm not interested in drafting someone just because he happens to be a local yokel."

He kept talking, but nobody heard much after the "local yokel" remark. The comment insulted the media and the community. The new coach was going out of his way to make sure they knew that he knew more about basketball than they did. He was quick to point out that three of Cousy's teammates—George Kaftan, Dermie O'Connell, and Joe Mullaney—had failed to star in the NBA. Plus the Cooz was only six-foot-one, a small player even in 1950.

Just as Auerbach was doubtful about Cousy, the Cooz was skeptical about the NBA. "The NBA was not a big deal at the time," remembers Cousy. "Frank Oftring and myself had just opened a gas station and a driving school in conjunction with it. Kerner offered me seventy-five-hundred dollars. Even then, frankly, I felt if I couldn't earn that much doing whatever else I was doing after four fairly productive years in school, that something was wrong. It just wasn't that big a deal. I had never seen an NBA game. The NBA was Mickey Mouse. So none of us harbored it as a dream. Oftring and I had gone to a couple of banks to find out how we could best exploit our New England notoriety in the business world. Two of them happened to say, 'Gas stations are the way to go,' so I was focused on that. I was thinking in terms of staying in Worcester with my family and capitalizing on my local notoriety."

Unable to sign Cousy, Kerner traded his rights to Chicago.

"That was it," remembers Cousy. "I wasn't going to play pro ball. I went on teaching ladies to drive and pumping my gas."

Then the Chicago Stags folded. The NBA called a meeting in New York on October 5, to divy up the Chicago roster. At the end of the day, the three higher-priced players, Bob Cousy, Andy Phillip, and Max Zaslofsky, were available with the Knicks, Warriors, and Celtics still bidding. Auerbach wanted Zaslofsky. His second choice was Phillip. The team argued over the players and finally, Commissioner Maurice Podoloff borrowed a hat from Syracuse owner Danny Biasone (later famous as the man who invented the 24-second clock) and wrote the three names on separate slips of paper. The Celtics had the right to select first, but Walter Brown (typically too nice) told New York's Ned Irish to go ahead. The Knicks drew Zaslofsky. Philadelphia's Eddie Gottlieb picked second and got Phillip. Brown grabbed the paper with Cousy's name and dropped it on the floor. Tactless Auerbach made no attempt to hide his disgust, and New England fans were further outraged. Brown offered Cousy nine thousand dollars and Cousy signed.

Cooper is the third entry in this turnaround Celtic season, and his input was more symbolic than statistical. In the second round of the 1950 draft, moments after Cousy was bypassed and shortly after Kerner selected Cousy, Walter Brown selected Cooper. No black player had ever stepped on an NBA court before—or been drafted. Brown's selection opened the gates. The Washington Capitals selected Earl Lloyd of West Virginia State in the ninth round, and the Knicks suddenly were comfortable purchasing the contract of Nat "Sweetwater" Clifton from the Harlem Globetrotters. As it turned out, Lloyd beat Cooper and Clifton to the floor. Lloyd played for Washington in a 78–70 defeat on October 31, 1950, and holds the distinction of being the first black to play in the NBA. But it was Walter Brown and the Celtics who took the bold first step.

Auerbach, Cousy, and Cooper suffered an inauspicious debut when the Celtics were bombed, 107–84, in their opener at Fort Wayne. Boston lost its next two games, and there was plenty of reason to believe that another last-place season, one that might put the club out of business, was in store. Wrong. The Celts ripped off seven straight, ten of twelve, and challenged Philadelphia for first place. Easy Ed Macauley averaged 20.4 points per game, and the team finished with a 39–30 record before getting bounced from the play-offs by the Knicks. Attendance was up almost two thousand per game, and Brown's investment was slowly inching out of the red. This was also the year that the NBA played its first All Star game, and, fittingly, Walter Brown and the Boston Garden served as gracious hosts for the league's premier midseason spectacle.

Bob Cousy was born in New York City on East Eighty-third street on August 9, 1928. The place had no hot running water, and when young Bob was five, his family moved around the corner to better digs. His father was a cabdriver, and his mother was a stickler for cleanliness. Bob grew up on the East Side, and French was the only language spoken in the household. When the family moved to Queens, young Cousy started practicing basketball on the asphalt playgrounds of St. Albans. He was cut from the junior varsity squad at Andrew Jackson High School but found competition in nonschool leagues on Long Island. A right-hander, Cousy worked on ball-handling day and night and became very adept with his left hand. He was a starting player on the Andrew Jackson varsity by his junior year, and as a senior won the city scoring championship. He accepted a scholarship to Holy Cross and was on the second string when the Crusaders brought an NCAA (National Collegiate Athletic Association) crown to Worcester in 1947. At the Cross, Cousy learned to move without the ball. He was a little too much of a showboat for coach Julian, but the climate improved when Julian went to the Celtics and Buster Sheary came to Holy Cross. Sheary didn't mind Cousy's no-look passes or his keep-away dribbling. His arms were disproportionately long, and he could throw a basketball farther and faster than most human beings could. He could also dribble higher than most guards and still control the ball. He could shoot off balance and he could fire long, one-handed set shots off the wrong (left) foot. He was the best middleman on the fast break anyone had ever seen. No doubt a couple of behind-the-back passes wound up in the expensive seats at the Worcester Auditorium, but Cousy was a first-team All America in his senior year, the most celebrated college player in the land.

Auerbach didn't make things easy on Cousy when he arrived at the Celtics camp. Still stinging from media criticism, and ever stubborn, Auerbach announced that the kid would have to "make the team," just like every other rookie hopeful. The great Cooz was getting an audition, nothing more. The Holy

Cross hotshot and the crusty young coach were naturally suspicious of each other at the start, and Celtics players sensed a problem. Auerbach viewed Cousy as a threat to his authority and was intent on establishing that *he* was the dominant personality, *he* was the boss, not this fresh kid from Holy Cross.

"I just showed up," says Cousy. "Red's never changed. He was never one for formalities—always very direct. I don't remember him welcoming me or having much to say about anything, other than my T-shirt. At Holy Cross, we wore T-shirts under our uniforms. So here I come and here's Arnold saying, 'What the hell is that? Get your ass downstairs and get that thing off.' "

The kid from Holy Cross was a little cocky but hardly a sulky wiseguy with a star complex. He slung the ball around a little in his early practices, but when his passes started clanging off the hands of Macauley and Cooper, Auerbach took him aside and told him to make sure his passes were caught. The no-nonsense coach would put up with a little razzle-dazzle but not if it was going to cause turnovers. Deep down, Auerbach sensed that Cousy held the keys to some championship drives, but the coach wouldn't let the kid know it. He wasn't going to let anybody slide by on reputation. Like a father who leans hardest on his most talented son, Auerbach did everything he could to keep Cousy from degenerating into a spoiled superstar. This probably wouldn't wash with the José Cansecos and Brian Bosworths of the 1980s, but in the early 1950s the tough-guy tactics worked. Cousy became the model teammate, the definitive point guard, and the player who kept the Celtics afloat until Bill Russell arrived to bring them to the promised land. Cousy was Rookie of the Year in 1950–51 and finished ninth in the league in scoring, averaging 15.6 points per game.

From 1951 to 1956 the Celtics were in the waiting room: waiting for a big man, waiting for championships. The team was neither great nor awful. They were entertaining, but they still didn't draw the way Holy Cross was drawing. Basketball was starting to gain new respect in greater Boston. The city schools were playing the game again, and the Crusaders of Worcester were still drawing big crowds and winning. Togo Palazzi, Tom Heinsohn, and Ron Perry helped deliver an NIT (National Invitational Tournament) championship to the Cross in 1954. Auerbach's Celtics made the play-offs in each of the six seasons before Bill Russell arrived, and there was never a sub-.500 season. The Celtics averaged between five thousand five hundred and eight thousand fans per home game—a far cry from today's obligatory 14,890 but much better than the 3,608 average turnout of 1946–47. The team wasn't making any money for Walter Brown, but with consistent winning and the star power of Cousy, it was a nice additional attraction for the Garden's winter nights. Brown's fraternity brothers in the other NBA arenas were also pleased. Cousy and the Celtics were a fine road show.

During these years Auerbach sculpted the style and the substance that would bring a row of championship banners. Deals were made, players were acquired, and the Redhead polished the seven-play system. Players who came and went during this period certainly cared nothing about future championships, which would be delivered by a young man from the Bay Area, and indeed there was no consciousness that the Celtics were in a waiting period. They tried to win the championship every year, but they were just one great player away from being a championship-caliber ball club.

Cousy was the real thing. There was no doubt. But he needed a supporting cast. Auerbach started putting the pieces together when he bagged University of Southern California's Bill Sharman in 1951–52. Like so many Celtics past and present, Sharman was a two-sport star. Today Celtics fans remember Danny Ainge coming from the Toronto Blue Jays to join the Celtics, but there have been many others. K. C. Jones tried out with the Los Angeles Rams before wearing the Green, and John Havlicek played preseason games with the Cleveland Browns before joining the champion Celtics. Chuck Connors, the original Celtics center, pinch-hit for the Brooklyn

Dodgers and played first base for the Cubs *after* his Celtic days. And of course, Gene Conley played for the Red Sox and the Celtics simultaneously—something we thought only organist John Kiley could do.

There is no record of Bill Sharman in the *Baseball Encyclopedia*. He doesn't even get the abbreviated mention of Archibald "Moonlight" Graham (one game with the New York Giants in 1905, no at bats). Sharman was an outfielder in the Brooklyn Dodger system, playing in St. Paul when he was called up to the big leagues for the final month of the 1951 season. The Dodgers were holding on to a lead that had once been thirteen-and-a-half games and planned to look at some of their kids after they clinched. Of course, Brooklyn never clinched, and Carl Furillo, Duke Snider, and Andy Pafko played every day, as the Giants roared back into the race, winning on Bobby Thomson's "shot heard round the world." Sharman was on the Dodgers' bench when Thomson beat Ralph Branca, and that was the end of Bill Sharman's big-league career. Sharman would get his rings playing another game.

While Sharman was sitting on the bench with the Dodgers, Auerbach was holding his NBA rights. Sharman had been a two-sport star at USC and was the all-time Pacific Coast Conference scoring leader when he signed a bonus contract with the Dodgers. Meanwhile, Auerbach had traded Charlie Share's rights (yes, the same Charlie Share he chose over Cousy in 1950) to Fort Wayne for Gabby Harris, ten thousand dollars, and the proverbial player to be named later. Drafted by the Caps in 1950, Sharman started his pro basketball career with Washington, but the Caps folded and the shooting guard was awarded to Fort Wayne. Sharman had played thirty-one games for the Caps but never reported to the Pistons because he wanted to get his baseball career going. The Pistons, fearful that the kid would never return to basketball, made Sharman the player-to-be-named in the year-old Celtics deal. Sharman came to Boston late in the 1951 baseball season and went to the Arena to check out the team that held his rights. Auerbach watched the kid pop a few jumpers, offered him fourteen thousand dollars to join the Celtics, and waited for the baseball season to end. When the Giants won the pennant, the Celtics won Sharman, and Sharman and Cousy combined for forty-four points in Boston's opening-night victory over Indianapolis.

Sharman and Cousy roomed together for eight years, and on the basketball court they formed the most complete backcourt in the history of the sport. Auerbach hadn't drafted either player, but through luck and guile he was blessed with a Hall of Fame backcourt. The Celtics went 39–27 in their first year together, but the Knicks beat Boston in a three-game play-off.

The Celtics didn't win a play-off series until 1952–53, the seventh year of the franchise's existence. This team compiled a glossy record of 46–25, then swept the Syracuse Nationals, winning the clincher, 111–105, in four overtimes. This game is remembered for a fistfight between Syracuse star Dolph Schayes and Boston strongman Bob Brannum, plus a fifty-point effort by Cousy, who played sixty-six of the sixty-eight marathon minutes. Cousy made thirty of thirty-two free throws. Brannum and Schayes were ejected, and another twelve players were disqualified on fouls. A handful of those who fouled out were allowed to continue, enabling the Celts and Nats to keep five men on the floor. An extra free throw was awarded when a disqualified player committed a foul. Walter Brown was happy to see 11,058 in his Garden for this one, and some in attendance no doubt became fans for life. This was the kind of NBA play-off excitement that the Celtics needed to acquire a larger following in New England.

Fights were common.

Dolph Shayes: "The Celtics were a blood rival and in almost every game there was a fight. I think Red was an instigator. He'd tell them, 'Go knock him on his kiester,' and 'Don't let them lay it up,' and that kind of stuff. There was bad blood, but it was good, tough, hard-nosed basketball. They were definitely our big rival. The Celtics were more like the tough guys and our fans definitely wanted to beat them the most. [Jim] Loscutoff was an instigator. Our fans would start yelling from behind their bench, and he'd get up and yell at them, and before you knew it, they started throwing things. It could really get out of hand. Syracuse and Boston probably had more fights than anyone."

There was a carnival atmosphere to the early days of the NBA, and it wasn't unusual for players and coaches to mix it up with the fans. Cousy remembers this story of the night he got revenge in Philadelphia: "There's one in every city that sits in the same seat and is a vocal and loud fan. This guy was not only vocal and loud, he was obscene. He was just bad news. He sat directly behind the basket within six feet of the floor. I don't know how long we put up with him—maybe two or three years. The bench was also sort of kitty-corner from where he sat, within about twenty-five feet, so when you came out you had to listen to his garbage. Nichols and I—Jack Nichols—set this up one day. While we were warming up, Jack stood on the court, directly in front of the fan. This guy had already gotten started before the game had begun. I was shooting foul shots at the line, and, at a signal—we didn't know that this was going to work, but thank God it did—I just wound up and threw my fastball at Jack. Of course, Jack just stepped out of the way. It fortunately got our friend right smack on the nose. It happened so quickly that it couldn't knock him out, but it stunned him and blood started gushing out of his nose. We went over immediately and started commiserating and telling him wasn't that a shame? What possibly could have happened, what a terrible accident. It was quite a while afterward before he realized what had occurred, but I think in this case it was very justified retribution because we had put up with him for two or three or four years. It was one of the best passes I ever threw in a thirteen-year career."

The Knicks ended Boston's 1953 play-off success, beating the Celtics three games to one in the division finals. Syracuse got revenge in each of the next three seasons, eliminating the

Celtics in two games in 1954, four games in 1955, and three games in 1956.

It was during one of these springs that Walter Brown came up short on the play-off cash. "He was literally going from month to month and from year to year, and he asked us to wait before we took our play-off money," says Cousy. "We went to the other players and said, 'The guy's in trouble. Let's give him a break.' "

Simpler times. No players' association. No grievances. In 1990 it is unthinkable to suppose that the Sacramento Kings might cut ownership a break if the checks are late. Big money breeds distrust and greed. Brown operated on the honor system, and it was a two-way street.

Frank Ramsey, a Kentucky forward, was Boston's first-round draft pick in 1953, even though he had a year left to play for the Wildcats. Ramsey had been red-shirted for a year, and that meant 1953 was his graduating class and that made him eligible. Auerbach has always had a way of using the rule to his advantage, thinking of things that no one else thinks of. This was the type of thinking that would later yield players Paul Silas, Larry Bird, and Danny Ainge. In 1954 the Celtics welcomed Ramsey, and another piece was in place.

Ramsey: "Professional basketball was not a big thing back then. I knew that after college I had two years to spend in the service, so being drafted wasn't really important. I knew Red. I'd met him at the Catskill Mountains when all the country clubs had teams up there. Red was a coach, and I was a busboy. . . . He was a nice guy, demanding, about like Adolph Rupp. They both believed in fundamentals and that you played as a team to win."

The 1954–55 Celtics dipped to .500, easily the worst record of Auerbach's Boston career. There was grumbling. Walter Brown complained about the salaries he was paying Cousy, Sharman, and Macauley. Angered by public criticism, Cousy went on the radio in his Worcester hometown and said he wanted to be traded. The Celtics were scoring plenty of points, but they weren't getting enough rebounds. The 24-second clock had been introduced in 1954–55, and it was more difficult than ever to control the ball without a big man. In an age when shooting 40 percent was considered good, rebounding was more important than ever.

Celtic fans were still green (that's green, not Green) and most did not know what the problem was. The basketball team was starting to take on the look of the Red Sox: high salaries, big numbers, unhappy players, and too many second-place finishes. By 1985 the Boston Celtics stood as the antithesis of their baseball neighbors, but in 1956 they were establishing the same kind of bridesmaid legacy that made the Red Sox infamous.

Auerbach knew what the problem was. The Redhead had been coaching basketball as long as anyone in the league and was very aware of what was needed. After the final play-off loss to Syracuse in 1956, Auerbach told the *Globe*'s Jerry Nason, "Damn it. With the talent we've got on this ball club, if we can just come up with one big man to get us the ball, we'll win everything in sight."

The big man was winning NCAA championships for the University of San Francisco. Auerbach first heard about Bill Russell during the 1953–54 season, when Russell was a sophomore at USF. Bill Reinhart, Auerbach's coach at George Washington and a man who worshiped the fast break, told Auerbach to keep an eye on the San Francisco center. Russell's Dons stomped GW at a tournament in Oklahoma City. The big (six-foot-nine) kid wasn't much of a shooter, but he could do everything else. Auerbach made contact with Russell's coach, Phil Woolpert. Red also had West Coast friends watch the kid and report back to Boston. Pete Newell, Freddy Scolari, and Don Barksdale phoned in with reports of Russell's rebounding, his defense, and his toughness.

Cousy remembers, "As players, we had very little to do with the college game. Even with San Francisco winning back-to-back. We were aware they had won the NCAA, and we were aware there was a guy named Bill Russell who was good. The fact that he did his thing on the West Coast minimized our exposure to him. However, I do have a recollection of Arnold coming to me in, like, December of that year [1955] and saying, 'I think we're going to get a guy at center that's going to turn us around' or 'that's going to fill the void we have.' I remember he was certain that he was going to try to get Russell. At least he was planning to at that point. And that was at a time when the jury was out as to whether Russell was going to make it in the league. He couldn't hit a bull in the ass. He wasn't an offensive threat, and shot-blocking was not that popular then."

Unfortunately for Auerbach, everybody in the country knew about Russell by the time he was eligible to be drafted in 1956. San Francisco won fifty-five straight games and two NBA championships in 1955 and 1956, and Russell was one of the most coveted players in the nation. Auerbach didn't have a low draft pick so he had to do some dealing, and he started by calling his old friend Ben Kerner. It was Kerner who'd employed Auerbach at Tri-Cities in 1950, and it was Kerner who'd made a trade against the wishes of coach Auerbach. The Redhead was hoping he could persuade Kerner to make another bum deal, but this time it would be a deal that would guarantee Auerbach immortality. Kerner was owner of the St. Louis Hawks and had second pick in the 1956 draft. He needed players and drawing cards to keep the franchise going.

If Red was to get the second pick, he needed to know what Rochester was going to do with its number-one selection. It wouldn't make any sense to give up the farm for Kerner's pick, then watch Rochester select Russell. Brown was friendly with Rochester owner Les Harrison, and he called Harrison to find out what the Royals planned to do. The Royals were strong up front with Rookie of the Year Maurice Stokes and feared Russell's twenty-five-thousand-dollar contract demand (a demand the Globetrotters had said they were willing to meet). Brown gave them additional incentive to stay away from Russell. According to Harold Furash, the Needham Insurance

Broker who has been a Celtic insider for forty-four years, "Brown made a deal. If Lester passed up Russell, he would arrange for Lester to get the Ice Capades for Rochester two weeks a year under Lester's promotion. It was then that Lester bravely announced that he didn't want to wait for Russell to make his Olympic commitment. Of course, Lester made more money from the Ice Capades than he would have made with Russell."

Auerbach: "What happened was this. Walter got him the Ice Capades, and he felt indebted to Walter. He said, 'Look, you gave me the Ice Capades, I'll give you my word that we won't take Russell.' "

Done. Rochester planned to draft Duquesne guard Sihugo Green. The coast was clear. Auerbach called Kerner and offered All Star Macauley for the number-two pick. Macauley was from St. Louis and had starred at St. Louis University. Auerbach also told Kerner that Russell planned to play at the Melbourne Olympics, which meant he wouldn't be available until December. Kerner sensed that he could get more and asked for Cliff Hagan. Auerbach agreed and the deal was struck.

In his autobiography, Russell later wrote, "That must have been a phone call to listen to. Here were two guys who were sharp, rough and tough, and really hated each other."

Suspicious of another angle, NBA Hall of Famer Oscar Robertson says, "St. Louis did not want black guys on their team, so they traded Russell for Macauley and Hagan. That was the difference. Red saw that. There're very few guys who understand what it takes to win."

On April 20, 1956, the Boston Celtics announced that they'd selected Bill Russell with the second pick in the NBA draft. Sihugo Green would play nine NBA seasons, averaging 9.2 points per game. He would play for Rochester, Cincinnati, St. Louis, Chicago, and Baltimore before landing in Boston for his final ten games in 1966. Bill Russell would go on to become the greatest player in the history of the NBA.

4
The Green Giant

WILLIAM Felton Russell was born February 12, 1934, in Monroe, Louisiana, the son of Charlie and Katie Russell. Bill's father worked in a paper bag factory, his grandfather was a champion logroller with wiry hands, and his great-grandfather left Louisiana for Oklahoma in the 1880s and took the family tree with him. Young Bill liked to watch trains, and he liked to pull gags on the adults. After he became a world-famous athlete, Bill Russell wrote lovingly of playing hide-and-seek in tall grass with his father, mother, and brother, Charlie. In *Second Wind*, Russell wrote, "When it was time to go home, my father would reach down and pick me up under one arm, my brother under the other, lean down so my mother could crawl up his back, and then run all the way home, carrying his whole family as if we weighed nothing."

It is a beautiful picture of youth, family, and innocence. But Russell also remembered the bad part about growing up black in the South. He did not like the racism he saw in Louisiana, and he was glad when his father brought the family to the northern section of Oakland, California. He was nine. The family settled in a housing project by the Cole School, and that is where Russell first played basketball. His mother died when he was twelve, leaving his father to raise two sons alone. Charlie Russell worked at a foundry for forty dollars per week and did the best he could. Charlie Jr. went to predominantly white Oakland Tech, and Bill went to McClymonds, a school that was 95 percent black.

Russell quit the football team and was the sixteenth player on a sixteen-man junior varsity basketball team, sharing a uniform with another inept hopeful. One of Russell's teachers, George Powles, gave Russell two dollars to join the Boys Club, and Russell started playing basketball twice a day in pick-up scrimmages. He was hardly a natural. When he started playing the tall man's game he was tall—nothing more. He was six-foot-five, weighed 160 pounds, and was as fast as the wind. He started getting better, almost good enough to keep up with a star player like Frank Robinson. By senior year, Bill Russell was a starting player, and when Hal DeJulio saw him score fourteen points against Oakland High, DeJulio offered the skinny kid a basketball scholarship to the University of San Francisco. It wasn't the kind of free ride recruits get today, but it beat working in a San Francisco shipyard. At USF, Russell had to wash dishes and wait on tables in addition to playing basketball. The university had no basketball reputation, but neither did Russell. His college roommate was K. C. Jones. His coach was Phil Woolpert. The Dons had no gym, no home court. They were the "Homeless Dons." Homeless, but hardly hopeless. They lost to Willie Naulls and UCLA early in their junior year, then ripped off twenty-six straight games to win the NCAA title.

K. C. Jones: "The first time I saw Russell was in the summer in the coach's office. We were there to go out and get a job. The coach introduced us and told us where to go to get a job, so we were walking down the street to get the streetcar. I wanted to walk on the other side. I was totally overwhelmed with this guy's height. I kept looking at the other side of the street. I just wanted to get to the other side. From there, we became roommates. He was an amazingly astute intellectual. And all I'd say was 'breakfast.' He just read and read and read. He never attended class that much, or paid much attention to it, but he got Bs. He was a loner. He chose you, you didn't choose him. He intimidates people. Russell is one of the most honest people you'll ever come across, almost to a fault, maybe to a fault. He's loyal and [he's] a psychologist. By the by, we became close, close, close."

At USF Russell also went out for track, and he high-jumped against Charlie Dumas and a San Francisco State student named Johnny Mathis. During the summer between his junior and senior years, he got a call from the university and was told that he had a letter from the White House. Russell initially didn't have the $1.50 needed for gas and tolls to get over the Bay Bridge and back, but three days later he drove to school and received his presidential invitation from Dwight D. Eisenhower. The president was hosting a physical fitness meeting and wanted Russell to represent college basketball. Gene Tunney, Ford Frick, Willie Mays, Hank Greenberg, and Bob Cousy were other invitees. Russell got some expense cash from USF and drove cross-country with his dad, his step-mother, and his wife-to-be, Rose Swisher. He met the president. His next trip east was in December, when the Dons won the Holiday Festival at Madison Square Garden. Among those getting their first look at Russell was Arnold Auerbach, who was also there to watch Holy Cross hotshot Tom Heinsohn.

"I didn't particularly have a good introduction to Red," says Heinsohn. "When I was playing at Holy Cross he was quoted in the papers saying I would not be able to make it and that I was too heavy and all that other jazz. I almost went to play for the Peoria Caterpillars. Anyway, in that game [against USF] we were up, and then I picked up the third foul guarding Russell, and we had to put another big guy in, and they ended

up demolishing us. He started blocking shots in the second
half. I mean, he really showed me something."

San Francisco beat Holy Cross, 67–51, and Russell scored
twenty-four with twenty-two rebounds. Heinsohn scored
twelve. The Dons won the tournament and every other game
they played that year. Twenty-nine–zero. Fifty-five straight.
Two NCAA championships.

Russell wanted nothing to do with the Harlem Globetrotters.
He was a proud young black man, never a clown. Word leaked
out that the Trotters would offer Russell fifty thousand dollars,
but the offer turned out to be seventeen thousand. Trotter
guru Abe Saberstein negotiated with Woolpert, and Russell
was insulted that the Trotter czar didn't think he was capable
of speaking for himself. Rochester wasn't appealing either,
and Russell took himself out of contention by asking for
twenty-five thousand. He did not know that Red Auerbach
and Celtics owner Walter Brown had paid off Rochester owner
Les Harrison by promising him the Ice Capades.

Draft day arrived. Russell was selected by the Celtics but
could not negotiate until he honored his Olympic commitment.
He went to Melbourne, won the gold (was there any doubt?),
came home, married Rose at the Taylor Methodist Church,
honeymooned for a week in Carmel, and joined the Celtics in
December 1956.

It was cold and slushy when Bill Russell first arrived in
Boston. Like Bob Cousy before him and John Havlicek after
him, he could hardly be impressed with the dingy Garden, the
laughable locker room, and the small-time Celtic organization.
He went to Walter Brown's office and signed for $19,500. He
took a pay cut because of the Olympic time he'd missed, but
Auerbach promised him that he would never discuss statistics
when negotiating future contracts. It was a promise that would
be unthinkable with any athlete today, but it was one Auerbach
kept. As long as Walter Brown was alive, Brown would ask
Russell how much he wanted, Russell would submit a figure,

and the contract deal would be struck. Frank Ramsey was so comfortable with Brown that he'd send the owner a *signed* contract and have Walter Brown fill in the amount. Try doing that with Donald Sterling.

Russell came to Boston with an attitude, and he left with the same attitude. He had a chip on his shoulder—a chip the size of Rhode Island. He never worried about being liked; he wanted to be respected. That was it. He would not play the fool, and people would just have to learn to live with him or lose him. He grew a goatee, something associated with beatniks. He was not keen on signing autographs. He did not have a warm personality, and fans in particular found it impossible to embrace the star center. He could be aloof or downright hostile. He was the only black man on the team when he arrived, and the lessons of Monroe, Louisiana, were always in his mind. He was totally uncompromising. Russell was never comfortable with Boston and its people. In *Second Wind*, in 1979, he wrote, "To me, Boston itself was a flea market of racism. . . . If Paul Revere were riding today, it would be for racism: 'The niggers are coming! The niggers are coming!' he'd yell as he galloped through town to warn neighborhoods of busing and black homeowners."

The 1956–57 Celtics were 16–8, resting in first place when Russell joined the team. It was two weeks after Larry Joe Bird was born in French Lick, Indiana. Rookie Heinsohn was doing a terrific job at forward, Cousy and Ramsey had it going in the backcourt, and Arnie Risen and Jack Nichols were doing reasonably well alternating in the middle.

Auerbach remembers, "A lot of people were not that high on Russell. I could name you some top basketball people. Ike Ellis, the sports editor of the [New York] *Post*—he didn't think Russell would really make it. He'd compare him to [Walter] Dukes. He figured he couldn't shoot as good as Dukes, and Dukes is about two inches bigger, and he's just about making it. Why would Russell make it, he can't shoot?"

"There wasn't much thinking about Russell being a great

player, I'll tell you that," says Heinsohn. "When he showed up nobody quite knew what to make of him. He was cocky in a way. He came in the middle of the season, and he was a strange guy. Roles had been developed, and he had to prove himself. He hadn't been to training camp or anything else. It wasn't that anybody was afraid of him. But very quickly, after a couple of games, everybody on the whole team could see what this guy could do. And what he could mean to the team. Off the court, he was just trying to feel his way around, you know. Get the lay of the land in Boston."

On December 22, Russell made his NBA debut in a nationally televised game against the St. Louis Hawks. Auerbach had the rookie on the bench at the beginning of the game but sent him in after five minutes of play. The Celts trailed by sixteen in the fourth period, but won by two on Sharman's jumper at the buzzer. Russell scored six with sixteen rebounds in twenty-one minutes. He also blocked three of Bob Pettit's shots during the crunch-time comeback.

Cousy says, "I think from the very first game—I don't remember that we developed this impression in practice probably because rebounding and shot-blocking you wouldn't notice in practice and Russell was never a good practice player—we came out of that game saying 'Uh-oh, we may have something.' We were already in first place in the league, but even being in first place, we didn't have the rebounder. I remember coming out of that St. Louis game thinking, 'Boy, we got a shot at doing something.' "

Later in the month, in Kiel Auditorium in St. Louis, Russell heard racial slurs from the crowd. He later wrote, "If one could query at what moment the string of world championships of the Boston Celtics was born, that would be the one moment that crystallizes in my memory."

Name another athlete who could use some incidental, ignorant hazing as a driving force for thirteen years. Russell stands alone.

The NBA had seen nothing like him. Just as Cousy brought

a new dimension to ball movement, Russell changed the game with his defense and rebounding. Opponents were forced to think about him every time they shot. He could jump, and he had an incredible sense of timing. This was something he had been studying since his days as an awkward teen at McClymonds. Because of his quickness and his smarts, he could stand several feet away from the man he was guarding and still steal the ball or block the shot. After NBA players got a load of this, intimidation came into play. People started thinking about Russell when they drove into the lane. His teammates could lay off, not worry about being beaten, funnel opponents into the middle, then sneak toward the other end of the floor. Russell was smart enough to control his blocks. He had a huge ego but would not compromise the objective to satisfy it. He didn't need the gratification of swatting a shot into the nickel seats—he'd control the ball and dish it to the wing where Cousy, Sharman, Ramsey, and Heinsohn were ready to take flight. This was the beginning of transition basketball. Boston's new center was also smart enough to save some of his block opportunities. He knew which shots to go after, and he usually got them.

Russell's rebounding prowess enabled the Celtics to control the ball at both ends of the court. And he could run. Running was something all of the Russells could do. His brother was a 10.4 sprinter, and Russell liked to tell of the time his father outsprinted his brother while wearing heavy work shoes. With Russell in the middle, the Celtics could play forty-eight minutes of aggressive defense and up-tempo offense. No one could possibly keep up. Russell was the first legitimate big man who could also run. He was what today we would call a "modern" player. Prior to Russell, NBA pivotmen were heavy-legged giants who stood under the basket and scored the points. Remember the chief in *One Flew Over the Cuckoo's Nest?* The chief could stand under the hoop, catch a pass, and drop the ball through the basket. Then he'd lumber down to the other end of the floor. Such was NBA pivot-play prior to 1956.

Russell was different. Russell could change a game even though he couldn't shoot. The only shot he had any confidence in was the dunk shot. He was not comfortable handling the ball, but he knew enough to keep it off the floor. He had fairly soft hands, could shoot a little hook, and could make more of his free throws than rival Wilt Chamberlain. In traffic, he could pass a little. His outlet passing was better than anyone's. Best of all, he knew his offensive limitations. He never took bad shots.

He wasted no energy. He wouldn't dunk during warm-ups—those points didn't count. He *walked* to the center of the floor when he was introduced with the other starters. It was an energy-conserving measure, and he knew it annoyed people. Russell enjoyed making fans uncomfortable, even his own fans. He didn't like to practice and often just went through the motions. But Bill Russell brought immense abilities and a great, rare sense of selflessness to the Celtics. During these years the Celtics would be the championship team that would never have a scoring champion. They kept running the same seven plays (with twenty-eight options) but fell back on that one big play—the fast-break lay-up. Russell was the rebounder, Cousy the passer, Sharman the foul shooter, Heinsohn the shooter, Ramsey the sixth man, Jim Loscutoff the bully, and Auerbach the coach. Players fulfilled roles, and if everybody did his job, the team would win. Auerbach assembled the proper parts, and Russell, of course, was the final ingredient to put the Celtics in the winner's circle.

"Russell totally disrupted everything in the other team's offense," says Heinsohn. "He made teams change their style of play. He took the low post away by himself. Everybody was playing low-post basketball. He was quick enough to play the guy he was guarding, then he'd be there if you gambled on your guy, and he got by you."

Auerbach was ahead of his peers because he had a team that could run, and he kept them in shape. The Celtics worked harder than other teams to get into shape, and this was always handy at the start of the season. Through the years, much of the Celtics success can be attributed to the simple fact that people like Russell, Cowens, and Havlicek were simply better endurance runners than their contemporaries. It took a while for the rest of the league to gain awareness of this, but in the 1970s, 1980s, and 1990s few teams win simply because they are in better shape than their rivals. The age of conditioning is upon us, and this might be one of the equalizers that explains why there are no more dynasties.

The Celtics never put Russell through the rookie hazing that has plagued everyone from Bob Cousy to Reggie Lewis. Russell didn't have to carry bags, get Cokes or coffee for the veterans, or pay cabdrivers. In one rookie initiation ritual, the team comes out for warm-ups and lets the rookie take the ball and lead them onto the floor. Hearing the introduction, the kid bursts out onto the floor while the rest of the team stands behind the curtain and laughs. Russell wasn't required to submit to these rites of passage. Nor was he ever one of Auerbach's whipping boys. Heinsohn was a perfect substitute in this case; Heinsohn was a rookie the same year as Russell, and he was the kind of player Auerbach loved to ride. Heinsohn needed to have a coach on his back, and he could also take it.

Russell took an immediate liking to Bill Sharman and Arnie Risen. Risen was the starting center but generously helped Russell along, knowing full well the kid was going to take his job. But there was no closeness between Russell and his other teammates. And if you read biographies of Russell, Cousy, Heinsohn, K. C. Jones, and Auerbach, it's clear that togetherness is not necessarily a component of a winning basketball team. The Celtics played well on the court. Away from the floor, they often went in separate directions.

No one was entirely comfortable with Russell when he burst on the scene just before Christmas in 1956, but it became clear that he was going to be the man to take the Celtics to the title. He belonged.

"They had built up tremendous frustrations by the time I

got there," says Heinsohn. "Cousy was so damn competitive. They needed rebounding. That team, when Russell and I showed up and then we got K. C. Jones in the same draft, had a young nucleus to go with experienced veterans. That's what always happened. It was push-pull. The younger players would push the older players, and the older players would pull the younger ones. And the nucleus of the team, Russell and Sam and K. C. and me, lasted a long time. Throw Cousy in there, and that was the nucleus of the team."

The Celtics averaged over ten thousand fans in Russell's first five games. Russell inhaled thirty-four rebounds in his fourth pro game. Boston finished 44–28 and wiped out Syracuse in three games to move into the championship finals for the first time. The Celtics enjoyed home-court advantage against St. Louis, and it turned out to be an important edge when the series was tied 3–3 after six games. There were a number of thrills in the first six games, but there could be no better moment than when Auerbach punched Hawks owner Ben Kerner before the start of Game 3 in St. Louis. Remember, these were two men who'd once been on the same side and who one year earlier orchestrated the trade that brought Russell to Boston. As a youth, Auerbach learned it's best to hit before the other guy hits you; the philosophy has served him well through the years.

On the Saturday afternoon of April 13, 1957, the Celtics and Hawks met to decide the world championship. There are some old-timers who'll tell you that this game solidified the NBA as a big-league sport in America. Sharman and Cousy made only five of forty shots, but rookie Heinsohn scored thirty-seven with twenty-three rebounds before fouling out. Russell scored nineteen with thirty-two rebounds and five blocked shots as the Celts won, 125–123, in double-overtime. During the final minute of regulation time, with St. Louis's Jack Coleman driving for a lay-up that would have given the Hawks a three-point lead, Russell beat everyone down the floor to block the shot.

Thirty-three years later, Heinsohn says, "The greatest play I ever saw in basketball was Russell blocking Coleman's shot. That sumbitch went by me like I was standing still, and I was near midcourt. He was the fastest man on the team."

The Hawks had a chance to send the game into a third overtime. Trailing by two with one second left, player-coach Alex Hannum, on an in-bounds play, heaved the ball the length of the floor, off the backboard, and into the hands of star forward Bob Pettit (thirty-nine points, nineteen rebounds). Pettit's shot clanged off the rim, and Russell and Loscutoff carried Auerbach off on their shoulders as many of the 13,909 fans flooded the Garden parquet. Teammates shaved Russell's goatee in the shower room, drank beer, and awaited their play-off shares of $1,681 per man.

It was a triumphant day for all the Celtics veterans who'd struggled through the formative years. Cousy, the man who rescued the franchise, finally had a ring. Auerbach had his first title after performing as the NBA's best coach for eleven seasons. For Russell, it was his third crown (NCAA, Olympic, and NBA) in thirteen months. But Walter Brown had to be the happiest man in the Boston Garden that day. Brown was the man who sold his house and hocked his furniture because he believed in the dream of professional basketball in Boston. And now he was the proud owner of the finest team in the country. The city of Boston hadn't had a champion since the Bruins won the Stanley Cup in 1941. The Red Sox hadn't won a championship since 1918. And now a team with the likable name of Celtics wore championship rings.

The Celtics were good, but that weekend in April 1957 there could be no way of knowing what was in store. In Boston, you did not think in terms of dynasties. Fans were happy with a championship a decade. No one could have predicted that the Celtics and their fans were in for the greatest ride in the history of professional sports.

But the players knew it was going to be good for a while. "Once we won the first time," says Cousy. "We were so certain that nobody would beat us. That, I guess, added to our ability to function. We had this inner confidence."

In the euphoric aftermath of championship number one, Auerbach immediately started plotting the future. Cousy and Sharman were in their prime, but Boston would need guard help before too long. When it came time to draft, the Celtics selected Sam Jones from North Carolina College. Seven teams skipped over Jones and chose immortals named Charles Tyra, Jim Krebs, Win Wilfong, Brendan McCann, Len Rosenbluth, and George BonSalle. Sam Jones was a slippery guard who liked to bank shots off the glass. Nobody had heard of him or his school, but Auerbach took the advice of former Celtic Bones McKinney (then a Wake Forest coach) and hoped he was getting some backcourt insurance for the future. These were years when Auerbach would keep the Celtics on top with draft selections and by picking up players with cash or through waivers. He was through trading for a while. In the thirteen years Russell played with the Celtics, Auerbach made only one player-for-player trade—Mel Counts for Bailey Howell. Sam Jones wasn't going to unseat Cousy or Sharman, but his day would come, and when it did, he would be ready.

The Celtics did not successfully defend their crown in 1957–58. They won their first fourteen games but lost Loscutoff to a knee injury early in the season. The Celtics again had the best regular season record (49–23) and beat the Warriors in five games to cruise into the finals, but Russell turned his ankle blocking a Pettit shot in the third minute of the third game of the finals against St. Louis. Adding insult to injury, Russell was called for goaltending on the play. He didn't play the next two games and was limited to eight points in twenty minutes of hobbling action in the finale, a 110–109 loss that turned the title over to St. Louis. Pettit scored fifty for the winners.

Dolph Schayes remembers, "It became apparent that Russell, with the blocked shots, and then with Cousy and Sharman and Heinsohn [and] Frank Ramsey, it became obvious that that team was going to be very difficult to beat. But the dominance wasn't apparent because St. Louis beat them, and we took them to seven games in 1959. So they weren't the dominant factor at that time."

This was a season when Russell was named Most Valuable Player, averaging 22.7 rebounds in his first full NBA campaign. It was not a bad year for a young man who'd had to share a uniform jersey for the sixteenth spot on his junior high basketball team. Starters Russell, Heinsohn, Ramsey, Cousy, and Sharman all averaged between sixteen and twenty-two points per game, and Cousy led the league in assists. They won more games than any team, but they were not champions. They were eliminated by the land mine that wounded many defending champs in future decades. It would have been easy to dismiss them as one-time wonders who would retreat to the role of runners-up. They had won one championship, then failed to repeat. They were like everybody else.

But not for long. There were some changes after the 1958 play-off loss, and the final pieces were being set in place. Arnie Risen, Jack Nichols, and Andy Phillip retired after the team breakup dinner, but there were some capable people waiting to take their places. In the fall of 1958, Auerbach had a pair of new players: K. C. Jones and Gene Conley. Jones was Russell's teammate/soulmate from the University of San Francisco who'd been drafted along with Russell and Heinsohn in 1956 (has any team in any sport ever drafted three Hall of Famers in the same season?). K. C. was Russell's roommate at USF, a fellow NCAA and Olympic champ. He was silent and wouldn't shoot the ball, but he was an exceptional defensive backcourtman and always seemed to be around when the championship trophies were handed out. After USF, he served in the army and got an invite from then-General Manager Pete Rozelle to try out for the Los Angeles Rams. Jones played defensive back in some preseason games but didn't like the NFL (National Football League) philosophy of playing with injuries. He called Auerbach to see if the Celts were still interested. Auerbach was interested. Cousy and Sharman were getting a little long in the tooth, and Sam Jones wouldn't be able to do it alone. Jones's Celtics teammates noticed that he liked to watch television all the time; they dubbed him "Square eyes."

When K. C. arrived at rookie camp, he befriended a twelve-year-old Jewish kid whose dad owned the campground. Years later, Jan Volk would be K. C. Jones's boss, but in 1958 they were just an odd couple, friends from the start. "I was just a kid and he was a grown-up," Volk says. "But he was a grown-up who was nice to kids. I also got to know Sam Jones. He also worked there. Sam was a quasi-grown-up. Sam had more fun than the kids. He had a wonderful time. He related to kids very well."

Conley was rare, even among two-sport stars. He was six-foot-eight, and he was the only man to win championship rings in two major sports. He was also the only player to star on two sports teams in the same city—and he did it twice. After going 0–3 for the Boston Braves in 1952, he joined the Celtics on the recommendation of Sharman, who had played against Conley in the minors and in the Pac Ten. When Conley was at triple-A with Toledo, and Sharman was at triple-A with St. Paul, Conley faced the University of Southern California hotshot and struck him out on a curveball. They remembered each other, and Sharman sent Conley to see Red. Conley signed for four thousand five hundred dollars and played thirty-nine games for Auerbach in 1952–53. He quit the Celtics to go into baseball full time and pitched in the 1957 World Series for the champion Milwaukee Braves. He did not pitch in the 1958 World Series when the Yankees beat the Braves, but he was in camp with the Celtics ready to take his place as Russell's backup. He went 12–7 and was an All Star with the Phillies in 1959. He was still with the Celtics in the spring of 1961 and went 11–14 for the Red Sox that summer. He won ninety-one major-league games and hit five career big-league home runs, three more than Toronto infielder Danny Ainge.

A proven All Star baseball player, Conley had some leverage when the Celtics came calling the second time. He remembers his salary negotiation going like this: "I came in to talk contract with him [Walter Brown] in 1958. I'd made the team. I'd already played a few years of baseball and made a couple All Star teams, and I said, 'Well, Mr. Brown, how about twenty thousand dollars?' And he said, 'Sure, fine.' Well, the season started, and after we played three or four games Red must have got ahold of the contract. He called me up and said, 'Conley, what'd you do to Mr. Brown?' I said, 'What do you mean?' He said, 'We can't afford to pay you that kind of money.' Well, he'd asked me what I wanted, and I didn't just get off a cabbage truck, you know. So then Red said, 'Well, Ben Swain and K. C. Jones are playing good ball, and I'm afraid I'm going to have to let you go.' And he did let me go! And about four or five days later the phone rang and Red said, 'You know, we might find an opening for you.' I said that would be terrific, and he said, 'The only thing is you got to take half your pay.' I said, 'OK.' "

Conley was no Bo Jackson, but he didn't get any time off, either. In the late 1950s and early 1960s, there was little of today's sports overlap, and Conley was usually able to play almost the full season for both teams.

"In the springtime, I'd bring my glove on Celtic road trips, but I had to hide it from Red," says Conley. "I'd get Ramsey to throw with me. One time we were throwing in the gym, hours before practice, but Red came in and started hollering at us. He told me to stick those baseball gloves up my ass. Trying to do both [sports] definitely hurt my baseball career. With no spring training, I'd rush into baseball games before I was ready, and it definitely hurt my arm."

The defensive back from the Rams and the pitcher from the Braves were ready to step into reserve roles for the 1958–59 season. Russell's ankle was healed and Loscutoff's knee was healed and Sharman, Cousy, Ramsey, Heinsohn, and Sam Jones were ready. The pieces were in place for the greatest dynasty in the history of professional sports.

5
The Greening of America

FROM 1958 to 1966, the Celtics played eight NBA seasons and won eight NBA championships. This was the era that produced the common catch phrases "Celtic pride" and "Celtic mystique." Extract this eight-year dynasty and the Celtics are just another very good franchise no different from the Baltimore Orioles, the Miami Dolphins, or the Los Angeles Lakers. The eight straight titles elevated the Boston basketball team to the top of the professional heap—above the Dallas Cowboys, Montreal Canadiens, and New York Yankees. Eight straight world championships hadn't been done before or since, and it's safe to state that it will never be done again. It is the 1990s and sports is moving toward parity. Television, money, free agency, injuries, complacency, and fatheads derail today's budding dynasties. If you win two in a row, you are the team of the decade.

The timing of Boston's dynasty served further to embellish the feat. The Celtics were the top team (for all practical purposes, the *only* team in the NBA) during the period when the league evolved from a bush league to a major league. The Celtics' reign spanned the dull years of Dwight D. Eisenhower, Kennedy's New Frontier, and all the way into LBJ's Great Society. Baby Boomers came of age during these yeas. Across America, the Boston Celtics were the symbol of dominance and excellence. Just as Bob Cousy was the pro game's first household name, Russell became the model for high school coaches across the land: Get your kids to play like Russell and they'll win like the Celtics win. The Celtics were the only basketball team on the planet.

They had their own traditions, their own look. The Celtics wore black high-tops so everybody wore black high-tops.

"That wasn't by design," says Cousy. "It was by accident. We just held on to 'em, I don't know for what reason. Maybe it was connected with some kind of superstition, but if that's the case, I was never aware of it."

"I got mad at Converse," explains Auerbach. "Of course, I got mad at a lot of people in those days. I was fightin' all the time on everything that I believed in. I found out that some teams were getting their shoes for nothing, and here was Converse right in our backyard charging us for shoes. This was before players had their own deals. So I got mad at them. Nothing to me looked worse than a canvas, white shoe that was dirty. So I figured, rather than go out there with dirty-looking shoes—we couldn't afford to change them like they do today—I figured if we had black shoes [they] wouldn't show the dirt, and that's the reason we wore black shoes."

Everybody wanted to be like Bob Cousy, "Mr. Basketball." Cousy's name was synonymous with the Celtics before the Celtics became international ambassadors of the sport. There were other Celtics trademarks. Russell threw up before every big game; this was more tradition than superstition—certainly more physical than spiritual. The Celtics went out West every February when the ice show came to the Garden. They always played a midweek day game during spring vacation. They never once sold out their home opener. Sellouts were reserved for select play-off games, and a Celtic sellout was 13,909, never more, never less. They'd pack eighteen-thousand people in and announce 13,909. Fire laws, you know. At the end of warm-ups, one Celtic would stay behind and make a couple of baskets. Jim Loscutoff first did this, and John Havlicek inherited the job in his rookie year.

"That was a kind of a superstition," admits Auerbach. "I always liked the last shot to go in before they came to the bench. I used to go crazy if a guy threw a ball and missed it or if a ballboy took a shot at our basket while we were going over to get ready for the introductions."

Havlicek says, "Loscutoff had been doing it and he said he was tired of doing it and that I was designated to do it. It didn't matter who did it as long as the last two shots were made. I continued to do it until I retired. When they had those giveaways and they'd give out basketballs, people would be firing them from all over the place. One time I'd taken my two shots and someone fired one in from the stands and I had to go out and take 'em again. Then they did it *again*, and this scene went on two or three times."

The players dressed like winners. Auerbach instituted a jacket-and-tie rule on the road, but after a time the players enforced it themselves. When you joined the Celtics you joined the family, and you lived by the family's rules.

In this world there are only a handful of former professional athletes who have trouble remembering specific details about a championship season. But when you win eight championships in eight years, they begin to blend together. *Let's see, was it the Warriors or the Lakers in 1964? And were they in Phil-adelphia or San Francisco? Which year did Havlicek steal the ball? Did Havlicek play on the same team with Cousy?*

This brain clutter doesn't exist with other professional ath-letes. It's safe to say that Elvin Hayes knows precisely where he was when he won his one and only NBA title. Ditto for

Julius Erving. Only the Boston Celtics have trouble isolating championship moments. These are the guys with more rings than Zsa Zsa Gabor.

"I don't know one from the other," Auerbach says. "I have to look it up if anybody asks me. . . . I had no 'best team.' They would change from year to year. When I had Cousy, Sharman, Ramsey, and Phillip, it was a great backcourt, then I had Cousy, Sharman, the Jones boys, and Ramsey, which was a great, *great* team. But then, when Cousy retired, Sharman retired, then I had the Jones boys and Havlicek instead of Ramsey."

Boston Globe reporter John Powers grew up with the championship Celtics. In his book, *The Short Season,* Powers wrote, "There were always tickets. While the losing Bruins filled the Garden, nearly 13,909 every night, the building was rarely more than half full for the Celtics. How many times did you need to be reassured, after all? I would rifle through the *Globe* to check the score—Boston 143, Chicago 99, eight Celtics in double figures—and nod, satisfied, like a Brahmin millionaire glancing at the financial pages. Yes, yes, very nice indeed."

This is the way it was. The streak started during the peacetime Happy Days of the late 1950s, when America was a nation of ponytails, bobby socks, Sunday barbecues, and two-car garages. The streak ended during the 1967 Summer of Love, when Hippies were protesting a senseless war. Celtics fans expected a championship every year. Every year, they got one.

1958-59

Soviet author Boris Pasternak finishes *Doctor Zhivago* and wins a Nobel Prize for literature. Pope John XXIII succeeds

Pope Pius XII. Elizabeth Taylor stars in *Cat on a Hot Tin Roof*. Fidel Castro's forces conquer Cuba. Charles de Gaulle takes over as president of France. Alaska becomes the forty-ninth state. Buddy Holly, Richie Valens, and the Big Bopper die in a plane crash in Mason City, Iowa. On April 9, 1959, Frank Lloyd Wright dies, and the Boston Celtics win the NBA championship with a 118–113 victory over the Minneapolis Lakers.

The Celtics roared out of the blocks and owned a 23–9 record by the first of the new year. The Celtics deflated the opposition before Christmas; they did it with their conditioning as well as with their talent.

They scored 173 points in a single game against the Lakers in February and won a league-record fifty-two games, averaging a record 116.4 points during the regular season. Cousy led the league in assists for the eighth straight year, Russell led in rebounds, and four Celtics (Sharman, Cousy, Heinsohn, and Russell) ranked among the top fifteen scorers. The Celtics drew Syracuse in the division finals and had to go seven games to get to the finals. Boston trailed by sixteen in the seventh game at the Garden and lost Russell on fouls in the fourth period. Conley played the game of his life, and Boston won, 130–125. The final series was anticlimactic. Ramsey scored twenty-nine in twenty-seven minutes of the opener, while only 8,195 fans watched at the Garden. Sharman extended his free-throw string to fifty in Game 2. Cousy scored twenty-three with fifteen assists in Game 3. The Celtics won Game 4 in Minneapolis, and Heinsohn, Loscutoff, and K. C. Jones carried Auerbach off the floor. The Celts became the first team in NBA history to sweep a final and extended their winning streak against the Lakers to twenty-two games. "We set a lot of records this year," crowed Auerbach. "And some may be broken, but that one won't be—winning the championship in four games."

This was an important championship. After winning in 1957 and losing in 1958, the Celtics had to win another title to get back on track. They knew they had the best team, and to come away with anything less than a championship might have stripped them of the cocky, winning attitude that carried them through the next decade.

1959-60

Vice President Richard Nixon and Soviet Premier Nikita Khrushchev argue while standing in a kitchen exhibit at the American National Exhibition in Moscow. Hawaii is proclaimed our fiftieth state. The Guggenheim Museum opens in New York. Ford dumps the Edsel. Charlton Heston stars in *Ben Hur*. Bobby Darin sings "Mac the Knife." Americans watch "The Many Loves of Dobie Gillis," Tuesdays at 8:30 on CBS. John F. Kennedy announces he will seek the presidency. Ebbets Field is demolished. On April 9, 1960, South African Prime Minister Hendrik F. Verwoerd is shot and wounded in an assassination attempt. That same day, the Boston Celtics defeat the St. Louis Hawks, 122–103, to win their second consecutive World Championship, four games to three.

The hot NBA story in the fall of 1959 was the unveiling of seven-foot-one center Wilt Chamberlain. This was Goliath come to life, and the day he arrived he was already the strongest and most dominant player in the league. He was nothing less than a circus freak, a giant who would ruin the game for everybody else. It was predicted that his presence would disrupt the balance of power in the NBA. The game wouldn't be fair anymore. Instead, Bill Russell became the Chamberlain antidote. Chamberlain's first meeting with Russell was November 7, 1959, at the Garden. Both teams were undefeated. "Wilt the Stilt" outscored Russell, 30–22, but Russell had more

rebounds, 35–28, and, typically, the Celtics won, 115–105. A
pattern was established.

Cousy says, "I don't remember the specifics, but I do remember we won the game, and it was obvious that if [Russell]
was not going to be able to neutralize Chamberlain, Chamberlain was not going to be able to dominate us. He might
have dominated many of the other teams. Chamberlain developed that fall-away bank shot because he didn't want to
take it in against Russell, and that was his least-effective
weapon because once he took the shot, he was out of the play.
I don't think he ever dominated the series in such a way that
we felt threatened. We always felt that any time Russell
wanted to dig in on him, he could neutralize him enough so
that we could win the game. We had respect for Wilt's
strength—I mean, Christ, he was the strongest man in the
world it seemed like at the time—but he didn't utilize that
strength against us because Russell got into his mind early."

Chamberlain averaged 37.6 points and twenty-seven rebounds in his rookie season with Philadelphia. These are eye-
popping numbers by any yardstick. The first-year center was
named Most Valuable Player and first-team all-NBA center.
But thanks to Russell, the Celts refused to cower, and they
went about their business, winning eleven of their first twelve
games and ripping off seventeen straight (tying a record set
by Auerbach's Washington Caps) during the holiday season.
Boston finished 59–16; again, the best record in the young
history of the league. Boston's whopping scoring average of
124.5 was another record in this year of runaway offense.
Russell's Celtics met Chamberlains's Warriors in the Eastern
finals, and Boston took the series in six games, a scenario that
would torture Chamberlain for the rest of his career.

Heinsohn and Chamberlain scuffled during Game 2, and
Chamberlain hurt his hand with a wild swing intended for
Heinsohn.

"We were running all the time," says Heinsohn. "We were
running off made free throws. We'd get it in quickly to Cousy.

Russell would take off and beat Chamberlain down the court for a lay-up. Finally, Chamberlain started to catch on. We get to the play-offs, and Red says, 'That play isn't working anymore. We got to make it work. Somebody's got to get in Chamberlain's way. Tommy, you got to step in front of Chamberlain.' I said, 'Fuck you, Red. Put Ramsey in there.' He said, 'No Ramsey can't.' So I was elected to get in Chamberlain's way. I did, and Chamberlain started getting pissed at me. There was a foul shot made, and he's trying to get to Russell, and I'm standing in his way, picking him off. He said, 'You do that again, and I'm going to knock you on your ass,' and I said, 'Bring your lunch.' Sure as hell, he knocked me on my ass the next time and came storming at me as I lay on the floor. As I started to get up, Tom Gola came in between us. Chamberlain lets a punch fly and hits Gola. [Chamberlain] broke his hand. So I immediately got up with the courage of a lion and started peppering lefts and rights, and he didn't know anybody was touching him."

The Celtics hooked up with St. Louis (coached by Ed Macauley) in the finals and went the distance. It was becoming increasingly clear that it would be impossible to beat the Celtics on the Boston Garden floor in the deciding game of any series. The Celtics had back-to-back titles. It didn't seem like that big a deal at the time, but there wouldn't be a repeat NBA champion from any city other than Boston for another twenty-eight years (1987–88, Los Angeles Lakers).

The champs were close-knit in these early years of success. Conley lived in the attic of Ramsey's Newton house during the 1959–60 season. Conley on Ramsey: "He's the one that would watch the money. If you had to rent cars and go to Syracuse when the weather was bad, he made sure everybody got in the right cars and paid their bills. He was like a general manager for the players. His favorite line was 'You guys are messin' with mah money.' "

1960-61

Ted Williams homers in his final at bat. Kennedy defeats Nixon by less than 120,000 votes. Clark Gable dies. Lillian Hellman publishes *Toys in the Attic*. Walt Disney releases *101 Dalmations*. The Tokens sing, "The Lion Sleeps Tonight." In Jerusalem on April 11, 1961, former Nazi official Karl Adolf Eichmann goes on trial for war crimes, and the Soviet Union prepares to send Yuri Gagarin into space. On that same date, at the Boston Garden, the Celtics beat the St. Louis Hawks, 121–112, and win their third straight NBA crown.

This may have been the best basketball team of all time. It was the last time the Celtics had all the major contributors from their first championship: Russell, Loscutoff, Heinsohn, Cousy, Sharman, plus a bench of Ramsey, Conley, Sam Jones, K. C. Jones, and rookie Tom Sanders. Name another team in any sport with three Hall of Famers (Ramsey and both Joneses) who didn't start.

Sanders was a six-six first-round draft pick from New York University, and his teammates chuckled when he arrived because he did not know how to drive a car. Talk to these Celtics thirty years later, and they remember one another's driving habits as well as they remember their playing strengths and weaknesses. Auerbach drove too fast, Walter Brown drove too slow. Native New Yorker Sanders couldn't drive, but he could play defense. Jack Moreland, Lee Shaffer, Fred LaCour, and Al Bunge are four of the players who were selected ahead of Tom Sanders, and all had forgettable careers. Sanders became famous for his great defense and for telling President Kennedy, "Take it easy, baby," when the Celtics visited the White House. Sanders had style. He was dubbed, "Satch," a nickname borrowed from Louis "Satchmo" Armstrong. Satch's fans liked the way he draped himself in towels when he sat on the bench. He was cool at a time when only beatniks were cool. Nobody wore towels like Tom Sanders.

The 1960–61 Celtics went 57–22 and won the East by eleven games. Chamberlain averaged 38.4 for the second-place Warriors, but they were eliminated by Syracuse in the first round of the play-offs. This was Sharman's last year (he still led the league in free-throw shooting with a .921 percentage) and the Celts gave him a resounding send-off. Boston beat Syracuse in five games, then routed St. Louis, 129–95, in the first game of the finals. It was over in five games, and a gloating Auerbach said, "This is the greatest team ever assembled."

He had a good case. The Celtics didn't have a player among the league's top fifteen scorers, but six Celtics averaged fifteen or more points. Russell won his second Most Valuable Player trophy. Nine of the players on the squad had their numbers retired. Seven playing members of the 1960–61 unit are in the Basketball Hall of Fame. Auerbach makes eight, and Walter Brown makes nine. Think of it this way: In 1989, the NBA was forty-three years old and had forty-seven players and coaches in its Hall of Fame; eight of those forty-seven members, or 17 percent, came from one team.

Auerbach explained his "greatest ever" boast, saying, "There are two reasons for it. One is the way these guys get along together and play as a unit. On some teams, the players get into each other's hair over a long schedule. That doesn't happen here. And the other reason we're so damned good is the quality of the people. We've always got somebody ready to explode. Any one of them can tear you apart. One night it's Heinsohn; the next night it's Cousy. Then Sharman. Or maybe it's Ramsey or Sam. And, of course, there's Russell."

Conley says, "You get a club like that, and if a team had you down by eight or ten points by the third period, you didn't worry about it. It was just a matter of 'in the next four or five minutes let's put the kill on 'em.' "

How close were the players? K. C. Jones taught Heinsohn how to dance. This is not the way we think of our pro ball players in the 1990s.

"Everybody had roommates then," says Heinsohn. "We used

to have parties together and go out after games together. We used to play cards a lot. On planes and after games. There was always a card game going on somewhere."

Ramsey says, "I think we were very close—the reason being we were together so much traveling. We traveled by bus, we traveled by car, we traveled by train. I know one trip from Boston to St. Louis took eight hours. We were playing cards, and there wasn't a whole lot to do so we were together constantly. I roomed with Loscy, then I roomed with Conley. I roomed with Sam once. There was always Sharman and Cousy. We had regular roommates, but that didn't mean a whole lot because we were always playing cards in somebody's room."

"I'll give you an idea," Conley adds. "That was in 1958–61 that all those guys were together, and I still hear from Ramsey once every two or three months. He calls me from Kentucky. Late at night he has some of that bourbon, and he calls to see how everything is. I see Loscutoff around. I got a letter from Satch Sanders four days ago, saying hello. Heinsohn I run into all the time. Maybe it's just that all of us got old, and we remember how it was."

1961-62

Roger Maris hits his sixty-first home run off Boston pitcher Tracy Stallard. Twenty-year-old Bob Dylan plays in a Greenwich Village café. Chubby Checker does the Twist, and Natalie Wood stars in *West Side Story*. John Glenn orbits the earth. NBC and CBS simulcast "A Tour of the White House with Mrs. John F. Kennedy." President Kennedy says America's soldiers in Vietnam are "not combat troops in the generally understood sense of the word." Byron White replaces Charles Whittaker on the Supreme Court. On April 18, Kennedy and

U.S. Steel are at war over a price hike of six dollars per ton. Meanwhile, in Boston, on the eve of the marathon, the Celtics beat the Los Angeles Lakers in overtime, 110–107, to win their fourth consecutive World Championship.

This was the first year of transition. Sharman was gone, and Sam Jones stepped into a starting role, averaging eighteen points per game. Few teams could lose a guard like Sharman and not feel the effect, but Auerbach had the deepest unit in the history of sports. Still, the Celtics were by no means the big basketball story in 1961–62. This was the season that Chamberlain averaged 50.4 points per game and scored one-hundred against the Knicks in a game in Hershey, Pennsylvania. Despite Chamberlain's gaudy numbers, the Celtics finished 60–20 and beat the Warriors by the usual eleven games. Russell again was Most Valuable Player, a significant award in a year dominated by a man with a fifty-point average. The play-offs were another story. A year earlier, the Celtics swept to the title in a pair of 4–1 series—both laughers. There was nothing funny about the 1962 play-offs. The Celtics came close to losing in the conference finals, and again in the championship finals.

The conference duel with the Warriors was a classic. Chamberlain had a pretty good supporting cast, players named Tom Gola, Guy Rodgers, Al Attles, Paul Arizin, and Tom Meschery. With the series tied 2–2, tempers flared during Game 5 in Boston, and Sam Jones picked up a photographer's stool to defend himself against a charging Chamberlain. A photograph of this episode can be found in any worthy Boston sports bar. Watching from the stands was college senior John Havlicek, a star at Ohio State. It was Havlicek's first night in that city, and he never forgot it. Eventually, Sam won Game 7 with a fifteen-foot jumper. In the finals, the Celtics and Lakers drew only 7,617 people for Game 1, a 122–108 Boston victory. K. C. Jones played the series with a broken nose, thanks to a Jim Krebs stray elbow. The Celts trailed 3–2 after a sixty-one-point effort by Elgin Baylor and had to win Game 6 in Los

Angeles to stay alive. Down by ten at halftime, they won, 119–105. The Celts almost lost Game 7, but with the game tied at the end of regulation, a wide-open, fifteen-foot buzzer-beater by the Lakers' Frank Selvy somehow rolled off the rim.

Selvy, a guard, once scored one-hundred points in a game for Furman University. He took the final shot because K. C. Jones was guarding Jerry West and "Hot Rod" Hundley couldn't get open. Cousy was guarding Selvy. Selvy remembered, "I had to get it off fast. I sort of hurried it, but I thought it was going in. I get the blame for missing that shot, but I don't think that was the ball-game."

Auerbach says, "We were cheated. The timer froze. There were three seconds to go. They took it out at midcourt and threw it to a guy at midcourt. He took a bounce, then he threw it all the way into the corner. Now that goddamn thing is three seconds there. Selvy takes the ball and goes up for a jump shot and misses it. The rebound goes in the air, and the clock still hadn't gone off. Baylor got the rebound and put it up and missed it. It was more than Selvy's shot."

Russell snatched the rebound, and it was into overtime. Ramsey, Loscutoff, Heinsohn, and Sanders had all fouled out by the end of the game, but Russell (thirty points, forty rebounds in fifty-three minutes) held the Celts together and Boston won in overtime, 110–107.

Laker Tommy Hawkins said, "Especially in Boston, they developed that invincible aura. Teams going in there were totally psyched out. Even athletes have a fear when they enter competition. They are in awe of certain things, and Boston had developed that in other teams."

"All of us get into trying to explain what Celtic mystique was," says Cousy. "We talk about how we always got together, and our wives would get together and socialize when we were on the road. And we did a lot of things together when we were on the road and stuff. And it's like it's unique to you. I'm not sure that every team in professional sports doesn't do the same thing. You're not aware of it because you're relating to your thing. First comes the success. When you start talking about what made the unit successful over the years, almost anything you say makes sense. Yes, we had a positive relationship. Yes, Arnold handled the racial situation from the beginning in, I think, the best possible way by throwing it out there. We used to kid each other in the locker room—the *schwarze* and everything. It was just out there for everyone to see."

The coach was trusted by the players because he would not tolerate any slights from the outside. If a writer got on one of Red's players, the scribe was an outcast; he was "against" them. If a restaurant refused to serve a player because the player was black, the restaurant served no Celtic players. Auerbach would pull the team out. Auerbach was a Jewish kid from Brooklyn, and he'd encountered discrimination. He would have none of it for his team. The team pulled together. The team could not be beaten in any close, important game.

1962-63

Marilyn Monroe kills herself in her Los Angeles home. Americans put water jugs in their cellars and brace for war during the Cuban Missile Crisis. Eleanor Roosevelt dies. Ken Kesey writes *One Flew over the Cuckoo's Nest*. Robert Frost dies. John Steinbeck wins a Nobel Prize for literature. National Football League stars Paul Hornung and Alex Karras are suspended for betting on games. Ford introduces the T-bird. "Blue Velvet" and "Puff the Magic Dragon" top the record charts, and on April 24, the Celtics beat the Lakers in Los Angeles, 112–109, for their fifth straight NBA title.

Bob Cousy's last year was John Havlicek's first. Could any sports town deserve this many riches? Sharman had been first to leave, but in 1963 Cousy hung up his black high-tops. Like Sharman, Cousy got a World Championship as a going-away present. Cousy announced his retirement before the start of the season. He was going to coach at Boston College and wanted to get a leg up on recruiting. This had to be good news for K. C. Jones. Like Sam Jones, K. C. had been pining away on the bench, waiting for a starting spot to open up. Sharman's departure had opened the door for Sam, and Cousy's retirement made room for K. C. Let it never be said that the Celtics of the early 1960s rushed kids into starting roles. Cousy had his usual excellent year, and on St. Patrick's Day, a rainy Sunday, he was honored in a tearful, forty-three-minute pre-game ceremony. The tribute was highlighted by a leather-lunged fan in the upper deck who interrupted a tearful pause, bellowing, "We love ya, Cooz." The event needed a light touch. Even the referees were crying.

It is impossible to overemphasize the impact Cousy had on the NBA and on professional basketball in Boston. He helped the Celtics and the league stay afloat during the 1950s, and he introduced a style of play that forever changed the pro game. In an age of Magic Johnson and Michael Jordan, it's easy to forget that a six-foot-one-inch white guy revolutionized the sport. Russell is duly credited as the center who delivered the championships, but when the NBA was learning to walk, Bob Cousy was the Man.

"I've never seen anybody pass like Cousy," says Tom Heinsohn. "They talk about Magic Johnson today and all these other guys. Christ, nobody ran an offense like Cousy. That's all I got to say. You had a half a step on your man, you got the ball. You cut to the basket, and Cooz would keep his eye on you until you were no longer a threat, and then he'd go on to somebody else. He was creative. He was the guy that put the fast break into fast-break basketball. He knew how to read the defenses. He would see the defense, and then make them react to him. Cousy was really the one that made the offense

work. We only had six plays and the fast break. Guys got free-
lance stuff off picks and simple plays. We moved without the
ball and went backdoor. He was such a great passer."

Havlicek was the final pick of the first round. Teams were
looking for treetops, and Bill McGill, Paul Hogue, Zelmo
Beatty, Len Chappell, Wayne Hightower, and Leroy Ellis
were selected before Auerbach picked Havlicek. Jerry Lucas
had been the star of Havlicek's Ohio State teams, which included starter Larry Siegfried and bench warmer Bobby
Knight. Auerbach liked the idea of selecting a player who'd
been number two on his college team—it made it easier to
accept a second-banana role in the pros. The Cincinnati Royals
were expecting to get Havlicek in the second round, but Auerbach pounced. Sam Jones and K. C. Jones had replaced Sharman, and Cousy and Sanders had replaced Loscutoff. A
replacement would be needed for Ramsey, and Havlicek fit
the mold.

Just as Auerbach fretted over Sharman's and Conley's baseball careers and K. C. Jones's tryout with the Rams, the Redhead had to wait to find out how Havlicek would do with the
Cleveland Browns. Fortunately for Boston, Paul Brown was
loaded with wide receivers, and Havlicek was cut. He became
a Celtic.

Joining the World Champs was quite a shock for the Ohio
State star. Like so many others, Havlicek came to Boston and
wondered, "Is this all there is?" His first experience was seeing
the drunks lined up outside the Hayes Bickford Cafeteria
across the street from the Garden. And who could believe the
Celtic dressing room? Each player had two hooks for his
clothes. There was one shower head for eleven players, the
shower floor was usually flooded, and the locker room had one
toilet with no door. Welcome to the major leagues.

"I'll never forget my introduction to the place," says Havlicek. "It was a dreary, rainy night with not too much going
on—the train tracks overhead and the rumbling. The grimy
scene of the Boston Garden in 1962 with the Hayes Bickford

across the street and that type of thing. The next thing I woke up and had breakfast with Red in the Madison Hotel. It was the first time I had met him. Red was very much what I thought he was going to be: a person who was sure of himself; an individual who was cordial and nice, but you could tell that he was the boss. He was interested in me as a player. A lot of his mind was on the game that afternoon. We went over to the Celtics office on the first floor of 150 Causeway Street. The only people there were Howie [McHugh], Mary Wayland [a secretary], Walter Brown, and Red. That was the office staff, four people. I was a little surprised that it would be as bad as it was, and the locker room was just absolutely atrocious. You had one large room with a coatrack. And three sides of the room were taken up by hooks on the wall, and that's where you hung your clothes. There was a bench in front of each one. The back part of the room was much lower than the front part of the room, so the taller guys would dress in the front part of the room and the other guys in the back. The area of the shower was no more than five feet by five feet. You sort of had to take turns. Then there was one sink and one hopper and one urinal. The training room was probably fifteen feet long and six or seven feet wide. Red refused to move out of there because he was very superstitious. Ohio State's facilities were much, much better, but I figured if those guys who had played there for so long a time could deal with it, I could deal with it."

The Celtics won fifty-eight games. Seven players averaged double figures, and Russell was Most Valuable Player for the third straight season. Boston fell behind the Royals, 2–1, in the Eastern finals, but won it in seven with Sam Jones scoring forty-seven in the clincher. Cousy scored twenty-one with eleven assists in the final game of the Royals series. Folks in Los Angeles were talking up their city as the basketball capital of the world because of UCLA's NCAA champions and a Lakers team led by Jerry West and Elgin Baylor, but when it came time for the finals, the Celtics won it in six games. Havlicek sprained his left ankle in Game 1. Russell had thirty-eight rebounds in Game 2, and the Celtics were up, 2–0. Baylor and West scored enough to give Los Angeles victories in two of the next three games. The Celtics wrapped it up at the Los Angeles Sports Arena. Cousy sprained his left ankle in the finale, but the Celtics were able to build a fourteen-point lead. Late in the game, when the Lakers cut the lead to one point, Cousy came in for Havlicek and quarterbacked the Celtics one last time. The Cooz had the ball at the end, dribbled out the final seconds, then heaved the ball to the rafters when the buzzer sounded. Fittingly, Cousy and Havlicek each scored eighteen points in the final game. Five straight titles. Ho-hum. There was no champagne in the clubhouse. The Celtics got to the airport for the long flight home, and Ramsey (known as "general manager for the players") bought a bottle of bourbon. Havlicek says, "We won, and I think people expected us to win. We had a breakup dinner, and we were gone within a day or two."

Ramsey says, "I don't think we realized then what we had. We just tried to win it year after year after year."

1963-64

John F. Kennedy is assassinated in Dallas. Teenager Frank Sinatra, Jr., is kidnapped and returned for a $240,000 ransom. Cassius Clay takes the heavyweight crown from Sonny Liston. The Beatles land in America. Fifteen-year-old Peggy Fleming is a member of the U.S. Olympic team at Innsbruck. Jimmy Hoffa is sentenced to eight years for jury tampering. Twenty-three-year-old King Constantine takes the throne in Greece. General Douglas MacArthur dies, and Arnold Palmer wins his fourth Masters. Sean Connery stars in *Goldfinger*, and Dionne

Warwick sings "Walk on By." On April 26, three days after the opening of the New York World's Fair, the Boston Celtics beat the San Francisco Warriors, 105–99, winning their sixth straight NBA crown.

K. C. Jones took over for Cousy in the backcourt. Havlicek moved into Ramsey's sixth-man slot. Willie Naulls, Clyde Lovellette, and Larry Siegfried were acquired to beef up the bench. Ramsey and Loscutoff announced that this would be their final season. Again, there was no letdown.

"I changed the philosophy," admits Auerbach. "My point production had to be lower, so I had to change and overemphasize the defense."

The Celtics went 59–21, took four of five to beat the Royals in the conference finals, then beat Wilt's Warriors in five games to win the championship. This was one of the more methodical campaigns, totally unremarkable except that it established the Celtics as pro sport's greatest dynasty. The Yankees won five straight World Series from 1949 to 1953 and the Montreal Canadiens won the Stanley Cup from 1956 to 1960, but no team had won six straight world championships.

There was much preseason speculation about Life Without Cousy. The Cooz hadn't been able to deliver championships until Russell came along; could Russell win without Cousy? Of course he could. The supporting cast was still very strong, and the Celtics had one of their easier championship seasons. Auerbach and Heinsohn later said that they felt Cousy's departure made the team more committed in 1963–64. They wanted to prove they could win without the greatest ball-handler of all time. K. C. Jones finished third in the league in assists, and Havlicek led the team in scoring (19.9 points per game), despite the fact that he never started a game. Russell later said this was his favorite team and his best season. With Russell, Sanders, and K. C. Jones starting and Havlicek coming off the bench, and given the ages of those players in 1963–64, this might have been the best defensive team assembled. It was also the first NBA team that put five black players on the court simultaneously. Heinsohn was the only white starter, and Naulls would frequently join Russell, Sanders, and the two Joneses.

To this day, it is difficult to pinpoint why Russell's teams invariably beat Chamberlain's teams. On paper, it made no sense, but it kept happening year after year.

"Chamberlain was a real threat," remembers Heinsohn. "There wasn't anybody in the NBA that was going to stop us. Then Chamberlain came in, and he was bigger and stronger than Russell. And Russell had to figure a way to beat him. That was really Russell at his best. Chamberlain would score all the points, but Russell would always do something to minimize Chamberlain. It was a tremendous challenge to Russell and Russell knew it. Those two guys—Russell and Chamberlain—are so far above all the other centers that ever played the game. And that includes Kareem Abdul-Jabbar."

Larry Bird takes the praise one step further: "Everybody now says, 'Yeah, this guy is the best.' There's gonna be a million guys come along in the next few years, and people will forget all about it. That's what amazes me, boy. You can't tell me that Bill Russell and Wilt Chamberlain weren't the two greatest basketball players ever. How can you say that—individually—Wilt Chamberlain wasn't the greatest basketball player ever? With just the stats. It's so much bullshit. Every five years they talk about somebody else. First it was me and Magic, and now Michael [Jordan] is thrown in there. Next thing you know Karl Malone is gonna be thrown in there with David Robinson. Hey, right now, in our time, we're good basketball players, but if you want to say that somebody's better than Wilt Chamberlain, all you got to do is get the record book out. It's right there. The man scored one-hundred points in one game. Led the league in assists."

K. C. Jones on Russell's impact: "Bill didn't do it all. We just used *team*. That's a word that's thrown out all over the place, but the total personification of team is what we used. We used everybody's ability, and everybody had a role out there that was natural for them. Whoever was guarding the ball had four guys back there helping his ass out. The whole is bigger than the sum of the parts; we wrote that without knowing the phrase. We knew how good we were. And we knew how to use one another because we knew one another. The most important part of it was the understanding that we had of each teammate—what this guy likes and what that guy doesn't like and who can't play defense and who shoots the ball well. But that was positive. We used all that. If a guy couldn't play defense, we were there, picking him up. Let each guy do what he does best. That's the famous story of Russell and Sam during the time-out in St. Louis. Russell went in the other direction, and we were thinking, 'Where the hell is he going?' but he was waiting for Sam to catch up. He said, 'Sam, how come you're not shooting?' Sam said, 'I missed five shots in a row.' Russ said, 'Sam, you're the greatest shooter in the world. Now when Red gets through with this shit, what play do you want? Take one-hundred shots.' That's just an example of knowing how good we were."

When the championship was won, Ramsey went home for good. He had two cars, and he wanted someone to drive one of them home for him, so Clyde Lovellette drove John Havlicek to Ohio, then drove Ramsey's car down to Kentucky. It was a one-way trip for Ramsey's car. The NBA's first sixth man was done. Like Sharman and Cousy, Ramsey got a championship ring as a going-way present.

1964-65

Bob Hayes wins the one-hundred-meter dash at the Tokyo Olympics. Julie Andrews stars in *Mary Poppins*. Herbert Hoover dies, and LBJ beats Barry Goldwater in a landslide victory.

Martin Luther King wins the Nobel Peace Prize. The United States confirms that 136 American soldiers died in Vietnam in 1964. Winston Churchill dies. Skateboards are the new rage. Princeton scholar Bill Bradley rejects the NBA and accepts a Rhodes Scholarship. Hundreds of blacks are arrested for protesting segregation in Selma, Alabama. On April 25, American-supported Dominican Republic President Donald Reid is deposed in a military coup. On that same day, the Boston Celtics beat the Los Angeles Lakers, 129–96, winning their seventh consecutive NBA crown.

Another transitional period. Another championship. Sharman, Cousy, Ramsey, and Loscutoff were gone. This would be Heinsohn's last year. Unlike most of the other stars, the thirty-year-old forward did not make his announcement until several weeks after the title was won.

Another member of the Celtics family was gone: Walter Brown died at his summer home on Cape Cod on September 7, 1964, just five weeks before the season started. The man who'd brought pro basketball to Boston was gone at the age of fifty-nine, and the Celtics wore a black patch on their jerseys the entire season. Russell dedicated the season to Brown before the first game.

"Everybody loved Walt Brown," says Heinsohn. "He was like your father. He didn't make any money. He savored the life at the Garden. You went in to talk contract with Walter Brown. You'd walk into the men's room, and he'd say 'What do you want?' And you'd say, 'What do you want to give me?' And it would be back and forth, and by the time you zipped up, you had a deal."

The Celtics did not want to be dethroned after losing their owner, and they were not. Boston rolled to a 62–18 record, best ever, averaging 112 points per game. Sam Jones averaged 25.9 points per game, shattering all Celtic scoring records. This team had five players over the age of thirty, but no one in the league matched up—until the Warriors and 76ers made a whopper trade two hours after the All Star Game in St.

Louis. On January 13, 1965, San Francisco dealt Chamberlain to Philadelphia, and a new threat surfaced in the East.

Philadelphia finished third in the East, twenty-two games behind the Celtics, but the 76ers were a different team when the play-offs started: They had Chet Walker, Luke Jackson, Hal Greer, Larry Costello . . . and Chamberlain. This series was a classic. Punch—counterpunch. Boston won—Philly won. It went back and fourth until the final seconds of the seventh game when a bucket by Chamberlain cut the Celtics lead to 110–109, with five seconds left. The Celts had never lost a seventh game and were on their familiar parquet. Auerbach had already lit his cigar. But a seven-point lead was down to one point, and when Russell went to inbound the ball, his toss hit a support cable and the 76ers were awarded possession. Earl Strom, working with Richie Powers, made the call.

Strom: "I had my hand in a huge cast. I had gotten into an altercation with a fan in Baltimore a few nights prior to that. He had hit me with something, and he ran away, and I ran after him, and when I hit him, I broke my thumb. I had a pin put in my thumb and had to referee that game in a cast. I called Russell for throwing the ball and hitting the wire; I'm sure it had happened prior to that, but I can't recall. But the call had to be made. That was a court rule, like a ground rule of the arena."

Strom handed the ball to Hal Greer. Greer's inbound pass was headed for Chet Walker when Havlicek hustled into history. Anticipating perfectly, Havlicek stepped in front of Walker and tapped the ball toward Sam Jones. Sam dribbled out the clock while Celtics radio maven Johnny Most screamed, "Havlicek stole the ball!" much the way Russ Hodges called, "The Giants win the pennant!" back in 1951.

Havlicek: "When Russell inbounded the ball and hit the guide wire, I don't think anyone thought that we weren't going to be able to get the ball back again and be able to inbound it. All of a sudden there was this controversy. The ball was given back to Philadelphia, and Red had been arguing the point the whole time, and before you know it, the ball was ready to be inbounded, so there wasn't much of a strategy type of thing. We figured they were going to Chamberlain. We figured we'd do everything we could to prevent him from getting it. We had a small lineup on the floor at that time with Sam and myself and K. C. and Satch and Russell. And they countered with Luke Jackson, Johnny Kerr, Chamberlain, Walker, and Hal Greer, and I said to Sam as we were going out on the floor, 'Let me take Johnny Kerr,' because I played in the frontcourt a little more and I'd keep him off the boards. He said, 'No, I can handle him on the boards.' So K. C. was guarding Greer, and I ended up guarding Walker. I knew that they had five seconds to put the ball in play. My thought was, as the official handed Greer the ball, to start counting, 'One thousand one, one thousand two, one thousand three.' Generally a pass is made within the first second or two, and I knew that he was having some sort of problem because that guide wire was in the exact same position as where Russell had inbounded it. So it may have been a thought on his mind, too. When he was having trouble putting it in play, I sort of had a vision as to where the ball was and where my man was, and I started to peek a little, and as I started to peek, I really got a clear view as to what was happening. I saw the lob pass coming out, and that was a surprise to me because I figured they'd be going to Chamberlain down low. So as it came out, I knew it was going to be a little short. So I was able to jump up in front of it and keep my body away from Walker and momentarily deflect it and control it and tip it over to Sam. I didn't realize it was that outstanding a play until I heard Johnny Most. The radio played that thing the next day probably every fifteen or twenty minutes. Then the record came. The play gets bigger as time goes on."

The Celts went on to the final and crushed the Lakers in five. The ease with which Boston took this series was startling. They scored a play-off record: 142 points in Game 1. Meanwhile, K. C. Jones held Jerry West to one basket in the first quarter and stole the ball from him five times in the first half. They split the next two games. Then Sam Jones hit for thirty-seven points as Boston went up 3–1. While the crowd screamed for blood, they ripped off twenty consecutive points in the Boston Garden Game 5 clincher. Russell wrote, "We were not just beating this team. We were destroying it. . . . It was my worst moment in sports. There was the horror of destruction, not the joy of winning. . . . We knew—and did not know—we sensed, and did not completely comprehend, that we had taken sports out of the realm of the game."

Sanders said, "We were just kickin' ass and takin' names out there."

Heinsohn's departure was somewhat of a stunner. He was only thirty, still a starter and ever the champion. But he had other things to do. In later years Heinsohn would return to coach the Celtics, then proceed into careers as a television commentator, an accomplished artist, and a businessman. In 1989, he addressed a new edition of the Celtics at a banquet and told them, "What's made this team unique over the years is the ability of its players to swallow their own egos. Nobody's ever been point-crazy here. All that counts is getting the win. The Celtic jerseys don't win games. The people *in* those jerseys win games."

1965-66

The Byrds release "Mr. Tambourine Man." Author Somerset Maugham dies. Ferdinand E. Marcos is sworn in as president of the Philippines. Ralph Nader goes toe-to-toe with the auto companies. Indira Gandhi becomes Prime Minister of India. Gemini 8 astronauts Neil Armstrong and David Scott make the first docking in space. Ted Williams is elected to the Baseball Hall of Fame. On April 28, 1966, the United States Supreme Court rules that General Motors violated antitrust laws. On this same date, the Boston Celtics defeat the Los Angeles Lakers in a seventh game on the Garden parquet, 95–93.

This one was special. Always, it seemed, the Celtics had a cause, something to prove. They wanted to prove they could repeat, and then they wanted to prove they could beat Chamberlain, and then they wanted to prove they could win without Cousy, and then they wanted to win one for the memory of Walter Brown. Number eight was for Red Auerbach. Russell wrote, "For a few years in there we couldn't think of anything special, so we won those on general principle."

The inimitable coach announced that 1965–66 would be his last year on the bench. He made the announcement before the season—in effect, challenging the rest of the league to beat him. He was forty-seven years old but looked and felt much older. It was time to relinquish some of his duties. Things had gotten tougher since Walter Brown died.

The Celtics finally looked beatable. Chamberlain would have an entire season with his new Philadelphia teammates, and the team that came so close to beating Boston was on a mission. Meanwhile, the Celtics were getting long in the tooth, and Heinsohn, who had been part of every championship team, was gone.

On the recommendation of Heinsohn, Auerbach snatched six-six forward Don Nelson off the waiver wire. Nelson had been a part-time player with Chicago and Los Angeles, and every team passed on him when his name surfaced. Nelson joined the Celtics, and Naulls moved into the starting lineup—giving Boston the NBA's first black starting five.

Predictably, the 76ers kept pace throughout the season and finished 55–26, one game ahead of Boston. It marked the first time since 1956 that the Celtics had not finished first during the regular season. The Celts had to play a first-round playoff series and went the distance, beating Cincinnati in a fifth game at the Garden. Philadelphia was next, and the Celtics took the 76ers in five. Chamberlain scored forty-six in the Celtics' clincher, but Goliath missed seventeen of twenty-five free throws. Philadelphia sportswriter Joe McGinnis asked Chamberlain if he thought the missed foul shots had cost the Sixers the game, and Chamberlain went after him.

K. C. Jones: "The other team had a large problem dealing with us 'cause when we played against them, we used psychology. Philadelphia, that year, had the best team in every way. Luke Jackson was running up and down the floor, and Willie Naulls was guarding him. Willie noticed Jackson hadn't gotten the ball yet. Jackson was bustin' his butt, getting rebounds, running, playing defense, diving after loose balls, and stuff. Willie finally said, 'You know, Luke, you haven't gotten a shot yet.' And he said, 'Yeah, you noticed that, too?' The next few times down the court, he got the ball and didn't give it up. That's using your brain, and it's what we did. It started with Russell."

The Celtics and Lakers matched up in the final again. After the Lakers won the first game, Auerbach announced that Russell would coach the Celtics in 1966–67. Buoyed by this news, Boston won three straight games. Los Angeles extended the series to seven games, but Auerbach was not going to lose a seventh game on the Garden floor. The last cigar yielded the eighth straight championship: Leading by six with sixteen seconds left, Auerbach allowed Massachusetts Governor John Volpe to light his cigar. The crowd surged forward and formed a human frame around the court's perimeter. Unfortunately, the Celtics kept turning the ball over, and Los Angeles cut the lead to two points with four seconds left before K. C. Jones dribbled out the clock.

Russell played all forty-eight minutes of Game 7, scoring twenty-five points with thirty-two rebounds. When Auerbach walked out the door, Russell was the last surviving member of the first championship team. Auerbach went back to his hotel room, ordered Chinese food, made himself some french fries, and sat by himself. Later, there would be days when he'd be tempted to return to the bench, but whenever the urge hit him, he'd look at a photograph of himself in 1966. He'd aged beyond his years. Eight straight and nine of ten had taken its toll. He left the coaching to the younger men, and some of them did a pretty good job.

The spoiled Boston sports fans had come to expect championships each spring. The Celtics treated Hub fans to eight straight. It was going to end soon, but there were other treats in other sports on the menu. The Bruins had a teenage defenseman named Bobby Orr. And the Red Sox were only a year away from a season that would forever alter the fortunes of the sagging, star-crossed Boston baseball club. The Bruins and the Red Sox were nearing the end of long droughts, but the Celtics had stepped into the breach and won more than anyone ever won. They were never fully appreciated for this greatness. They never averaged ten-thousand fans during the championship streak. From 1959 to 1966, the Celtics won eight straight world titles, but the average regular-season crowd during the eight-year span was 7,803.

The word "great" has been diluted beyond recognition in today's era of instant fame and fortune, but those who patronized the 1959–66 Celtics know what they saw.

(Dick Raphael)

Red Auerbach as coach: Giving an earful to an official and lighting up a victory cigar.

(Dick Raphael)

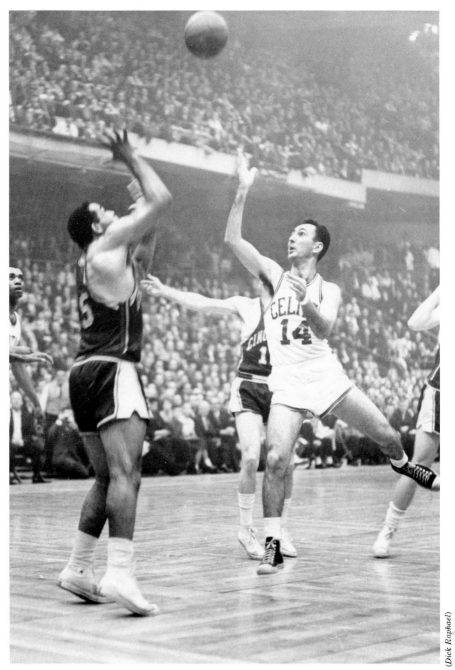

Bob Cousy.

(Dick Raphael)

Two sides of Bill Russell's game: Stuffing arch-rival Wilt Chamberlain and grabbing a rebound.

(Dick Raphael)

(Dick Raphael)

Sam Jones.

Tom "Satch" Sanders.

Future Celtics coach K. C. Jones drives past Chamberlain.

John Havlicek moves on Laker guard Jerry West
as Bill Russell looks on.

(Dick Raphael)

Tom Heinsohn, quick-shooting forward
and Tom Heinsohn, Celtics coach.

(Dick Raphael)

Don Nelson.

Paul Silas.

Dave Cowens.

Jo Jo White.

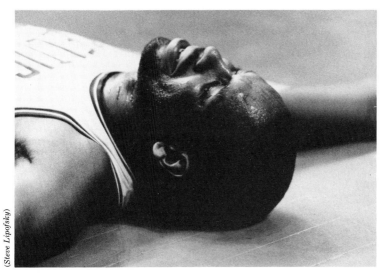

Cedric Maxwell.

Danny Ainge.

Dennis Johnson.

(Steve Lipofsky)

Robert Parrish, The Chief.

(Steve Lipofsky)

Kevin McHale posts up.

(Dick Raphael)

Bill Walton.

(Dick Raphael)

Bill Russell scoring over Wilt Chamberlain.

(Dick Raphael)

John "Hondo" Havlicek drives
past New York Knick Walt
"Clyde" Frazier.

Red Auerbach
today.

(Steve Lipofsky)

he 1966–67 Celtics never lost their dignity. They were
eated by one of the most powerful NBA teams in history.
e 1966–67 Celtics won sixty games, only two games off their
4–65 record, but Philly's powerhouse went an NBA-record
-13. The 1967 Sixers are often cited as the greatest team
NBA history (Auerbach snorts whenever he is confronted
th this claim). The 76ers had a new coach, Alex Hannum,
d Hannum got Chamberlain to play a team game. Wilt's
oring dipped to 24.1, but he finished first in rebounding and
ird in assists. His supporting cast included Chet Walker,
uke Jackson, Billy Cunningham, Hal Greer, Wali Jones, and
arry Costello. The 76ers won forty-six of their first fifty
ames. Chamberlain took only fourteen shots per game, and
ix Philadelphia players averaged in double figures. Celtic fans
ecognize all of this as a prescription for a championship.

Auerbach paid player-coach Russell $100,001, one dollar
more than Chamberlain. Russell was the first black head coach
in major American professional sports, and he was hardly your
basic whistle-and-clipboard guy. He never liked practice when
he played for Woolpert or Auerbach, and now he could give
himself a day off any time he wanted. Russell the coach went
very easy on Russell the star center. He sat on the sidelines,
drinking coffee and reading newspapers, while his players
worked on those seven basic plays.

The star player–rookie coach, however, was never too big
to take a tongue-lashing from Auerbach.

Auerbach: "One night there was a blizzard. And [Russell]
had no assistant coach, so I came out of the stands to coach
the team. He didn't show up. Everybody else was there. With
about fifteen seconds to go, we're ahead by 12–14 points, he
walks in, looks at the score. He grins. We walk back into the
dressing room after the game, and he's having fun. I laid into
him like you wouldn't believe. I said 'Goddamn it, what happened to you?' He said there was a blizzard outside. I said,
'Havlicek walked three miles. His car got stuck. You and your
goddamn Lamborghini with six carburetors—you can shove

(Dick Raphael)

Dave Cowens defending
against Kareem Abdul-
Jabbar.

Larry Bird posts up against
Dr. J, Julius Erving.

(Steve Lipofsky)

Larry Bird.

T
def
The
196
68
in
w
an
sc
th
I
I
g
s

6
Final Green W

EVERYTHING ends. Lou Gehrig missed a ga
Maggio's fifty-six-game hitting streak was stop
Keltner's glove. Walter Cronkite stepped down f
chor desk at CBS. The Beatles broke up.

On April 11, 1967, at Convention Hall in Philad
76ers beat the Boston Celtics, 140–116, winning th
Conference finals in five easy games and ending th
championship winning streak in the history of pr
sports. It was cold and windy back in Boston on this
Red Sox had been scheduled to play their home ope
it was postponed due to thirty-degree temperatures ar
mile-per-hour winds. This would prove to be the turr
season in Red Sox history, one that restored basebal
proper place at the top of the Boston sports agenda. T
three years later, it seems fitting that the Sox opene
postponed in deference to the Celtics burial. The Celtic
been carrying the torch of Boston sports for eight str
years.

it! When you're not here, it's two people who are not here: Bill Russell the player and Bill Russell the coach.' At this point, Don Nelson touched my arm. He knew I was burning. He said, 'You know, he's the coach, and some of these young players might get the wrong idea.' I said, 'I don't give a goddamn. To me, he's just a player and I'm his coach and I'm going to blast him.' What was my purpose? My purpose was for him to owe me one. I want the next game. The minute that game was over and I walked into that dressing room, I wanted a reason, a motivating force to win the next game."

Relieved of the everyday burden of coaching, Auerbach had more time to make deals in smoke-filled rooms (Red's favorite arena). Boston's general manager swapped seven-foot Mel Counts to Baltimore for Bailey Howell. Two weeks later, he got Wayne Embry from Cincinnati for cash and a draft choice. Auerbach wasn't dealing just because he had some free time; age was creeping up on the Green. Russell was thirty-three, Sam Jones thirty-four, and K. C. Jones thirty-five. Loscutoff, Ramsey, Sharman, Cousy, and Heinsohn were retired, and K. C. would be the next to go. But the Celts gave Boston fans hope. They won three of every four games they played and convinced their fans that Philadelphia could be handled. There was no cause to worry. Russell had never lost a play-off series to a Chamberlain team, and Boston won five of nine regular-season contests against the muscle-flexing Philadelphians.

Coach Russell led the Celtics to a 3–1 first-round victory over the Knicks, but the series with the 76ers was over early. Philadelphia had the home-court advantage and took the first three games easily. Averting the indignity of a sweep, the Celtics beat the 76ers, 121–117, in a nationally televised Sunday game, then went to the City of Brotherly Love to watch the dynasty finally fall. Long-suffering Philadelphia fans chanted, "Boston is dead, Boston is dead!"

Russell said, "The best way to be a good loser is to shut up."

K. C. Jones: "When we lost to Philly, it was thought that

we would just slump down, but we said, 'They won.' We went into their dressing room and congratulated them. We had no hanging heads. We'd done the best we could. They beat us on our court, and that did a lot for them."

In his autobiography, Havlicek wrote, "We never again played another team with that much power and depth."

The Sixers were simply better than the Celtics. "No doubt about it," admitted Satch Sanders.

Boston's coach had been outplayed by Chamberlain in the finale. Wilt outscored Russell, 29–4, outrebounded him, 36–21, and had thirteen assists to Russell's seven. The estimable Leonard Koppett wrote, "He was better than Russell now. Hard for Russell to handle. His quickness sapped by age, Russell resorted to strength and psychology, manhandling Wilt, talking to him, trying to talk him out of it, but Wilt now was not listening to him."

Boston sports fans didn't know quite what to do. This was an introduction to reality. There were high school-age basketball fans in New England (author included) who did not remember a spring when the Celtics were not World Champions. It was just something that always happened. There was St. Patrick's Day, Easter, then the Celtics winning the championship.

Naturally, this defeat inspired overreaction. Russell later recounted how fans walked up to him on the street asking, "What happened" and stating, "I knew it wouldn't last. You guys don't have it anymore." The player-coach silently nodded and congratulated himself for ignoring the comments when he was on top; that made it easier to disregard the stupid statements when the Celtics finally fell.

Apart from the shock and hysteria, there was legitimate concern that the golden days were over. The Celtics were old, and Chamberlain looked unstoppable. He was younger, stronger, and, finally, better than Russell. It appeared likely that more payback was in store.

In the autumn of 1967, there was new commitment at the

Celtic training camp based at Boston State College. K. C. Jones was gone. After winning eight rings in nine seasons, he decided it was time to get a job and make some real money. National Basketball Association players in the 1960s were not wealthy people. Jones was a starter and had won eight championship shares, but, like Heinsohn, he felt he could make more money on the outside. Larry Siegfried took over for K. C., and Howell started with Sanders up front. Havlicek was still content to be the best sixth man in history, certainly the best since Frank Ramsey turned in his sweats.

Don Nelson had a different perspective. He'd graduated from Iowa in 1962 and played three seasons with Chicago and the Lakers before Los Angeles waived him in 1965. Auerbach took Nelson off the junk heap and Nelson was part of a championship season in 1965–66. Nelson wasn't devastated when he didn't win a second ring in 1967. Only longtime Celtic watchers *expected* to win every year. Nelson was happy to have a job and impressed with the people on his team. Nelson and Havlicek would be the only Celtics who would win championships playing for Auerbach, Russell, and Heinsohn.

Nelson: "I was waived by the Lakers, and I thought it was over. I remember waiting around [for] forty-eight hours to see if anybody'd claim me, and they didn't. I went home, and a couple of days after that I got a call from Auerbach, and he said to come to Boston and wait there for a few days because the team was on the road. . . . I looked at the roster, and I knew the guy I had to beat out was Ronnie Watts. I was listening to the game on the radio. Somehow I got it [from] Illinois because I think they were playing in the Midwest somewhere. And it was a garbage game, and Ronnie got in the game. I was rooting against him. It was my only chance to really make it. Then I waited in Boston for three or four days until the team came back, and I made the team. The reason Red picked me up was because we went to the finals the year before in L.A. and Elgin Baylor had fractured his kneecap and I had an opportunity to play some. I had to play in the backcourt. They played me at two-guard, and a couple of times I even had to bring the ball up. They put K. C. Jones on me, and I lost the ball three straight times. But anyway, Red saw me play in that series, and I think liked me a little bit. The Celtics were an awesome team. I didn't even dream about playing for 'em. Little did I know I'd be playing there a long time. When I got there they were closer than I expected. I knew Havlicek because I played against him in college. But I found out that it was fairly cold when I first got there because I had to make the team. I was an outsider, trying to bump somebody within the structure off the team. But once I did that, and once they saw me play and liked my game and I made the team, it was totally different. I was a member of the team, and I was welcome."

Bailey Howell: "I was happy about coming to Boston. The Celtics had won eight championships in a row so I thought this was an opportunity for me to accomplish a lifelong dream and play for an NBA champion. The Celtics were getting older. As a group they were kind of all getting older at the same time, and Philadelphia had put together a great young team. The year before I got there, Philadelphia had won the regular season. My first year we lost it, so the story was that Boston was dead and the dynasty was over and it was now all Philadelphia, but we turned it around the next couple of years."

The 1967–68 Celtics opened the season with six straight victories and were 25–7 by Christmas. The Celtics again finished second in 1967–68, trailing the World Champion 76ers by eight games with a 54–28 record. In the first round of the play-offs, Boston fell behind Detroit, 2–1, and Russell moved captain Havlicek into the starting lineup. Havlicek scored eighty-four points in three games, and Boston eliminated the Pistons in six games.

The emergence of Havlicek as a superstar could not have been more timely. He was six-foot-five, 205 pounds; he could play guard or forward; he could start or come off the bench; he could shoot and defend; and he could run full speed for forty-eight minutes. He was cerebral and instinctive. He was also one of the neatest and most fastidious persons in the history of the planet. Roommates claimed Havlicek put his socks on a hanger when he unpacked his suitcase on the road. His wife, Beth, admitted that at home he hung his shirts one-half inch apart in his closet. His locker was tidier than a shelf at CVS. Shampoos, deodorant, colognes, and so on, were arranged according to height and sequence of usage. He believed in doing things sensibly, orderly. He never left his sweater inside out when he took it off—that would add time when he went to put it on, and he might be in a hurry then. He always washed the toothpaste out of the sink, and he always folded his towels neatly. He was a jump-shooting Felix Unger.

Havlicek was ready. Russell was ready. The Celtics were ready. Hello Philadelphia.

In Philadelphia, on April 5, one day after Rev. Dr. Martin Luther King was shot by James Earl Ray at the Lorraine Hotel in Memphis, the Celtics defeated the 76ers, 127–118. There had been talk of postponing the game, but since no funeral arrangements had been set, the Celts and Sixers played, agreeing to wait five days before playing Game 2. The Sixers roared back after the break, winning three straight. The Sixers' streak was especially impressive in light of the fact that Philadelphia was playing without sixth man Billy Cunningham, who had broken his wrist.

Only one of the final three games was scheduled for Boston Garden, and fans resigned themselves to defeat. No NBA team had ever won a series after trailing, 3–1.

The Celtics knew that the Sixers were less committed than they had been a year earlier. The Sixers were afflicted by the championship blues—a malady that struck every NBA winner except the Celtics. The first sign of trouble in paradise came when Chamberlain skipped training camp just a few months after the victory parade. Then, during their title defense season, coach Hannum soured and decided he wanted out. General Manager Jack Ramsay wanted to become coach. There was grumbling about money and who was getting the credit. Egos and greed struck down the Sixers. Everybody knew Chamberlain was gone when the season was over. Ever conscious of his place in the record book, Chamberlain had decided to go for the assist crown and was getting mad when his teammates missed shots. Meanwhile, the big guy was passing up easy baskets for himself. Wilt didn't get it. He still doesn't get it.

Down to its last breath, Boston put its psychological arsenal to work. Havlicek and Wayne "the Wall" Embry wrote "Pride" on the team bulletin board before Game 5. Russell kidded Nelson about an early trip home to Moline, Illinois. Russell was a better coach than he had been a year earlier. He could call shots, motivate, and still concentrate on his own game. A decision was made to run the age-old, pick-and-roll play all night long, and it worked. Havlicek scored twenty-nine with ten assists in forty-eight minutes, leading the Green to a 122–104 victory at the Spectrum in Philadelphia. The series moved to Boston where the Celtics won by twelve, then back to Philadelphia.

Prior to Game 5 in Philly, Havlicek and Nelson had eaten sausage sandwiches and gone to the movies. They repeated the ritual before Game 7. The Celtics took the final, 100–96. Chamberlain took only two shots (both taps) in the second half of the final game, his last as a member of the Philadelphia 76ers. His teammates gave him the ball only four times in the final twelve minutes. The Celtics had never lost a seventh game; the Sixers had never won one.

The Lakers were tanned, rested, and ready to go at the Celtics in the finals, but the Celtics won it in six games, taking the clincher, 124–109, in Los Angeles. Boston trailed by fifteen in the third quarter of Game 1, then beat Los Angeles, 107–101. Mel Counts, the man Auerbach traded for Bailey Howell, led the Lakers to a Game 2 victory. Larry Siegfried's twenty-six points led the Celtics to a Game 3 victory, but the Lakers came back to win Game 4 in Los Angeles. Nelson was the surprise star of Game 5; he scored twenty-six, including four in overtime in a 120–117 extra-inning victory. Havlicek, the new star, scored forty in the clincher. He played 291 of 293 minutes in the final series. Howell, about to be fitted for his first ring, led the team in prayer after the game. Embry, excited about his first championship, celebrated all night and wound up falling asleep in the hallway of the team's hotel.

Howell: "The game has to be won on the court. You try to block out all the hype that's going on and all of that. You just concentrate on your job and play as good as you can and see what happens. Bill, I thought, was real wise as a coach. He was always open to any suggestions that you might have. Most of the guys didn't try to coach the team, but if you were a little weary or tired, you'd say, 'Bill, I need a blow,' and he'd get you out of the game and get a fresh guy in there. We had a strong bench, and everybody played as hard as they could when we were on the floor. It was a good situation. We had a lot of veterans, and you would do what needed to be done to win the game."

The 1968–69 season was perhaps the most magical of all Celtics campaigns. Conventional wisdom was that 1967–68 had been a last gasp, or perhaps an aberration. In either event, the Celtics certainly had done as much as they were going to do in this generation, and it was time to yield the throne. The next time the Celtics lost, it would not be considered an interruption. It would be the end of the dynasty. It was widely assumed that 1968–69 would mark the end of Russell's reign. Russell was thirty-five, Sam Jones thirty-six, Howell thirty-two, and Sanders thirty. At midseason, Russell made up his mind that this was it (he didn't tell anybody until long after the play-offs ended). Sam Jones had already announced he was retiring at season's end.

League power shifted when the Lakers sent three players to the Sixers in exchange for Chamberlain. Los Angeles had Jerry West, Elgin Baylor, and Chamberlain. It was an unthinkable glut of superstars. There are only three major positions in basketball—guard, forward, and center—and it was arguable in 1968 that West, Baylor, and Chamberlain were each the best-ever at their position. Auerbach sat back, puffed on a stogie, and noted, "You still play this game with only one basketball."

The Celtics finished fourth with a 48–34 record. It was Boston's lowest finish in twenty years. Russell knew he had an old team, and he knew he had to play three play-off series no matter where he finished, so he took his foot off the accelerator and settled for fourth. The player-coach averaged a career-low 9.9 points per game. Baltimore, Philadelphia, and New York beat Boston in the East. The Lakers, of course, led the West with a 55–27 record. No team had ever won a championship without having home-court advantage in at least one play-off series, and the Celtics knew they'd be on the road all the way.

Havlicek says, "One of the reasons we finished fourth was that Russell missed a lot of games near the end of the season, and that was a blessing because he had two or three weeks where he didn't play. He sort of came back to the play-offs rejuvenated, and being that we had won so many championships, we knew that anything could happen in a short series, and we . . . felt that we could still win it. New York was a team that was coming along strong, but we knew that we could do a job on them if we played to our ability."

Russell's old team took on a new look once the play-offs started. Again, the Celtics were forerunners of a new philosophy. Knowing what he had and didn't have, Russell concentrated his effort on the play-offs. Gaining home court was not worth exhausting his grizzled veterans. This thinking works well today: Due to overly long seasons and expanded play-offs, it matters more to be playing well at the *end* of the year. You can afford to conserve some energy during the season. Take your time getting your act together. It doesn't matter how you play during the regular season, as long as you win enough to make the play-offs, then get hot at play-off time. Super

Bowls, World Series, and NCAA championships have been won with this attitude. The best team didn't always win; the team that was playing best at play-off time did. The 1969 Orioles (109 victories, lost to the Miracle Mets in five games) learned this lesson a few months after watching the cranky Celtics beat the flossy Lakers.

Howell remembers, "We were underdogs not only against the Lakers but against *all* the teams. The Knicks had beaten us pretty bad all year. But in a short series we could make the plays and do the things we needed to do to win. Those other clubs—it wasn't quite their time yet."

When the 1969 play-offs started, the Celtics were ready. Turn back the clocks. They faced the Sixers (sans Chamberlain) in the first round, and Sam Jones and veteran publicity man Howie McHugh were thrown out of Game 1 by Jack Madden. The us-against-the-world mentality was at work. Emmette Bryant replaced Jones, and the Celtics beat the 76ers by fourteen points. Boston KO'd Philadelphia in five games. New York was coming on strong with Walt Frazier, Willis Reed, Bill Bradley, and Dave DeBusschere. The Knicks had won six of seven games against the Celtics during the regular season, but the Celtics stunned the Knicks in six. Russell destroyed Reed and gave Willis some pointers on the way out the door.

Los Angeles was next. This was going to be the Lakers' revenge. The Celtics had made fools of the Lakers for more than a decade—Los Angeles playing the part of the Washington Generals to Boston's Globetrotters. Against the combined talents of Chamberlain, Baylor, and West, the fossils from Boston stood no chance. West scored fifty-three in Game 1, and the Lakers took the opener by two points. Baylor scored thirty-two in a six-point Los Angeles win in Game 2. No team had ever lost the first two games of a championship final, then won the title, but this was a year for firsts. The Celts rebounded to win a pair in the Garden. Siegfried came off the bench to score twenty-eight in a Game 3 victory in the Garden, and Sam Jones delivered victory in Game 4 with an off-balance buzzer-beater. Jones's shot came courtesy of the famed "Ohio" play, brought to Boston by Havlicek and Siegfried. "Ohio" calls for a shot off a triple pick. Sam got the shot off, fell down, and watched it go through the basket to tie the series.

Home court held in Games 5 and 6. West scored thirty-nine, and Chamberlain outplayed Russell in the Lakers' thirteen-point, Game 5 win. They came back to the Garden and the Celtics won by nine, while Nelson hit for twenty-five and Garden fans said good-bye to Sam Jones. Nobody knew it was also time to say good-bye to Russell. The Celtics returned to Jack Kent Cooke's Forum for Game 7 on May 5. Cooke had the celebration planned. There were five-thousand balloons suspended in nets on the ceiling of the Forum. Cooke planned to shower the Laker fans with balloons in a festive victory celebration. The University of Southern California Marching Band was on hand, giving the new Forum an electric, collegiate ambience.

Cooke hadn't done his homework. This was the twelfth time the Celtics played a deciding game of a series. The Celtics were eleven for eleven in such situations. Chamberlain had squared off against Russell in seven play-off series and had lost six.

In the Celtics locker room, Havlicek got hold of a postgame program of activities that explained every detail of Cooke's celebration. The band from USC would play "Happy Days Are Here Again," just like at the Democratic National Convention. Balloons would fall. Champagne would flow.

Nelson remembers, "Red mentioned that before the game, and you could see the balloons by the thousands, and he just let his feelings be known. It was definitely a mistake on their part to do that."

The Celtics had incentive, and they had a plan.

"I knew that if we were running, we were always effective,"

says Havlicek. "Oftentimes we didn't have the whole team running because Russ was a little older and a little more tired, and the same with Sam Jones. . . . The key to every win that year was our running. So I said, 'Get me the ball because I'm going to do nothing but run, and if you give it to me you're going to have to stay up with me.' That worked for the first half, and we came out with a pretty good lead."

Boston built a seventeen-point fourth-quarter lead. Chamberlain banged his shin and took himself out in the fourth. His coach, Butch van Breda Kolff, would not let him return. Russell was miffed. He wanted Chamberlain on the court at the end. His competitive spirit overwhelmed his quest for victory. He wanted to earn the win. He didn't want it handed to him. The Celts held on for a 108–106 victory. The clinching basket came on a foul-line jumper by Nelson that hit the back rim, bounced straight up in the air, then crashed back down through the net with 1:17 remaining. Havlicek says, "I was sort of driving to the center, and Keith Erickson came around behind me and poke-checked it, and Nelson happened to be right there at the foul line, and he got it and shot it, and it went up in the air and hung there and came down through."

Nelson says, "That was the luckiest shot I ever made in my life. . . . I remember everything about that because it's been replayed and overplayed. I haven't watched it myself too many times, but it's been on TV and so on. It was one of those games that it looked like we were going to blow 'em out. Chamberlain went out and they started making this comeback. We couldn't score a basket, and they couldn't miss one. We couldn't stop the blood from flowing. It looked like they were going to keep the blood flowing and beat us. The twenty-four-second clock was running down, and Havlicek made a move. Somebody from behind hit the ball, and it came right to me. I was cutting across the paint. I just grabbed it and shot it very poorly, and it made that crazy bounce and went in. I was in the paint right around the foul line. It was probably a twelve- or fourteen-foot shot. I just shot it too hard. I was trying to get it off before the clock, and I shot it very quickly and it hit the back of the rim and went up real high and came back through. There was no time to chuckle. It was like I planned it that way."

Sam scored twenty-four. Russell had twenty-one rebounds, playing forty-eight minutes. The great Russell had won twelve of twelve seventh (or deciding fifth) games, and four of four seventh games against Chamberlain. Russell closed the door to the locker room, called his players, and said, "We are each other's friends."

While Russell and Company were sipping champagne, and Auerbach was blowing smoke upward and pointing at "all those goddamn balloons," Chamberlain was calling his coach a liar and van Breda Kolff was calling his center a quitter. West, who had scored 556 points in the play-offs and forty-two in Game 7, said this one hurt more than any other. He was awarded a new car for winning the play-off Most Valuable Player. The car was green.

"We carried that champagne from coast to coast," said Baylor. "By the time we lost, the labels had come off the bottles."

It was over. Russell announced his retirement in a magazine article for *Sports Illustrated*. Auerbach made no attempt to talk him out of it. Russell had given thirteen years to the Boston Celtics and no one dared suggest he owed any more. It would be nineteen years before another team would win two consecutive NBA championships.

Auerbach says, "That was very traumatic. I didn't believe those mothers. When Russell told me he was going to retire and Sam says, 'Yeah, I'm going to retire, too,' I didn't believe 'em because I know they can still play. The reason Russell retired was the mental aggravation, but physically he could still play. I told them to keep their mouths shut about it because you never know what might happen. What I admired about Russell doing it was that he didn't have any money when he quit. He had blown it on legitimate investments."

An editorial in the May 7 *Boston Globe* read (in part): "Some day in the far-off future, there'll be other great teams, no doubt. But they'll have no statue in Boston, where people will sneer 'Aw, you shoulda seen the Celtics.' "

Auerbach has sixteen championship rings. He wears the 1969 ring. He says it's because it's lighter than all the others.

7
Fall and Rise of the Green

FOLKS in Los Angeles, Philadelphia, Baltimore, New York, and Cincinnati waited a long time for this. Pro basketball people from coast to coast had footprints on their faces—footprints from black, high-top sneakers. They had smoke in their eyes—smoke blown by that annoying man called Red. This was the way it had been for thirteen years, but now Bill Russell was gone and it was payback time.

The Celtics had delayed the moment for as long as possible. It was said they'd fold when Cousy left, and again when Auerbach left. They were dismissed when St. Louis defeated them in 1958, and again when Philadelphia trounced them in 1967. Each time, the Boston Celtics came back throwing knockout counterpunches. In the autumn of 1969, the Celtics had nothing left to throw at their rivals. Russell was gone. Sam was gone. The NBA was getting stronger each year. The New York Knicks were a team on the rise, and a rookie named Lew Alcindor was going to make the Milwaukee Bucks instant contenders.

Oscar Robertson, who would finally win a championship with the new big man in Milwaukee, remembers, "As long as the Celtics had Russell, he dominated and they were going to win. Look at the record when he was out. They had a great team, and he was the cement for their team. He made it go for them. I knew the Celtics. They were nice guys. They wanted to win like we wanted to win. But everything in sports goes in circles. Finally, it was just someone else's turn to win."

Russell's departure left Auerbach without a coach. Red turned to Worcester, where Heinsohn was making a killing in the insurance business. Auerbach wanted to keep the coaching job in the family, and Heinsohn was the best available option. He'd been a headstrong player, one that had jousted with the coach quite often, but he was tough and he knew the game. The new coach was going to need thick skin. Auerbach knew Heinsohn could handle the topple from the top. Unfortunately, there was a widespread perception that Heinsohn was still Auerbach's whipping boy. "Tommygun" had zero coaching experience. Neither the press nor the public took the new coach very seriously at first.

Around the NBA, everybody was looking forward to getting a shot at Boston.

They got their wish. The Celtics were bad. Boston lost its first four games, eleven of its first fourteen, and plummeted to the bottom of the Eastern Division. Havlicek still remembers players from other teams laughing at the Celtics when Boston would fall behind by twenty or thirty points. They missed Sam Jones's shooting. They missed Russell's defense, his rebounding and his passing—they missed his passing more than they thought they would. In February, Sanders hurt his knee and was lost for the year. When it was over, the Celtics were 34–48, three games ahead of the last-place Pistons and out of the play-offs for the first time since 1950. In twenty years, this was the first time Auerbach was associated with a Celtics team that did not make the play-offs. The Knicks won the championship (oddly enough, the Celtics beat New York four times in seven meetings), and, of course, provincial New York were quick to declare the Knicks the new dynasty. Books were churned out, and the Knicks immediately became one of the best teams in NBA history—maybe *the* best. The Celtics could only look back and laugh; they were going no-where for a while.

The rebuilding of the Boston franchise stands as one of Auer-bach's great accomplishments. He'd proven he could coach. He'd won with Cousy and Russell. Big deal, said the critics; let's see him start from the bottom and make it back. Auerbach did. But there were rough years in the interim, particularly 1969–70.

Heinsohn didn't have much to work with. Havlicek was in his prime, but Sanders, Nelson, and Howell were aging for-wards. Siegfried and Bryant were the returning guards. Ide-ally, these were role players, not starters. In the middle was Henry Finkel, a gentle seven-footer from Dayton, Ohio. Finkel could shoot, but his game was limited (six-foot-five-inch Hav-licek would be the leading rebounder even though he played in the backcourt for two-thirds of the season). Replacing Rus-sell was impossible. Finkel had been a part-time player with Los Angeles and San Diego. The Celtics got him for cash and gave him the job. It was unfair; he was an easy target. His name was perfect for sophomoric jokes. He was painfully thin and looked awkward. His hands weren't the greatest, and some of Havlicek's fastball feeds clanged off "High Henry's" hands. Finkel remains sensitive about the criticism and ridicule he endured when the team went to pieces. This depressing time is often referred to as the "Finkel Era," but it certainly wasn't his fault. He wasn't Russell, but there were 200 million other Americans who also were not Russell. Why blame High Henry? Finkel's backup was no better. Jim "Bad News" Barnes was Finkel's relief, and they didn't call him Bad News for nothing. In moments of desperation, Heinsohn inserted six-six Nelson into the pivot. It was just like the old days of pro basketball. The possibility existed that Nelson was, in fact, Boston's best center.

Nelson: "I played some pivot. We knew it was going to be bad. We'd finished fourth the year before, and that was with Russell. It was only going to get worse."

The Celtics tried to run even though they could not run. Too many of them did not know the plays. Finkel got booed. Heinsohn got booed. Some nights, there weren't enough fans for a respectable chorus of boos. The Celts drew fewer than five-thousand fans six times, and only 3,944 showed up to see the Lakers play them in Boston in December. They did not sell out a single game in the 1969–70 season.

Boston Globe basketball writer Bob Ryan, author of six books on the Celtics, believes that without Havlicek in 1969–70 the team might have won only ten games instead of their lofty total of thirty-four.

What was it like to play Boston in this first post-Russell season? "The difference is simple," said Cincinnati veteran Johnny Green. "Now you can get lay-ups."

"I knew we were going to have some problems," remembers Havlicek. "But we still had a pretty veteran team. If we could get someone to replace Russ we would be all right. During the regular season we still held the advantage over the Knicks, so we figured we could still hang in there with a lot of clubs. I think we lost fifteen games by two, three, or four points. And if you just get Russell in there for half of 'em, you win 'em."

The Celtics came back with help from three terrific first-round draft picks. In 1968, basking in the glow of championship number ten, Auerbach had selected Houston guard Don Chaney. Chaney was a quiet, defensive player with long arms and no shot. He was a bigger, 1970s' version of K. C. Jones. Like K. C., Chaney played in the shadow of a collegiate superstar: Elvin Hayes. Auerbach had had good luck taking role players from high-profile college teams (Siegfried played with Jerry

Lucas, and Havlicek and K. C. with Bill Russell), and Chaney seemed like a good gamble.

In 1969, after the eleventh championship, Auerbach again addressed his backcourt needs. K. C. was gone, and Sam Jones was retiring his bank shot. Red selected Jo Jo White, a shooting guard from Kansas. White was an outstanding college player, but teams were scared to select him because they believed he was obligated to spend two years in the military. Auerbach picked White and went to work on his vast Washington connections. Suddenly Jo Jo was in the Marine Reserve program and missed only training camp and the first twelve games of the season (this is the kind of special-interest power play that infuriates many Auerbach-haters). Soon White was getting his feet wet with the struggling Celtics. Rookies, especially rookie guards, hadn't played much in Boston during the golden years. Sam sat. K. C. sat. But Jo Jo played, and so did Chaney. The Celtics no longer had the luxury of letting their youngsters watch and learn. Everybody was tossed into the pool. On January 28, 1970, White hit twelve of twenty-two shots in a 112–100 victory over Philadelphia. It was a harbinger, and one of the few highlights of a dreadful season.

On the recommendation of Nelson, Auerbach had selected no-name forward Steve Kuberski of Bradley in the third round of the 1969 draft. Kuberski was a Moline (Illinois) neighbor of Nelson. Once the season was lost, Chaney, White, and Kuberski got a lot of playing time.

Heinsohn battled with some of his veterans. Dissension was nonexistent during the championship years, but losing breeds discontent, and Bryant and Siegfried weren't happy with their reduced roles. No one would have dared challenge Auerbach or Russell, but this was a new era. The Celtics were suddenly like everybody else. The Celtics were losers, and they had morale problems. Celtics-haters everywhere rejoiced.

Finkel: "It was a rough year mainly because the fans got against me. Anytime you play at home and the fans boo you, it's rough on you personally, and I'm a very sensitive guy. I took it very badly. As a matter of fact, I contemplated retirement for a while. I was twenty-six or twenty-seven years old. Tommy Heinsohn and Red Auerbach called me into the office after the season was over and told me to calm down and play my own game, and they told me that help would be on the way."

There was some necessary subtraction, and it came in the form of the expansion draft. Auerbach knew who to hold and who to let go. Buffalo, Cleveland, and Portland beckoned, and Siegfried, Bryant, and Howell were gone. This meant that Havlicek, Nelson, and Sanders were the only survivors from a championship won one year earlier.

A single, great reward came with the 34–48 record. For the first time since 1956, the Celtics had one of the top four draft picks in the country. Detroit selected Bob Lanier, San Diego Rudy Tomjanovich, and Atlanta Pete Maravich. This was one of the strongest draft crops in NBA history. Sam Lacey, Geoff Petrie, Calvin Murphy, and Nate Archibald were still available when it came time for Boston to select, and Red Auerbach leaned forward to the microphone and said, "Boston drafts Dave Cowens of Florida State." Fortunately, the Celtics had finished two games behind Cincinnati. Royals coach Bob Cousy coveted Cowens but had to settle for Lacey.

"There was a lot of speculation that Cincinnati was going to draft me," says Cowens. "That was the area that I was from. But because I was a left-handed center, I was always a big Bill Russell fan. When I'd play one-on-one, everybody was a player and I was always Russell."

Cowens was 6-feet-8½-inches and, like Havlicek, could run all day. He was something of a secret because Florida State had been banned from the NCAA tournament for recruiting violations. Former Celtic Mal Graham scouted Cowens and gave Auerbach a glowing report. The Redhead went to see the redhead and started to get nervous; Cowens was so good that Auerbach was afraid somebody would select him before Boston picked fourth. In typical Red fashion, the Celtic guru stormed out of a Florida State game, leaving the impression that he was disgusted with what he saw. There were certainly questions about Cowens's size. Cowens was a muscular young man, but at his height he was at *least* a half foot shorter than the new dominant force, Lew Alcindor. At six-foot-nine, Russell had been able to neutralize seven-foot-one Chamberlain, but Cowens would be giving up more than six inches, and he didn't jump as high or run the court as well as Russell. And the Celtics knew their hole was in the pivot position. After looking at Finkel and Bad News Barnes for a year, it was obvious the Green had to find a new center.

Heinsohn wasn't sure whether his number-one pick was a center or a forward. Cowens won Most Valuable Player in the Stokes game at Monticello, New York, then reported to Celtic rookie camp and wore out everybody with his hustle and stamina. It was John Havlicek all over again—a very big John Havlicek. Heinsohn designed an offense that would accent Cowens's abilities and minimize his limitations. Cowens was instructed to outrun the big guys and overpower the smaller ones. He played away from the basket more than most big men. It worked. He scored sixteen points with seventeen rebounds in his NBA debut against the defending-champion Knicks. He scored twenty-seven in his second pro game. Heinsohn moved him to center, and, utilizing his quickness, Cowens held his own against Abdul-Jabbar, Nate Thurmond, Willis Reed, Walt Bellamy, Wes Unseld, and Chamberlain. He shared Rookie-of-the-Year honors with Portland's Geoff Petrie.

"I wasn't thinking much about what had happened there the year before," says Cowens. "I just wanted to make the team. You go from one basketball court to the next, and you want to be tough and make people believers."

Havlicek remembers, "Dave wasn't projected as a center at the time, but he was an individual who was really going to be playing hard. He was fearless, he had speed, he could jump, he could run. He'd get out of control every now and then, but after the mystery man [Garfield Smith] didn't pan out as our center, the only guy we had that could come close to being a center was Cowens."

Nelson: "I could tell he was special. When he came in I befriended him right away. He lived in my house. He was really dedicated. We would play every day here and go out in the summertime and play one-on-one. When I started with him, I was just kicking his behind and he couldn't beat me. About a month later, I couldn't beat him. He was really going to be special, I could tell. But I didn't know he could play center at his size. I knew he was strong, and I thought he was more of a power forward."

The Celtics won ten in a row early in the year and finished 44–38. It wasn't good enough to make the play-offs, but it was a ten-game improvement. Meanwhile, Havlicek said the team was dumb, and the number of season ticket holders was down to 850. Could anyone have guessed that the Celtics were only three years away from winning the championship again?

Cowens was not your run-of-the-mill NBA talent. He had more intellectual curiosity than most professional athletes. He lived in a one-room cottage on an estate in Weston, Massachusetts, enrolled in a course in auto mechanics, attempted to learn sign language, and later took time off to drive a taxicab on Boston's rugged streets (in 1990 he announced candidacy for Massachusetts Secretary of State). He was frugal. He drove an Oldsmobile and wore flannel shirts. He hated phonies. He was a hardwood Thoreau who heard his own drummer. He raised Christmas trees on his Newport, Kentucky property. He was not into hero worship. Never a basketball fan, he was a *player*. On the court he was absolutely fearless and tireless, and he had a crazed look that scared many of his opponents. He was left-handed and could shoot from the perimeter. He could also jump. The black guys had never seen a white center who could jump like Cowens. And there was no big man who could run with him. National Basketball Association centers weren't used to working this hard for their points. They could

reach over young David, but they could not get around him
or beat him down the floor. He was prone to foul trouble. Like
many NBA rookies, he got called for stuff that veterans got
away with, but there was also a form of reverse racism at work
with the officials. One ref admitted that Cowens got called for
many fouls he didn't commit because officials simply couldn't
believe a white player could jump as high as Cowens did. When
he'd block a shot, they'd figure he must have fouled the other
player. Cowens was charged with 350 personals and fouled out
fifteen times in his rookie season.

"My attitude was, 'Let's see what these players are all
about,'" Cowens says. "I knew a Wilt Chamberlain could over-
whelm me on offense, but I said, 'Let's just see how hard these
guys want to work.' I think they got pissed at me because I
wanted to work hard. They weren't used to somebody who
played the way I did. I'd be running them, and after a while
they'd think, 'The hell with this.' That's intimidation. . . . Heinsohn and other people said I had to be enthu-
siastic and emotional out there or else I'd be just another white
guy. It's basketball. . . . You get involved. You shoot it, you
pass it, you rebound, you try to run faster than the other guy
and get yourself in the right place. You test everybody's
strength, their ferocity."

Finkel was delighted. "Cowens turned it around completely," says the 1969–70 scapegoat. "When you win, the fans
love everybody, and I happened to fall into that category.
Suddenly, the fans liked me because I was on a winning team.
It was a complete 360 with the fans."

The cast was getting stronger. Jo Jo White averaged
twenty-one points in 1970–71, and White and Chaney were
developing into a steady backcourt. Havlicek was the designated superstar, and Nelson contributed fourteen points per
game. Sanders played only seventeen games because of a knee
injury, but he was ready to come back strong in 1971–72.

The 1971–72 edition won the East Division with a 56–26
record but was wiped out by the Knicks in five games in the

conference finals. Cowens had a sensational season. He cut down on his fouls and was the East's starting center at the All Star game. The Celts were still a little too young, and they lacked a rebounding forward. Heinsohn often started four players under age twenty-five, and Nelson, Havlicek, Sanders, and Kuberski needed a beef brother to help Cowens on the boards.

Enter Paul Silas.

Drafting pro basketball players is an inexact science, and Auerbach has always been a long-range thinker in this area. His team usually finished too high to give Boston a top pick. The Celtics never had to worry about a coin flip. Auerbach had to be creative when it came time to draft. After Havlicek in 1962, the Celts went dry for five years—Bill Green, Mel Counts, Ollie Johnson, Jim Barnett, and Mal Graham. Counts brought Howell, but the rest didn't bring much of anything. The next five years were good ones. Auerbach selected Chaney, White, and Cowens before stumbling with Clarence Glover in 1971. He recovered by getting Paul Westphal in 1972 (the last good first-rounder until Cedric Maxwell in 1977), and in the fall of 1972, he got another player because of something he did in the 1970 draft. The Celtics got Phoenix forward Silas for the rights to Charlie Scott.

Scott was a dazzling guard from North Carolina who went to the ABA in 1970. Knowing he couldn't get him, Auerbach drafted Scott's rights with his seventh pick in 1970. A seventh-rounder is a throwaway pick, anyway, and what the heck? You never know. In 1972, Scott was set to jump to the NBA. Phoenix wanted him very badly, and Scott and the Suns agreed on a multiyear contract. There was only one problem: the little redheaded man in Boston was holding his hand out, saying, "What's in it for me?" Auerbach had Scott's NBA rights. The Suns delivered Silas.

Paul Silas was excellent compensation for a seventh-round draft choice, and it was Silas who put the Celtics over the top in 1972–74. He was an eight-year veteran, and he knew how to get the ball. He lost thirty pounds of excess baggage the year before reporting to the Celtics. Not much of a leaper, Silas said, "It's not how high you go, it's how much space you take up while you're up there."

Silas says, "When I came to the Celtics I was coming off my best year, and I really didn't want to come from Phoenix. I had settled out there, and I was apprehensive about the whole thing. I'd heard so much about the Celtic mystique and the way they carried themselves. I guess I kind of took a wait-and-see attitude. The first month was kind of a feeling-out thing for me. The training camp was the toughest training camp I ever encountered in my life. Tommy was coach at the time, and there was something very different about them—how hard they practiced and their general knowledge of the game. And it all kind of started to fit. We weren't very big but won sixty-eight ball games that year, and should have won the championship if Havlicek hadn't got hurt. It was something special. I remember that this was just the beginning of teams starting not to dress well. Satch Sanders was still on our club, and he went to Red and said, 'Listen, I don't care what the rest of those clubs do, we're gonna wear a shirt and tie or turtleneck, and we're going to be a class act.' It was just those little things that kind of won me over."

The natty 1972–73 Celtics went 68–14. It was six more wins than any Celtics team and still stands as a franchise best. The 1966–67 76ers went 68–13, and the 1971–72 Lakers went 69–13. Those are the only better records in NBA history, and both teams had Wilt Chamberlain at center. This Celtics unit was a lean and hungry team, a team that could never take a night off. They won their first ten games, then took nine straight in December, and finished by taking twenty-four of their final twenty-six games, the final eight in a row. They won nine of ten on the West Coast and finished eleven games ahead of the New York Knicks. They ran as much as any Celtics team, no small boast. Cowens was Most Valuable Player, and Havlicek, ageless at thirty-three, remained at the top of his game. The city of Boston was turned on by this team.

The Celtics drew a club record 10,852 people per home game. It was undoubtedly the best Boston team that *did not* win a championship. It is possible that no NBA team ever got more out of its talents than this unit. The players and fans remember this one as the one that got away. For years the Celtics left fans in other towns grumbling about injuries and hard luck, and finally it happened to Boston. They struggled to get past the Hawks in six games (Havlicek hit for a Boston play-off record fifty-four points in Game 1), then drew the Knicks.

The 1973 Knicks were a cagey, veteran group, much like the 1968–69 Celtics. They felt they had another championship in them and were not afraid of the young legs from Boston. The Celtics won the first game, 134–108, a stunning number considering the defensive prowess of the early 1970s' Knicks. The series was tied, 1–1, when Havlicek hurt his right shoulder fighting through a Dave DeBusschere pick early in the final period. The Celts led by two points when Havlicek went out, but the Knicks won by seven. Because of a partial shoulder separation and tearing of the joint capsule, Havlicek did not play Game 4, and the Knicks went up, 3–1, taking a 117–110 decision in double-overtime. Havlicek watched the game in his street clothes, his right arm in a sling, while Heinsohn cried about the officiating team of Jack Madden and Jake O'Donnell.

Boston fans will always remember Game 5 at the Garden when Havlicek came off the bench to score eighteen points (eight of them left-handed) in a one-point victory that took the series back to Madison Square Garden. "Hondo" was at his Audie Murphy best in this one. The assistant trainer had to comb his hair for him. The Celtics won Game 6 by ten points in New York, and one of the great ticket crushes of all time preceded Game 7 in the Boston Garden. Fans lined up overnight, and the train station was packed early Saturday morning. It was so crowded that ticket buyers at the front had to be hoisted over the crowd after they made their purchase. The Celtics hadn't played a seventh game since Russell and Company popped Jack Kent Cooke's balloons in 1969. The Celtics had never lost a seventh game, and they obviously had the hoop gods on their side. Havlicek was the picture of heroism, and, after all, Boston had already proven it had the best team by winning sixty-eight regular season games.

It is impossible to say why the Celtics were more appealing to Boston in 1973 than at any prior time. We are left with many theories. Certainly the town was becoming more sophisticated in terms of basketball appreciation. A generation of greater Bostonians had grown up with a championship basketball team, seen it fall, and now there was a hoop revival. The 1972–73 Celtics promised a return to the good old days. There was much more media coverage than there had been when the Celtics were perennial champs. Boston newspapers did not start to travel with the Celtics (except for play-offs) until the final years of the Russell era. In 1972–73, there was a glut of Celtics coverage, home and away.

At the secondary level, Boston basketball was bigger than ever (remember, the sport was not part of the Boston school curriculum when the Celtics were formed in 1946). High school basketball was thriving, and in 1972, former NBA official Ken Hudson helped put together the first Boston Shootout, featuring All Star high school teams from across the land. Boston won, thanks to the play of city talents King Gaskins, Bobby Carrington, Wilfred Morrison, Billy Collins, Ron Lee, and Carlton Smith. All six went on to major universities, five in the Boston area. Lee became an NBA star, and Carrington played briefly in the league. Meanwhile, the city of Boston was rounding up corporate sponsorship to promote the Boston Neighborhood Basketball League, a program designed to give inner-city youths a chance to play organized ball throughout the summer. Basketball was big in Boston—at every level.

Havlicek says, "I think in 1973 and 1974, interest started to turn around a little bit. I think it was because the championships came harder. Prior to that, they always thought we were going to win. Then, when we hadn't won, they said, 'Well, maybe this team has a chance to win. They're playing hard and they're a small team. They had a couple of guys who run around and play as hard as they can.' We were sort of over-achievers, I think."

No discussion of Celtic popularity is complete without an amateur assessment of the ever-changing/never-changing ra-cial climate in Boston. The city is approximately 10 percent black, and there are still plenty of neighborhoods where white children are taught to hate blacks. At its benign best, Boston is a quietly segregated town. Blacks know where they are not welcome and do not go there. Ditto for the whites. You won't see many black faces at Fenway Park or Quincy Market, for example. Forced busing came to the city in the mid-1970s, and in some ways the climate is better today, but generations of hatred and ignorance cannot be wiped out by court orders.

Across the land, many American sports fans have learned to identify with the Celtics as a team with a larger proportion of white players. Auerbach and Company are justifiably miffed when this point is raised and will always cite: (1) the Celtics were first to draft a black player (Chuck Cooper); (2) the Celtics were first to play five blacks at one time (Russell, Sam Jones, K. C. Jones, Sanders, Naulls); and (3) the Celtics were the first team of any major sport to name a black head coach (Russell), beating the NFL to the punch by a whopping twenty years. The Celtics have had three black head coaches (K. C., Sanders, Russell). Despite all of the above, the Celtics tra-ditionally *do* have a larger proportion of white players than other NBA teams, and it is impossible not to wonder if that was part of their appeal in Boston during the 1970s and 1980s. There can be no doubt that Dave Cowens, and later Kevin McHale and Larry Bird, satisfied the inferiority complexes of some of the white population thirsty for "white man's re-venge." Conversely, some black players on other teams resent the Celtics' image as a "whiter" team. Gerald Henderson played five years in Boston, then toured with the Supersonics, Knicks, 76ers, Bucks, and Pistons. Asked why teams get pumped up to play the Celtics, Henderson, a black man, says, "Well, they do have that reputation as the team with all the white players."

Boston mayor Ray Flynn, who grew up in South Boston, a hotbed of racial tension, says, "I really have been one of those people who have defended the Celtics, because I know more about it than the average person. I tried out for the team, and I know that the name of the game is to put the best players on the court, and I feel that that has been the case. As a result, I think they've helped the image of Boston. Some of the players have been a great inspiration to the young people of the city of Boston."

Paul Silas says, "When I first got here [1972–73] there was not that much enthusiasm at all. I recall that when we played the Knicks, the Knicks would have as many fans as we would have. That used to really upset us, but I think after our championship in 1974 we began to win the fans over. It was amazing because we won sixty-eight ball games, and they still weren't believers."

Tom Sanders adds, "Race was never an issue. I think they're more popular now because of all the marketing that's done. If you look back at it, it started in the early 1970s when corporations owned the team. That's when they went out to corporations for ticket sales. It was something they'd missed all those years. They started selling the product, and now you see what we've got."

Boston sports radio's Eddie Andelman says, "I don't buy the racial thing. I remember when the Knicks came in and first had black players, people turned out, much like they did when Jackie Robinson first came through Boston to play against the Braves. And people here really liked the Globetrotters. It's just that in those days the NBA had centers that were plodding, and you didn't see the great athletes that you have today. . . . Those were the days when the most prominent shot was the two-handed set shot. There was no twenty-four-second clock, there weren't that many great dribblers, and it was dull. It was a whole different kind of a show than it is now."

K. C. Jones, another black star from the 1960s and the Celtics' coach in the 1980s, says, "Cousy retired and then attendance dropped, but we still won more championships. Then Havlicek sort of blossomed. Then there was the Phoenix game [1976 play-offs], and the explosion hit. That just put it right over the top. That's when the popularity came. I think it has to do a lot with identification. A lot of blacks identify with Magic Johnson. The white population identifies with Larry Bird. It's not a question of race, it's a question of identification with someone who has something in common with you. So who fills the stands? Ninety-five percent white. When they come to the game, they see Havlicek and Larry, and you can't buy a ticket. . . . When I was in Seattle, a writer came up to me and said that he knows for a fact that Red Auerbach wants white players only. If that was the case, then I would have been totally insulted because I was the coach, which means Red was giving me players I didn't want to have. Well, I'm the one who chose the players, and if I ever chose a player because of his color then I'd never be a winning coach because my mind would be more on issues outside basketball rather than on the court. It was a big issue between Rick Carlisle and David Thirdkill in 1986. They were making a big lottery thing that we had to keep Thirdkill or we wouldn't have enough blacks. It was like it can't be right if you have all blacks on the team, and if you got all whites there's something wrong, too. Whatever you do, you can't be right, so why worry about it?"

When Dennis Johnson and Cedric Maxwell started for the World Champion Celtics in the 1980s, they played a private game watching the Boston newspapers. DJ says, "Whenever we'd lose, they'd use a big picture of me or Robert [Parish] or Max [Maxwell] on the front of sports. Check it out. When we won, they'd use Larry [Bird] or Kevin [McHale] or Danny [Ainge], but when we'd lose it'd be one of us."

Auerbach has been reluctant to plunge into this area. "My standard answer is this: Ever since Walter Brown owned the team, and he and I saw eye to eye, every player we get is a player we feel can do the best for this team. We don't care anything about his religion, his color, or anything, and that's where it's at. People are always trying to start trouble and look for trouble. I don't pay any attention to that. I refuse to even discuss it."

Racial overtones aside, Cowens was clearly a more likable superstar than Russell. Russell had a chip on his shoulder and was considered unapproachable. He liked it that way. Cowens was a 6-foot-8½-inch everyman. He went to work the way a hockey player went to work. Boston fans liked that.

And so there was a crush to see the Celtics do what they had done so easily eleven previous times. This time, the slipper wouldn't fit. On Sunday, April 29, the Knicks dismantled the Celtics, 94–78, in the Garden. Silas had warned, "Tradition won't be suiting up for this one. We have to go out and do it ourselves." New York did it. The crafty Knicks exploited Havlicek, taking the ball from him and stealing his passes. They let him take all the southpaw shots he wanted. The Celts were beaten in a deciding game for the first time in their history, and another player from the golden days said good-bye. This was Tom Sanders's last game.

"That year we would have won the championship if I had not hurt my shoulder. I'm sure of it," Havlicek says.

Star Knicks guard Walt Frazier remembers, "We were confident, but our fans were not. We could have ended it in a sixth game in New York. After they beat us, our fans were all saying, 'Oh, that's it; you'll never beat them up there.' But the players really didn't feel that way. We knew it wouldn't be easy. What Red always did, when you'd come to Boston it would . . . take you twenty minutes to find someone to let you in the locker room. Once you got in the locker room it's too hot or too cold, and there are no towels and no tape. They send you through all this aggravation before the game. This time, for that seventh game, they put us in a locker room we'd never been in. The tall guys had to duck. That kind of spurred us on. It really upset us a lot, and I think that was kind of a motivating point. It was the final straw that broke the camel's back, and we beat them, and it totally erased the invincibility that they'd had over the Knicks and the Knicks fans. They were stunned, and I can recall that going off the floor."

Lessons learned in the spring of 1973 came in handy when the Celtics went after championship number twelve the following spring. Coming off a 56–26 season, the Celtics beat Buffalo in a tough six-game series, wiped out the Knicks in five, then won a seventh game on the road to upset the Milwaukee Bucks and bring another flag to Boston.

The glory was spread around, but no one was happier than Auerbach. For a long time he'd been hearing "You never won without Russell." Finally, he won without Russell. He had built a team from bottom to top in five seasons. This stands as one of his great achievements. The 1974 team featured four starters who were Celtics first-round draft picks. He'd done it without the big bankrolls that existed in New York and Los Angeles. The 1974 title also signifies the beginning of a second period of Celtics success. If you toss out Boston's first eleven championships, and start from scratch in 1969–70, the Celtics have won five of twenty-one titles. The Lakers have won six and the Knicks and Pistons two. No other NBA teams have won more than one championship in that period. Yes, the Celtics proved they could win without Russell and they have been doing it for more than twenty years.

Heinsohn introduced a new wrinkle at the start of the 1973–74 season. Nelson returned to the starting lineup, and Silas became the sixth man. They won twelve straight early in the year, and were 29–6 in mid-January. There was some discontent with Heinsohn, and they didn't finish particularly strong.

It took Silas a while to get used to the idea of coming off the bench. Like any player from another team, he did not initially embrace the sixth-man role. It's only special in Boston. You grow up playing basketball, and you want to be a starter. The best players start. Auerbach's logic was, "The best players are on the floor at the finish."

"I was very upset about it early on," says Silas. "I had known about Havlicek being a sixth man, and Ramsey, but it wasn't a big deal to me. I had started in Phoenix and really done well. So I came here, and Tommy grabbed me one day and said, 'We're going to make you our sixth man.' I was wondering what the deal was. It took me a while to see. It was sort of like the sledgehammer effect. When I would come in, usually I was a little better than the guy that was coming in to guard me, so we would have an uplift as I did go in. And 'Nellie' and I had a competitive thing. He wanted to prove he should be starting, and I wanted to prove the same thing. So it really helped both of us."

Boston drew Buffalo in the first round of the play-offs, and the one-two punch of Bob McAdoo and Ernie DiGregorio presented a formidable obstacle. The Braves proved to be tougher than the Knicks, but everybody knew the Bucks were the team to beat. Abdul-Jabbar was at the top of his game, but guard Lucius Allen had ripped up his knee slipping on a warm-up jacket, and an aging Oscar Robertson was the Milwaukee quarterback. The Bucks won fifty-nine games during the regular season and had the home-court advantage.

This was one terrific series. Rival coaches Tom Heinsohn and Larry Costello matched wits and had the benefits of excellent scouting reports submitted by John Killilea (Boston) and Hubie Brown (Milwaukee). Two of the games went into overtime, one double-overtime. The visiting team won five times, including the final four games. Neither team scored one-hundred points in regulation, until the Celtics did it in the final game. The Celtics led, 3–2, and expected to wrap things up at home. On May 10, in a nationally televised drama, the Bucks took Game 6 in double-overtime, 102–101, to force a seventh game in Milwaukee. Game 6 has been a magical number in

Boston baseball lore. It was in Game 6 in 1975 that Carlton Fisk hit his midnight shot off the left-field foul pole. It was in Game 6 in 1986 that Mookie Wilson's ground ball slithered between the legs of Bill Buckner and into history. Game 6 in 1974 remains a Celtic masterpiece. It wasn't a victory, but it awoke the Boston fandom and gave the region new appreciation of the Celtics heart. Thirty-nine million people watched the game, and it is considered a pivotal moment in the NBA's climb toward "major" sports status.

Cowens was battling Abdul-Jabbar, just as Russell had dueled Chamberlain. Cowens's corner jumper and a last-minute steal forced the first overtime. The score of the first overtime was 4–4. In five minutes of white-knuckle basketball, these explosive teams scored four points each. Havlicek later called it the best five minutes of defensive basketball he'd ever seen. Cowens fouled out in the second overtime, and Havlicek took over. He hit a pair of killer jumpers, and the second, a rainbow over Abdul-Jabbar's extended arm, gave the Celts a 101–100 lead with eight seconds left. Havlicek scored nine of Boston's eleven points in the second overtime.

Kareem wasn't done. He got the ball on the right side of the key, and with five seconds left, standing seventeen feet from the basket, let fly with a sky hook over Henry Finkel. As the ball crashed down through the net, the clock struck :03. Jo Jo White's buzzer-beater fell short, and the Celtics were scheduled for one more trip to Milwaukee for Game 7.

Late after the historic loss, Auerbach huddled with Heinsohn, Killilea, and old friend Bob Cousy. Cousy was done with the Royals and was living back in Worcester. The four men decided to employ a new strategy for the final game. The Celtics would focus their entire defense on Abdul-Jabbar. Let one of the other guys win it. Most teams did this on a regular basis against the Bucks, but the Celtics had let Cowens play the big guy straight up for six games.

Silas: "I remember Cooz being around and telling Tommy, 'You've got to front Kareem.' I was supposed to let my man roam and play in front of Kareem with Dave in back. The amazing part to me was that Tommy changed his whole defensive scheme for that one particular game, which not a whole lot of coaches would do."

Cowens, meanwhile, was steaming. He thought he'd let the team down and was committed to winning Game 7. Today Cowens says, "I can remember walking and pacing until twelve, one o'clock at night in Milwaukee in the spring—walking around the streets too nervous to go to sleep and then getting up early in the morning wanting to get to the gym, anxious to get started 'cause I was wearing myself out worrying about it. Let's go, you know? Thank God it was an early game."

Celtic fans thanked the hoop god for Cowens. He wore his maniacal look throughout Game 7. The redhead hit eight of thirteen first-half shots, finished with twenty-eight points and fourteen rebounds, and (with help from Silas) held Abdul-Jabbar scoreless for an eighteen-minute stretch, while the Celtics built a big lead at the Mecca. A weary Oscar shot 2–13, and the Celtics cruised to victory. Havlicek, Cowens, White, and Chaney were celebrating on the bench when the game ended. The subs were on the court, and the Mecca was silent. This was the Celtics team everybody had danced on four years earlier. Now, they were back. They celebrated. Don Chaney drank his first can of beer in years. Silas walked up to Auerbach, hugged him, and said, "You know, Red, when I first got here I really believed all that stuff about tradition and so on was a lot of bullshit. But I know better now. It's real, all right, and I'm awfully proud to be a part of it." Auerbach beamed.

Silas: "When I became a believer, I think it did Red all the good in the world because I think I was about the only doubter."

Paul Westphal got into some champagne and passed out. Havlicek, remembering Bailey Howell in 1968, called the team together for a brief prayer before they boarded the flight home to Boston. When they touched down, Cowens went out and somehow ended up sleeping on a park bench in the middle of the Boston Public Garden. People who saw him while on their way to work Monday morning were probably thinking, "Hey! that looks a little like Dave Cowens. Naaa. No way." What a civic promotion; ride the Swan Boats and see a championship NBA center.

Cowens: "We were in Milwaukee and we came back after the game. When we got back, a crowd met us at the airport. By the time I got home, it had to be eight o'clock at night. My brother met me at the airport, and we went back to my place and sat around talking. I was so hyped up I had to go out, so I just went out and started visiting people that I knew all around the city. It got to be two, three o'clock in the morning. I just got tired. My car was within eyeshot, but I was in the Garden so I just went to sleep on one of the benches. When I woke up a lot of people were walking past me, sort of looking at me. I just had on a T-shirt and shorts. It was warm out, and we had a parade to go to that day around noontime."

Cowens also notes, "I was so sorry when that game and that series were over. It had been such a great series, such great basketball. The reason it was so good was that we had contrasting styles. One of our styles was going to win, one of our tempos."

"I can't ever remember being any happier than after winning that game," Havlicek says. "That championship brought me peace of mind. It was really great to have the knowledge restored . . . that we could play the game correctly."

Mayor Kevin White hosted a victory celebration at Boston City Hall, and Havlicek stood up and told the masses, "There were times I worried whether Boston would ever accept us. And I wondered if I wouldn't have been better off in New York or Los Angeles where pro basketball is really big."

The pro game was finally big in Boston. Like a great marriage, the partners didn't know how good they had it until there was a temporary separation. Boston sports fans had been spoiled, and the five-year drought made them appreciate what it means to have the best basketball team in the world.

A bumper sticker appeared on cars throughout New England: PASS THE WORD, THE CELTS ARE BACK.

They weren't back for long. In 1974–75, Boston went 60–22, winning the East. Cowens missed the first seventeen games because of a broken foot, but the Celtics finished fast, winning fifty of their last sixty-four games. They continued to play great defense. Boston wiped out Houston in the first play-off series. In the conference finals, the Celtics were pitted against the Washington Bullets, coached by K. C. Jones. Washington had Wes Unseld, Elvin Hayes, Mike Riordan, Kevin Porter, Phil Chenier, and streak-shooting Nick Weatherspoon. They played great defense and they ran. They were a lot like you-know-who. Ex-Celtic Sharman had won as coach of the Lakers, and Jones was doing it with the Bullets.

The Celtics were convinced they had the best team, but the Bullets were young and hungry. Unseld matched Cowens, Hayes scored with Havlicek, Chenier was a pure shooter, and the annoying Weatherspoon torched Boston with an array of weird shots, all of which seemed to go in the basket. Washington was 36–5 at home in 1974–75. Jones did not think his team could beat the Celtics, but he changed his mind when Washington overcame an eight-point halftime deficit and beat Boston, 100–95, in the Garden to open the series. The Celts were blown out in Game 2 and never recovered. Washington took the sixth and final game in the Cap Centre, 98–92, and the Celtics were dethroned.

Chaney was leaving to join the Spirits of St. Louis of the ABA. Auerbach reacted by trading Westphal to Phoenix for Charlie Scott, the same Charlie Scott who brought Silas in 1972. There was some doubt about the combination of White and Scott—both were shooters—but Auerbach didn't worry. Nelson was ready to hang up his black high-tops and announced that 1976 would be his last year. Nobody knew it at the time, but this would also be the end of Silas's Celtics career. Havlicek was thirty-six and had plenty of miles left, but he played much of the season with a torn fascia in his right arch. He carried a rectangular, turquoise-colored dishpan with him throughout the play-offs; this common household item enabled him to ice down his foot on airplanes, buses, and in hotel rooms. Havlicek today keeps it in a closet in his home as a memento of his final championship season.

The 1975–76 Celtics won fifty-four games. The most memorable moment of the regular season came when Cowens intentionally blindsided Houston guard Mike Newlin after Newlin twice had drawn phony offensive fouls by flopping to the floor. Livid, Cowens spotted Newlin dribbling up the right side and plowed into the trickster. Boston's raging bull then turned to referee Bill Jones and announced, "Now that's a foul!" Cowens no doubt enhanced his image as the little man's big man, but he was criticized in the press and responded to the *Boston Globe* with a letter—a position paper on the epidemic of phantom fouls.

The 1975–76 Celtics won another championship, banner number thirteen. In the final series with the Phoenix Suns, they participated in a triple-overtime game that is always included when the "best-ever" lists are drawn. The entire front-court—Cowens, Silas, and Havlicek—was named to the NBA's first-team all-defensive unit (this hasn't been done before or since). Scott took over for Chaney. White was better than ever and took the play-off Most Valuable Player award.

There was luck involved. The Celtics were sluggish in the spring of 1976, and going into the play-offs, the teams they feared most were the Sixers, the Bullets, and the defending champions, the Warriors (fifty-nine wins). With help from Buffalo, Cleveland, and Phoenix, Boston didn't have to face any of the three. Havlicek hurt his foot in the first series and missed three games against the Braves. Boston beat Buffalo, then Cleveland, winning the sixth and final game on the road in both series. The highlight of the Cleveland series came in Game

5, when Heinsohn was ejected by Richie Powers and Auerbach left his seat in loge seven, moving to the press table just to the left of the Celtic bench. In the final quarter against Cleveland, Boston assistant coach John Killilea had the greatest coach in NBA history sitting two feet on his left, just in case. The Celtics won it, 99–94.

The Suns were a third-place team that had finished just two games over .500. Under their young coach, John MacLeod, they finished strong, and they were almost impossible to beat at home. They upset the defending-champion Warriors to gain the finals against Boston. In the 1976 finals, the home team won each of the first four games.

Cowens says, "All I remember is they were bellyaching about how physical we were. It was supposed to be me beating up Alvan Adams and Westphal and Van Arsdale. It worked. They called a lot of fouls on us. Things went back and forth. We beat them at home two in a row, and they beat us out there. It was a pretty close series, but it seemed like we either beat them by quite a bit or we lost a close one."

Silas adds, "They did say we were beating up on 'em, and we probably were. They claimed we were dirty ball players and that kind of thing. Dave and I had a little thing going where we knew we had to come out and hit the boards hard every night in order to be successful. We had this little thing where Dave would come over and pat me on the rump right before we started each game, and we knew at that time that— hey, we had to go get it. In this one particular game in the play-off against Phoenix, he waited until the last possible moment. When we finally got ready to walk the court, he gave me my slap. It was a lot of fun. We had quite a few characters on that team. And we had a lot of smart players."

On June 4, 1976, Phoenix came to Boston for Game 5, and the Celtics won a close one—a game for the ages.

America was getting its Bicentennial celebration in gear. The Tall Ships were coming to Boston, and Pops conductor

Arthur Fiedler was preparing for his annual Fourth of July celebration on the Esplanade. Millions of tourists were en route to observe the nation's 200th birthday. It was already warm and muggy in Boston. Summer had arrived. But first, the winter sport had to finish its business.

Havlicek: "I went down that afternoon to the Garden. I took my son, who was six years old, and I had him rebound the ball. I hadn't been practicing at all because of the injury. I remember shooting a little bit because I had to find a way to get some shots up in a short period of time. Since I couldn't run and my shooting wasn't on, I would work out a little bit and get the feel for the ball again. I came to the game thinking I'd play twenty minutes, and I ended up playing fifty-eight."

The Celtics led, 42–20, in the second period, and still held a nine-point lead with 3:49 to play. Westphal got hot and put the game into overtime. At the end of the second overtime, the Suns led by one point with seconds to play when Havlicek banked in an off-balance leaner off the drive with two seconds left.

Havlicek: "Nelson was inbounding the ball, and we set up an emergency score play. Generally, I was the first option, but because of my foot, I became the third option. Jo Jo was covered. He was the first option, and Cowens was the second option. Cowens was covered. Having taken the ball out-of-bounds early in my career, I knew that that's the most crucial part of any last-second heroics. They've got to get it inbounds to someone. He had probably gone through about four seconds in his mind, and there was no one to pass it to. I said, 'Hey, I remember this situation, I got to go to the ball and give him an outlet.' He gave it to me, and I started driving down that left side, and all I wanted to do was get in some traffic, where I could hopefully get some contact and have someone foul me. But I went up and I kept my elbows out, and they just backed off and I was sort of hung out to dry. I realized they weren't going to foul me, and I'd left myself wide open. I said, 'Oh no, now I gotta make the shot.' And, fortunately, I had the good angle and was able to bank it in. It wasn't a particularly long shot."

The clock went down to 0:00 as all hell broke loose. The crowd stormed onto the Garden floor, some of the Celtics went to their locker room, and referee Richie Powers was trying to get one second put back on the clock when a fan punched him. Havlicek was in the trainer's room when somebody came in and told him he had to fight through the crowd and get back out on the court. Order was restored. Sort of. Powers stayed in the game. The Suns were preparing to inbound from the far end of the court when Westphal cleverly called an illegal time-out. Phoenix didn't have any time-outs, but Westphal knew his team would get to inbound from halfcourt if Boston shot a technical free throw. Jo Jo (thirty-three points in sixty minutes) hit the free throw to give Boston a two-point lead. Phoenix inbounded, and the immortal Garfield Heard hit a twenty-two-foot turnaround over Nelson to put the game into a third overtime.

Cowens, Scott, and Silas were all on the bench with six fouls before the game ended, and in the third overtime, White teamed with unlikely heroes Jim Ard and Glenn McDonald (six points in the third overtime) to ice the game. Scott was furious after the game because he'd fouled out on some questionable calls. Auerbach went to the star guard before the press got in and told Scott to shower, go home, and prepare for Game 6. They flew back to Phoenix, where it was 100 degrees outside. Scott scored twenty-five in Game 6, and the Celtics won it, 87–80. They had won all three series on the road. Flag number thirteen. It was a lucky one.

8
Dark Green

THE Celtics were headed for another fall, an over-the-cliff tumble that would be even worse than the one following Bill Russell's retirement. The Celtic family was going to be traumatized by the realities of greed, impatience, jealousy, and selfishness. Things that had been happening to other franchises for thirty years finally happened to Boston, and this would be the true test of Celtics pride. The 1976–79 period stands as the low point in franchise history—worse than the pre-Auerbach days when Walter Brown couldn't make the payroll and worse than the sounds-of-silence days of the Finkel era. The Celtic mystique was put to the test as never before, and there were times when it appeared that the long, happy reign was forever over. The low point came when irresponsible ownership almost forced Auerbach to take a job with the Knicks. Surely, that would have been the end.

There wasn't much favorable fallout after the 1976 title. Nelson retired immediately after the City Hall Plaza celebration. Norm Cook was drafted and would prove to be a player with zero impact. On October 12, Sidney Wicks was purchased from Portland, and eight days later, after a protracted contract dispute, Silas was traded in a three-way deal that brought Wicks's UCLA running mate, Curtis Rowe, to Boston. The Silas deal came one day before the start of the season. Silas was dealt because Auerbach wouldn't cave in to his demand for a three-year, one-million-dollar contract. He would not pay Silas more than Cowens or Havlicek; it went against his lifelong code.

There was another reason for dealing Silas: As in the case of Westphal, Silas was traded because the Celtics feared they might lose an arbitration, which would declare him a free agent; if this happened, the Celtics would get nothing for him. Mistakes had been made involving option clauses before. A blunder of this nature expedited Jan Volk's ascension in the Celtics hierarchy. Modern contracts were far more complex than in the days of Walter Brown's handshake agreements. Volk was a lawyer and the Celtics needed some expertise to keep abreast of the times.

Silas: "Red was really under the gun because I was asking for quite a bit of money at that time, and he felt it would disrupt the whole money scheme. And quite often when players get a lot of money, they quit competing. Years later, Red told me, 'Listen, if I had it to do over again, I probably would have done it differently. But at that time I had to do what I had to do.' I understood that perfectly."

At the start of the 1976–77 season, only Havlicek, Cowens, Kuberski, and White remained from the 1974 champions. They won their first two games, but something was missing—the poise and presence of Paul Silas was missing. After eight games, Cowens stopped by Auerbach's office and told the coach that he wanted a no-pay leave of absence. The team issued an appropriately cryptic press release, and Cowens was gone, into the night. Rumors flew, but it turned out it was nothing more than one of Cowens's transcendental periods. He had lost the fire. Many of his friends, particularly Silas, were gone, and he needed time to think, time to be alone.

Years later, Cowens says, "He was the whole reason we started winning in the first place. When he leaves, a lot of your capability of winning goes with him. We completed each other, we got along; we're still good friends. That always helps. I think if I had looked at it just from a business standpoint it wouldn't have made any difference at all. But my most memorable thoughts are about the people I played with—those relationships."

Cowens missed thirty games and came back in January. The night he returned, Scott broke his forearm and was out until April. The Celts won forty-four games, then beat San Antonio in the first round of the play-offs. *Sports Illustrated* put Wicks on the cover under the headline THAT OLD CELTIC MAGIC. They went to Philadelphia, and there was some magic when White's last-second jump shot gave the Celtics a 1–0 lead. It turned into an old-fashioned seven-game brawl with the Sixers.

Moments after Boston won Game 6 to take the series back to the Spectrum, Philadelphia coach Gene Shue said, "There is no mystique."

There wasn't. Philadelphia won Game 7, 87–73. Lloyd Free (before he became "World B. Free") did some styling at the end, and a Sixers fan taunted radio announcer Johnny Most: "How do you like it, Johnny? Huh? How do you like it?" Given everything that happened, Heinsohn thought this 1976–77 team represented his best coaching job. The Celtics were a team in transition, suffering from internal decay, yet they had extended a good Philadelphia team to a seventh game.

The Celtics did not make the play-offs in either of the next two seasons, finishing 32–50, then 29–53. Unlike the Finkel year of 1969–70, no one was prepared for this fall. The Celts had won forty-four a year earlier, and that was done despite Cowens's odd sabbatical and Scott's broken arm. The big guns were all back, and the team added number-one pick Cedric

Maxwell, a rubberband forward from the University of North Carolina, Charlotte, and Tom Sanders was brought in as assistant coach. Heinsohn was working with a new two-year contract. Veteran guard Dave Bing was signed to beef up the depth in the backcourt.

This was the proverbial "strong team on paper." They had seven players who'd been All Stars, but they also had problems. Cowens came to training camp and said he wanted to go on a nautilus program and skip practice every other day. Wicks held out until opening night, then finally signed for $1.5 million over five years. White was having trouble with his heels. Wicks was out of shape, and the Celts were flabby at the start and went 1–8. Auerbach ripped the team behind closed doors, calling them quitters, singling out Havlicek and White. White was livid. He was already sulking because meddlesome owner Irv Levin had reneged on a new contract. Now Auerbach was calling him a quitter. Havlicek knew it was just Red being Red. White quit for a couple of days and missed at least one practice. Before the next game, he met with Auerbach and returned to the team. Heinsohn reacted by benching everybody except Cowens. Morale was at a new low. When Auerbach hosted the annual team Christmas party, Havlicek, White, and their families were the only families to attend. Gifts had been wrapped for all the others, and it was the saddest of sights to see Auerbach walking around after the party, gathering up the unopened gifts of the ungrateful absentees.

Dave Bing, an NBA Hall of Famer, grew up in Washington, D.C., and remembers, "I'd known Red Auerbach since I was a kid. The opportunity to play under him and to play for such a great organization was a fine way for me to end it up. Unfortunately, Red sold me a bill of goods and told me I would have a chance to play on a championship team—we had all those names: Rowe and Wicks and Cowens and Charlie Scott and Jo Jo—and it didn't work out that way."

Levin went over Auerbach's head. As owner, he was certainly entitled to this privilege, but it had never been a winning formula with other Celtics owners. If Red Auerbach was your basketball boss, it was best to leave him in charge of all organization matters. Levin couldn't resist. He took star players to dinner at the Algonquin Club. He encouraged them to air their gripes. Levin asked Auerbach to take over a couple of practices. He put pressure on his venerable general manager.

There was one regrettable day when the owner ordered Auerbach to run practice while coach Heinsohn watched from the sidelines. Levin made sure he was present for this embarrassing session. Heinsohn sat in a corner while Auerbach changed all the plays. Heinsohn was humiliated, but he wasn't stupid enough to quit. Levin wanted Heinsohn to quit; it would have gotten him out of his two-year contractual commitment. Heinsohn refused.

Scott was traded to the Lakers for Don Chaney, Kermit Washington, and the Lakers' second pick in the 1978 first round. Wicks became the goat of goats. He was a sixth man, making a lot of money after holding out. Fans perceived him as something less than a Celtic. Comparisons with Silas made Wicks look bad. Sidney wanted the ball and this was a team that spread the scoring around. Wicks became a scapegoat, and Heinsohn said, "I wish people would get off Sidney Wicks's ass and let him play. They're doing the same thing to him that they did to Finkel, and it's not fair."

Finally, on January 3, Heinsohn was fired, and Sanders became head coach. This marked the first time in the twenty-two-year history of that franchise that a Celtics coach had been relieved during the season. They were 2–20 on the road by the end of January. Rowe scripted a new Celtics slogan when he said, "Hey, man, there's no Ws and Ls on the paycheck." The only break they got all season was when they were lucky enough to be in Kansas City during New England's blizzard of the century in February 1978. Silas, then a Supersonic, said, "To see them play like that—the guys not really caring—it was really sort of frustrating for me. I really didn't enjoy playing against them. The fight, the spirit, it wasn't there.

When you played the Celtics, you'd be in a battle and you enjoyed it. You hoped it would always be that way. This year, it was almost as if they were a laughingstock." Eighteen players wore Celtics uniforms before the season ended, including Ernie DiGregorio and Zaid Abdul-Aziz.

They finished 32–50, winning their last game, 131–114, as John Havlicek scored twenty-nine points against Buffalo in his final game, Hondo game number 1,441, a record. Havlicek came to the Garden in a rented tuxedo and received a fifty-thousand-dollar mobile home from the team. After the game, there was a telegram waiting for him in the locker room: "Havlicek, Hondo is watching. Congratulations, John Wayne."

It was an inglorious ending to the career of one of the great players in Celtic history. Cousy kept the franchise afloat. Russell took the Celtics to the promised land. Cowens brought the spark that started a new generation of winning. And Bird came to the rescue when the franchise sagged to its lowest point. Havlicek is the bridge connecting each generation. He played with Cousy, Russell, and Cowens and easily could have stayed around long enough to play with Bird. "I would never have retired if I had known there was a chance to play with someone like him," he said later.

But even Havlicek couldn't escape the bad feeling that engulfed the Celtics. In his 1988 book, Heinsohn included Havlicek among the problems when he wrote, "John was getting ready to retire, and frankly he was more interested in going out with his Big Day than he was in rebuilding the club."

The retirement of Havlicek came as the Celtics ownership was again about to change hands. Irv Levin was preparing to sell to John Y. Brown and Harry Mangurian.

There has been no mystique surrounding Celtics ownership since Walter Brown owned the team, from 1946 until his death in 1964; and during that time the stock was as honorable as the product on the floor. The Celtics were a family, and Brown was Papa. Players negotiated contracts with him. Some players, like Ramsey, just sent him a blank contract and let Brown decide what he was worth. There was rarely an argument. Heinsohn got into a dispute with Brown when he was running the NBA Players Association, but all was forgotten when Heinsohn led the Celtics to another championship. After Brown's death, the team was transferred to Marvin Kratter/ National Equities (1965–68); then to Ballantine Brewery (1968–69); then to E. E. Erdman's Trans-National Communications (1969–71); then to Investors Funding Corporation (1971–72); then to Bob Schmertz–Leisure Technology (1972–74); then to Schmertz and Levin (1974–75). When Schmertz died, Levin had the team all to himself, from 1975 to 1978. It was in 1978 that Levin sold to John Y. Brown and Harry Mangurian.

Nice lineage. After 1964 the Celtics family was run by a succession of corporations and businessmen, all attracted by the Celtics name, none familiar with the NBA or the Celtics tradition. These were carpetbaggers, guys looking for tax shelters and a connection with greatness. It was a nice write-off and a great calling card. Celtics owners could do a lot of nifty name-dropping, borrowing greatness. Meanwhile, the players and fans had as little to do with them as possible. Without local ownership, it was hopeless to think of any owner as permanent. It was hard to think of E. E. Erdman's Trans-National Communications as akin to Thomas A. Yawkey or Walter Brown.

And so, there was Irv Levin, standing at midcourt April 9, 1968, proudly presenting gifts to Havlicek and getting booed like a politician who'd been accused of stealing money from parking meters. Levin had claimed he had nothing to do with the firing of Heinsohn or the trading of Scott or the acquisitions of Wicks and Rowe. Celtics fans are great sports fans, and great sports fans can't be fooled by out-of-town owners in leisure suits. Levin was an owner who took road trips, who tried to show the team off to his friends. Heinsohn believed that Auerbach set up the owner for this embarrassing ballyhoo on the final day of 1978. It was Auerbach who talked Levin into buying Havlicek the expensive gift and Auerbach who suggested that Levin make the presentation. Red no doubt knew what would happen. Levin was hooted; Auerbach was cheered.

Always, Red was the only constant. He dealt with a succession of owners, educating them on the simple points of basketball while trying to keep them at a comfortable distance so they would not meddle with the product on the court. He'd always publicly back the men in suits, even when he found them odious and repugnant. A photograph of the Celtics owner-of-the-hour was always next to Auerbach's desk. When the owners changed, the photograph changed. Red never told you what he really thought of these gentlemen until they were gone. Bob Cousy wrote, "For thirty-eight years, the essential duties of a Celtics owner have been to kiss Red's ring, sign the checks, and be ready to accept the championship trophy."

The spring and summer of 1978 was a difficult time for Auerbach. A large corps of the Celtics fandom was beginning to believe the game had passed him by. Clunker draft choices Steve Downing, Glenn McDonald, Tom Boswell, and Norm Cook were tossed in his face. Meanwhile, Silas was in the NBA finals with the Supersonics and Westphal was an All Star guard for Phoenix. What did the Celtics have to show for Westphal?—just Scott, who was gone; and Scott had brought only an old Chaney, Kermit Washington, and a draft pick.

Auerbach was kept in the dark while Levin and John Y. Brown worked out a whopper of a deal. They swapped franchises. Brown took over the Celtics and Levin took over the Buffalo Braves, moving them to San Diego, where they became the Clippers. As part of the transaction, the Celtics would send Wicks, Kevin Kunnert, number-one draft pick Freeman Williams, and Kermit Washington to Buffalo for Marvin Barnes, Nate "Tiny" Archibald, and Billy Knight.

Volk remembers, "Red and I went down to Washington to meet with agents representing [Kermit] Washington and Kunnert, both of whom were being traded in this transaction. Red and I were not aware that this was happening at all. We went down and finalized the deal. The next morning, the franchise swap was announced. Apparently the franchise swap was contingent on these contracts having been negotiated, finalized, and signed. And we were given that responsibility. We were like the Japanese ambassador who was meeting with Roosevelt while Pearl Harbor was being bombed. We were absolutely in the dark."

John Y. Brown was the antithesis of his namesake, Walter Brown. John Y. was in it for the short haul, for the money, for the glory. He'd folded his ABA franchise in Louisville and run the Buffalo team into the ground. He bought out Colonel Sanders then sold Kentucky Fried Chicken to Heublein. Brown liked to say that he'd been in basketball for seven years and that if he'd been in medical school for seven years he'd be a brain surgeon. He started making calls to people around the league, trying to glean knowledge from Auerbach's friends.

Auerbach was crushed by the announcement of the Brown-Levin transaction. He'd been humiliated and his draft picks and trade maneuvers had gone up in flames. It was the first time in Boston that a player transaction had been made without his knowledge. The Celtics were suddenly being run in George Steinbrenner fashion, and Red looked like one of the Boss's general-manager buffoons. His contract was up August 1, and he went to New York to discuss a job offer from the Knicks. The Knicks were reorganizing and wanted Auerbach to be president. They offered him a four-year contract at the highest salary ever offered an NBA executive.

The people of Boston rallied and implored Auerbach to stay. His wife, Dorothy, cast the deciding ballot. "I told him he was a Boston Celtic and not a New York Knickerbocker," she remembered. "I told him if he was finished in Boston, I wanted him to come straight home to Washington. I didn't want him stopping in New York for a few years first. He was not a Knick or anything else. He was a Celtic."

Brown gave his word that he would include Auerbach in

basketball decisions. What followed was a season worse than the one before, a season littered with dumb, dizzying moves. Havlicek and Bing had retired. Kevin Stacom and Tom Boswell had played out their options. The Celtics acquired Earl Tatum in July and traded him to Detroit for Chris Ford in October. Dennis Awtrey was purchased from Phoenix.

Ford: "When I was in Detroit, I always thought of the Celtics as having that winning tradition. In Detroit we had a continual parade of coaches and players. There was never any stability. I looked at the Celtics as a team that kept their players together, and they always managed to be able to add to it. We never thought we were going to win when we went to the Garden, and I don't know that we ever beat them when I was with the Pistons. I was happy to be traded here because my wife and I had made a list of the places we'd like to go and Boston was at the top of the list. They were back East, and I had always loved the Celtics, even when I was a kid growing up in New Jersey. I liked Russell and what the Celtics did as far as team play. My game was team oriented. When I was traded it was only the third game of the year, so I didn't really know what I was getting into. . . . When I got here, it was utter chaos. It was the exact same thing I had left. It was a turnstile in terms of coaches, players, owners, everything."

The owner couldn't help himself. Cousy was witness to one of Brown's particularly cruel moments. After a loss in the Garden, John Y. was waiting for Red in Auerbach's office. The place was filling with the usual postgame guests, and when Auerbach entered his chambers, all heard Brown say, "Well, well, well, here comes our great leader now. Say something intelligent, great leader." Cousy was ready to duke it out with the imposter from Kentucky. Auerbach ignored Brown and let it pass.

Cleveland, coached by Bill Fitch, beat Boston, 115–101, in the Garden on opening night. It was the only sellout at the Garden all season. They lost twelve of their first fourteen games, and Sanders was fired, replaced by player-coach Dave Cowens.

"It was obviously unfair," says Sanders. "But the reality of the situation was that we weren't winning, and the crowds weren't what they were supposed to be, and they decided they needed a coaching change."

Sanders left one farewell gift. He'd recruited K. C. Jones as an assistant coach, and Jones would eventually lead the Celtics to a pair of championships in the next decade.

There were more personnel transactions. Knight went to Indiana in exchange for center Rick Robey. Marvin Barnes was waived after playing lethargically in thirty-eight games. Jo Jo White was traded to Golden State for a draft pick. A draft pick? This was something the Celtics had studiously avoided through the years. Messrs. Sharman, Cousy, Jones, Jones, Heinsohn, and Sanders were allowed to start and finish their careers in Boston. White was one of the finest Celtic performers of all time, and he was tossed aside at the end of his career in exchange for a draft pick. The Celtics were not acting like Celtics. Boston made six trades and signed three free agents by Valentine's Day. After a game in New York on February 10, Brown and his fiancée, Phyllis George, went to dinner with Knicks General Manager Eddie Donovan and Sonny Werblin. George (who quickly went from Miss America to misinformation) liked McAdoo's style, and Brown wanted to please his woman. Two days later, it was announced that the Celtics were shipping three first-round draft picks to New York for Bob McAdoo.

Auerbach: "He made one great big deal that could have destroyed the team, without even consulting me. He did ruin it. We just happened to put it back together again, luckily. One wrong guy can ruin it so fast your head will swim. John Y. Brown had an ego like most people who are successful in what they do. He always felt he knew a lot about everything. I'd get calls from coaches and general managers around the league, and they'd ask about this John Y. Brown calling them and asking them questions. He'd call them up and try to pick their brains, and then he'd come back to me with this information. And all these guys knew it, and they were giving him all crazy things. Finally, I said, 'John, why don't you stop talking to these guys? Hey, we can't get along. One of us has got to go. You're the boss. You can fire me. I'll leave tomorrow. Otherwise, you got to sell your part of the team.' I told him he had two weeks to sell the team or I was gone. I told him there was no way I was going to work for him anymore. That's when he sold the team to Harry."

General Manager Jan Volk remembers this about Brown: "He was not here that often, but when he was here he was exceptionally disruptive. He tended to call late in the day to start things going that he wanted to get done. Like at four-thirty in the afternoon. I think he was a very creative guy who was not interested in nailing down the details of what he was doing. There was often a lot of housekeeping chores to follow the deals that he would do. I think he enjoyed making deals for the sake of making deals. I think he was challenged by that."

Brown was planning on running for governor of Kentucky. It was a blessing for Boston basketball fans. Auerbach warned the voters of Kentucky, "Watch out for that guy. He'll trade the Kentucky Derby for the Indianapolis 500."

Mangurian wanted to be a low-key owner, and he and Auerbach hit it off. Auerbach told *Boston Magazine*, "He [Mangurian] reminds you a lot of Walter Brown because he is low-key. He doesn't have the great big ego, and yet he's human like the rest of us. He's a businessman, but he's also a sportsman. They're very seldom in combination."

On March 9, 1979, the Detroit Pistons beat the Celtics, 160–117, at the Pontiac Silverdome. M. L. Carr scored twenty points for Detroit and remembers, "You don't like to question certain things, but it looked to me like the guys were laying down on the job. They had just come off a West Coast trip.

They were trying to send a message, I think. . . . Guys really weren't playing. There just wasn't any effort at all. There are certain times when you know that guys don't have it physically or just aren't clicking, but this was beyond that. Our guys loved it. This was the best. It would have been fine if it was Atlanta or somebody else, but the fact that this was the Boston Celtics, this was like paying them back for all those years they'd beaten Detroit. It was almost like going into the Garden and ripping down one of the flags."

The *Boston Globe*'s Bob Ryan wrote, "The Celtics used to stand for something. Now all they stand for is the anthem." Boston finished 29–53, last in the Atlantic Division.

The names Sidney Wicks and Curtis Rowe have come to symbolize this dark hour in Celtics history. Coach Cowens on Wicks and Rowe: "It was only because of the lack of sustained effort. People used to tell me, 'I can't believe you throw a lead pass and he would just stop running and let it go out of bounds.' But in a way it was unfair. If they had been brought in in a better environment in terms of having a real solid group, they probably could have fit in real well and really helped our team. But at the time they were asked to be leaders because they were better players coming to a new situation, and there was just turmoil. They probably didn't feel real welcome or comfortable. They knew what winning was all about and what you're supposed to feel like, and so I think maybe that didn't help their attitude."

Cowens announced he was through coaching after the final game of the season, a Garden victory over the New Jersey Nets. "Red was a little bit upset, I think," says Cowens. "I didn't tell anybody. At the end of the game reporters asked me what was going on and I said I'd resigned. I smoked my little cigar and that was it. Going into that game, I figured, 'Let somebody else do it.' I was just a stop-gap anyway. I had no coaching experience. It was like running a day care center. It was making sure that people were going to show up on time. We had a few people that really worked hard. Maxwell's first year we ran a lot of stuff to him because at least he could get us on the line. Jeff Judkins and Chris Ford and other guys who wanted to play would play hard. They just really liked basketball. But we had a lot of guys who forgot what it took to get to that position. It was tough for those guys to stay in top shape. It was one of those years where we did a lot of experimenting because we lost so many guys. There's so many holes to fill. We tried to do it with Curtis Rowe, Sidney Wicks, Tom Boswell, that whole routine, but none of those players worked out so we had to start over, and the first real quality guy we got was Bird."

While the Celtics were diving to new depths in March 1979, Larry Joe Bird was leading the Indiana State Sycamores to the Final Four. Indiana State lost the championship final to a Michigan State team led by Magic Johnson, Greg Kelser, and Jay Vincent. Celtics fans looked at Bird and wondered if they had a chance.

Let the record show that the fortunes of the Boston Celtics forever changed for the better on June 9, 1978, when Arnold "Red" Auerbach gambled and drafted Larry Bird with the sixth pick of the first round. The Celts knew they couldn't have Bird for a year, but it gave everybody something to look forward to. Bird-watching was better than Celtic-watching during the 1978–79 basketball season. In fact, Indiana State (33–1) won more games than the Celtics (29–53). Boston fans knew that Auerbach had drafted the six-foot-nine-inch forward as a junior eligible.

It is interesting that Auerbach would make this gamble during one of the darkest hours in franchise history. Bird was eligible for the 1978 draft because his original senior class was graduating. Bird had entered Indiana University in the fall of 1974. He dropped out of IU after only a few weeks, but he was eligible to be drafted with that class in 1978, even though he was only a junior (this rule has been changed, one of many that was changed after Auerbach exploited it). Auerbach was always a visionary when it came to draft gambles. He was the man who thought to draft Charlie Scott even though Scott was committed to the ABA. Holding Scott's NBA rights two years later, Auerbach was able to get Paul Silas, in effect, for nothing.

Auerbach heard of Bird when assistant coach John Killilea came back from a scouting mission and reported, "I think I found another Rick Barry."

It was a year or two after the new collective-bargaining agreement. Prior to this 1976 agreement, if you drafted a junior eligible, the player was your property only until he went back to school. Some people in the Celtics front office felt that the new agreement would give them a year to negotiate with Bird. Others disagreed. Finally Satch Sanders suggested someone call the league office, so Volk called the NBA in New York and spoke with legal counsel David Stern (now commissioner). There was some fear about tipping off the rest of the league, but Volk felt Stern could be trusted, and the question had to be answered before they wasted a draft pick.

"It didn't take much thinking," says Sanders. "We had two first-round draft choices. It was philosophical. Red was always looking at the Celtics in terms of the long range."

Selecting Bird was a gamble because the player had the option to sign or play his senior season and plunge into a second draft. Auerbach had hopes that the Celtic mystique might get to this kid. He also had two picks in the top eight, thanks to the Scott trade to the Lakers. Boston needed a shooting guard. Everybody needed Bird. Portland picked first and selected forward Mychal Thompson. Kansas City took guard Phil Ford, and Indiana took Kentucky center Rick Robey. The Knicks went for guard Michael Ray Richardson, and the Warriors took Purvis Short. In the Blades and Boards Club at the Boston Garden, the Celtics brain trust was assembled in front of the New England media. Vice President Jeff Cohen, son of Sammy Cohen, the friendly newspaperman who helped launch the franchise, leaned toward Auerbach, and Auerbach whispered in his ear. Cohen grabbed the hot line to New York, where NBA

Commissioner Larry O'Brien was waiting, and announced, "The Boston Celtics draft Larry Bird of Indiana State."

Portland, Kansas City, Indiana, New York, and Golden State could have selected Larry Joe Bird and taken their chances. Why not the Pacers? Bird was from Indiana. Why not the Knicks? New York's pocketbook was bottomless.

Portland was the team Boston was worried about. The Blazers, like the Celtics, had two picks in the top eight. Portland had number one and number seven.

Volk remembers, "We thought that the only people who might be interested in taking a risk on him, because he had said outright that he was going back to school, would be teams with two picks. Portland had seven. And that's why we picked him with our first pick [number six] and not our second [number eight]."

No one dared throw the dice. You look bad if you've got a top-six draft choice and come away empty-handed. Teams are always looking for a quick fix. Only Auerbach was bold enough and secure enough to take a chance on Larry Bird. And he made this move at a time when he was on shaky footing with his owner and the fans. The spring of 1978 was a troubled time for Boston's Redhead. It was just before the dark days of John Y. and the lucrative offer from the Knicks. Despite all of this distraction, Auerbach was able to see clearly and stay the course. He did the right thing. The Celtics picked Bird with the sixth pick and shooting guard Freeman Williams with the number-eight selection. Williams was sent packing in the Levin-Brown swap, and Auerbach had nothing to show when the Celtics stumbled through 1978–79.

After the heartbreaking loss in the NCAA finals, a group of four Terre Haute businessmen and coach Bob King convened to help Bird select an agent. Bird was willing to talk to the Celtics before the 1979 draft, but he needed a heavy-hitting negotiator. The search committee came up with two finalists— Reuven Katz, the man who would later represent Pete Rose when Rose was banned from baseball, and Bob Woolf, a Boston-based agent who had handled many professional athletes and many Celtics. Woolf was a little down on his luck when he bagged Bird, and Bird has hinted that Bob Woolf rose to the top of the list because he offered his services for free. Bird has since stated that he was somewhat intimidated by Katz's intellect and that he preferred Woolf because Woolf didn't seem as smart. In any event, Bird had his agent. Woolf and Auerbach were familiar foes. Bird had leverage. He was a great college player, he was six-foot-nine, white, and had tremendous drawing power. Attendance for Celtics games in 1978–79 was at its lowest in seven years. The team was bad, and the town was suddenly sour on them. Auerbach had some leverage. If he couldn't meet Bird's price, he could trade his negotiating rights to another club before the 1979 draft-day deadline.

Auerbach explains, "It was a gamble, but I had to do it. I've always had the philosophy that you take the best kid that's available in the draft. Worry later. I felt that the reputation of the Celtics was such that every kid would want to play here."

Auerbach and Cowens went to see Indiana State play a game in Cincinnati. Auerbach met with the shy forward and told him he could play for the Celtics after he finished with the Sycamores. Bird could have been the first player to play in the NCAA championship and the NBA in the same season. Auerbach promised he'd pay him for a full season, but Bird was annoyed because Red didn't seem to think Bird's team would last very long in the NCAA tournament. Bird decided to stay in school. During these spring months, while the Celtics were going down the drain, Bird enjoyed his local celebrity, waited to hear how Woolf was doing with negotiations, and played a little softball on the side. He was playing left field one day when his brother Mike hit a long fly. Larry was camped under the ball but made an error in judgment and the ball crushed his right index finger. The knuckle was shattered, and he had to learn how to shoot a basketball all over again.

Negotiations were tense for a while. Woolf still tells a story about getting lost in Worcester, asking a man for directions, and having the man give him the finger. Auerbach thought the agent was asking for too much for the rookie. Red pointed out that no *forward* had ever been a franchise player. Auerbach was hoping that the Celtics reputation would help him bag Bird, but this was not a typical NBA fan the Celtics were courting.

Bird says, "The first game I ever went to was when I was in the sixth grade. It was in Kentucky, and Kentucky and Indiana were playing, and I thought it was a college game. When we got out of there, my brother told me it was a pro game, and I was pissed off because I didn't know it was a pro game. I would have been more serious watching it. I'd seen the Pacers play Kentucky in the play-offs, and I'd seen Dr. J play against the Pacers one time. Other than that, I didn't have any contact. I had heard of Bill Russell and Wilt Chamberlain. That's really the only two I can think of. When I was in the fifth grade, me and my cousin used to play ball all the time, and the goal was probably seven foot high. He was either Russell or Chamberlain, and I was the other one. I met Red one time when I was in an All Star game in Atlanta. The second time was when he came to Indiana State to watch me play. He said when the season was over we'd get together. Then he came down to the play-offs in Cincinnati. We were talking, and he said when the season was over he would like to sign me and have me play the rest of the year with the Celtics. It pissed me off because he thought we was gonna get beat. But I was very impressed by him. After I got drafted by the Celtics, everybody started telling me about the Celtics. I respected him from the very first time I'd seen him. But it's really funny about that whole situation. I could care less about playing professional basketball. I was playing college basketball and planning on getting that over with and going through the summer and just see. My way of thinking at that time wasn't that I couldn't wait till I got there."

With the contract talks at an impasse, owner Mangurian intervened and Bird agreed to a five-year contract that would pay him $650,000 per year. At that time, he was the highest-paid Celtic and the highest-paid rookie in the history of professional sports. Mangurian, the quiet owner, was not afraid to spend money as long as he believed he was spending wisely. This turned out to be the best sports investment since Yankees owner Jake Ruppert bought Babe Ruth from the Boston Red Sox for $100,000 after the 1919 baseball season.

9
The Green Bird

IN August 1979, the Red Sox were the hottest team in Boston. They were one summer removed from a memorable pennant race and still had the corps of players who made it to the seventh game of the World Series in 1975. The Sox trailed the Baltimore Orioles throughout the summer of 1979, even though center fielder Fred Lynn was having his best season at Fenway. The Olde Towne Team played before more fans (2,353,114) than in any year of its seventy-nine-year history.

Meanwhile, the Celtics were down, but there was help on the way. Larry Joe Bird came to Marshfield in August 1979 to see what this Celtics tradition was all about.

Camp Milbrook in Marshfield, Massachusetts, was hardly a shiny, state-of-the-art training facility. It was a former lumber mill, a place where middle-income families sent their young sons for summer basketball camp. The courts are outdoor asphalt, the backboards are made of metal, and the sleeping quarters are old, dusty, and damp. The place reeks of mildew. There are only a couple of air-conditioning units. The food is like all camp food: you go back for seconds only if you are incredibly hungry. The camp was started by Jan Volk's father, Gerry, in 1938. Auerbach began hosting his basketball camp there in 1960. The camp was in poor shape by the late 1970s, and Jan Volk now admits, "I was embarrassed that we [the team] had anything to do with the place."

Marshfield is a swampy beach town, a half hour south of Boston. It is a town everybody passes through on the way to Cape Cod. It is famous for Daniel Webster, the Marshfield Fair, and the Celtics rookie camp. In the early 1980s a Chinese restaurant was built not too far from the camp, and some say it was built just to accommodate Red Auerbach.

It was in August 1979 that Bird and his girlfriend, Dinah Mattingly, found Marshfield, walked into Auerbach's dark, humid campground office, and heard the man with the cigar say, "What's *she* doing here?" Bird walked outside, looked at the baskets, and noticed that one was too high and the other too low. He said to himself, "Here I am. The Boston Celtics are supposed to have won all these championships, and the baskets aren't even the right height. What am *I* doing here?"

Volk says, "We took care to make sure he wasn't over-whelmed by the big city, and I think it worked."

Bird worked out with the other rookies, free agents, and camp counselors during afternoon sessions at Camp Milbrook. Public scrimmages were held at night in the Marshfield High School gym, and Dave Cowens, Rick Robey, and Tiny Archibald played in some of the games to check out the rookie hotshot. Veterans were not required to participate in the summer sessions, but Celtics fans have learned to measure the hunger of the upcoming Celtics edition by the number of vets who show up in Marshfield.

Bird got Auerbach's attention right away. In his book *On and Off the Court*, Auerbach wrote, "The day he walked into our rookie camp was the day my eyes were opened: the way he shot the ball; the way he passed it around; the way he crashed the boards; the way he raced up and down the court;

the way he controlled the tempo and action; the way he seemed to make no mistakes. As I sat there watching, all I could think of was the day Havlicek first showed up seventeen years earlier. It was the only thing I could compare it to. My first thought was simply that this kid was worth every nickel we ended up giving him."

Bird's presence in a Celtics jersey consummated a marriage of two great basketball traditions. Indiana is without doubt the capital of amateur basketball, and Boston is where professional hoops gained its identity. Hoosiers follow their basketball religiously, and Terre Haute was giving its greatest gift to the most prestigious basketball team in the world.

Bird was not the only new face in camp. The man blowing the whistle was Bill Fitch, an ex-Marine who'd done a fine job with the Cleveland Cavaliers and who represented the first nonfamily member to coach the Celtics since Auerbach came to town in 1950. Russell, Heinsohn, Sanders, and Cowens followed Auerbach to the bench, but when Cowens resigned, Mangurian and Auerbach agreed it was time to go outside for a head coach. Fitch was experienced, innovative, indefatigable, and he knew the league. He was the kind of authority figure needed in the post-Wicks/Rowe era. He was even Irish.

Not given to reading the *Sporting News*, or anything else for that matter, Bird had never heard of Bill Fitch. But Fitch was an ideal mentor for the rookie Bird. They hit it off immediately. In Bird, Fitch saw a hungry raw talent he could mold. He also saw the rarest of the rare: a superstar kid who would take instruction. Bird was raised to respect authority. He always did what his coach told him. He might have floundered under a so-called player's coach if he'd had too much freedom when he joined the league. Fitch was perfect. Bird also respects people who work hard, and Fitch worked harder than any NBA coach.

Fitch ran Bird into the ground at rookie camp and again when the veterans and free agents arrived in September. The coach tried to crack the kid and couldn't do it. The coach liked this. Others didn't react as well. Fitch had been granted control of the entire basketball operation, and he used this power to send a message to the team during the first day of practice. Fitch spotted Rowe jogging at half speed and yelled, "Just take that jog up there by the door on the left, take a shower, and get out of here. You've been cut."

That was an eye-opener. Cowens didn't have that kind of clout when he was coaching. Bird was stunned. So were Maxwell and Archibald. The gravy train had been derailed. This coach meant business and had the power to play God.

There was another key personnel move two months before the start of the season. On September 6, 1979, Auerbach fleeced the Detroit Pistons in a deal that would supply Bird with frontcourt running mates for more than a decade. Dealing with affable and emotional Piston coach and General Manager Dick Vitale, Auerbach signed free agent forward M. L. Carr and offered McAdoo as compensation in return for two 1980 first-round draft picks. Small wonder that Vitale was destined to make millions babbling on television; he was no match for Red Auerbach in a smoke-filled room.

Carr was a physical player and a talker. He brought spirit and charisma to the Celtics locker room and found a soul mate in Maxwell, who was beginning to enjoy his status as a young senior statesman. Meanwhile, Cowens, relieved to be a player instead of a player-coach, showed up in great shape and was recharged by the influx of youth and enthusiasm. In the backcourt, Ford was proving to be a dangerous three-point threat, and Archibald had recovered from a career-threatening Achilles tendon tear. He had been the only man in NBA history to lead the league in scoring and assists in the same season, but due to injuries he'd played only thirty-four games from 1976 to 1978 and needed the summer of 1979 to rest his Achilles. Archibald's career was resurrected by Fitch and the new supporting cast in 1979.

"I knew that the Celtics had been down many times before," says Carr. "But the fact that they had Red meant that they weren't going to stay down much longer. The guy won in the past, and the history of the Celtics told me that this team eventually would get back. I just felt it was a situation where it was more attitude than anything else."

The Celtics had forgotten their dietary staples of defense and running. Fitch made them start thinking again. The bread-and-butter stuff worked in the 1950s and 1960s, and it would work again. The cast was good enough to run and young enough to shut down the opposition. It was a matter of application and dedication, and Fitch was the taskmaster this team needed. The bumper-sticker campaign for 1979–80 was the best ever: NO MORE GAMES.

Meanwhile, there was considerable doubt about Bird's ability to star in the pros. New Englanders remembered Holy Cross's Jack "the Shot" Foley who simply could not get his shot off in the NBA. What would happen to Bird? For all of his strengths, he was afflicted with the NBA malady known as "white man's disease." He was not fast and could not jump. Until he proved he could play with the NBA thoroughbreds, it was possible that Bird might suffer the fate of other great college players with insufficient tools to make their mark in the NBA. His NBA debut smothered the doubts. On October 12, 1979, in a 114–106 victory over the Houston Rockets, Bird hit six of twelve shots, snatched ten rebounds, and handed out five assists. Seven Celtics scored in double figures, and 15,320 fans roared in approval.

Bird was an instant star. He could shoot, rebound, and pass as well as any player in the league—right from the start. He was a six-nine Cousy. He made everyone on the court a better player. If you were open, you got the ball. He had tremendous vision and seemed to see the game in slow motion. He was ferocious on the backboards. He wanted to take the important shots. He was the consummate teammate. He loved to play the game and cared only about winning. Fans couldn't get enough of him. In an era when marginal talents and events were advanced with a tonnage of excess hype and hysteria (think of every Super Bowl), Bird had actually turned out to be better than his billing. The Celtics and the Boston media had talked of him as a savior, but even Auerbach admitted later, "I had no idea he would be that kind of rebounder."

"It was hard to tell," says Cowens. "I hadn't seen him play all that often. . . . Nobody was going to tell him he couldn't play. The guy was putting up some impressive numbers. But it was a weak conference, and he was kind of slow. All I knew is he had quick hands and quick feet. Even though he's not fast, he's got a lot of quickness, and that's all you really need. I knew he had good hands."

"There were tremendous expectations for Larry," says Carr. "I don't think many rookies came into the league with more. Red was saying he was going to be a great player. People felt this was the guy that was going to bring in the new era. We tested him, no question about it. Everybody was saying this guy was getting all the play and all the pub—but can he really play? I was convinced when I started watching those passes in rookie camp. I'd never seen a guy come into the league and try to invent situations the way Larry would. He would create situations, and he would try any type of pass, and 90 percent of them were working, so you knew it wasn't a fluke. I remember talking to guys from other teams about Larry, and they'd say, 'No, they're just trying to build Larry up there in Boston,' and I'd say, 'This kid can play.' He came in with a strong court presence and a sense of awareness of where players were that was really unparalleled."

Chris Ford remembers, "I went home that summer, and I didn't comprehend what could happen as far as making the move with Larry the following year. I didn't know you could turn the thing around that quickly. I didn't sense anything until we actually started playing. Bill was very strict, and I think it's what the organization needed at that time because it had become so chaotic. I didn't know how good Larry could be. I hadn't really followed him. But when you saw him out there on the floor, you saw what he brought to the team. It was team play; the type of game I liked to play. The ball was moving and guys were hitting the open man, and all the little things were working. That's what Larry Bird brought."

Bird was the new superstar, and the Celtics were back. Just like that. Bird averaged twenty-one points and ten rebounds, made the All Star team, and won Rookie of the Year honors. Archibald came back to average 14.1 points and 8.4 assists. Maxwell led the league in shooting percentage (61 percent). Ford ranked second in three-pointers made (1979–80 was the first year of the three-pointer). Cowens was bothered by foot problems but was buoyed by Bird and the return to winning. Boston won its first four games, ten of twelve and twenty of twenty-six. They wound up 61–21, an improvement of thirty-two games, easily the best turnaround in league history. They won as many games in one season as they'd won in the previous two seasons. Attendance shot up 46 percent, including thirty sellouts in thirty-nine Garden games. There was not a seat to be had after January—a sellout streak that would continue though the 1980s and clear into the 1990s. Twenty-seven of their forty-one road games were sellouts. They added Pistol Pete Maravich for the stretch run, and he averaged 11.5 points in twenty-six games. There were a lot of paybacks along the road. Teams had enjoyed dancing on Boston's grave in 1977 through 1979, none more than the Pistons and coach Vitale. Boston beat Detroit in Pontiac in overtime.

They swept Houston in the first round of the play-offs, then encountered the team that would be their nemesis for the next six years: the Philadelphia 76ers. Philadelphia won fifty-seven games in 1979–80, and the Sixers were a veteran cast with Julius Erving, Caldwell Jones, Bobby Jones, Darryl Dawkins, Steve Mix, and Henry Bibby. The wily Sixers overpowered the Celtics inside and took the series in five games.

"They were better," concedes Cowens. "You lose in five games, you've got to say the other team was better."

Draft day in 1980 ranks as one of the pivotal days in the history of the Celtics franchise. The 1979–80 Pistons finished

16–66, which meant Detroit's first-round pick was the number-one pick in the land. Auerbach owned this pick. Boston dealt the number-one pick, and the number-thirteen pick to Golden State for center Robert Parish and Golden State's number-one pick, which was the number-three pick overall. The Celtics would settle for Minnesota's Kevin McHale over Purdue's Joe Barry Carroll. Everybody liked Carroll as the top pick, and even Auerbach has admitted that he'd have taken Carroll over McHale. The bottom line is this: Boston got Parish and McHale for Joe Barry Carroll and Ricky Brown. Fitch should get credit for this deal, but he never does, and that is one of the reasons Bill Fitch could not stay in Boston. Auerbach was widely applauded for the Parish trade even though Fitch was the man behind the move, and this was the kind of regional mentality that bothered Fitch. Ever the outsider, Fitch could not stand seeing Red get credit for his deal. Heinsohn, Sanders, Cowens, Volk, and K. C. Jones were all family members who could not be jealous of Red. Fitch was.

The 1980–81 Celtics were a year wiser and a couple of feet taller than the 1979–80 edition. Parish and McHale gave Fitch a team that could compete up front with Philadelphia. Fitch made Parish run. The quiet seven-footer had been a sulky underachiever at Golden State, but Fitch saw Parish as a big man who could run like Bill Russell. Parish started running the day he got to Celtics practice at Hellenic College in Brookline. Parish kept running, and Fitch smiled his sadistic smile. Robert Parish was destined to evolve into an All Star center for more than a decade in Boston.

McHale almost didn't make it to Boston. He felt he was not being offered money commensurate with his draft status and flew to Europe to check out an offer to play in Italy. Fitch said, "Let him eat spaghetti." McHale finally signed with the Celtics and brought his shot-blocking to Boston. He had the arms of a seven-foot-four-inch man and the personality of a kid who spent a lot of time in detention. McHale was a big kid, and he drove Fitch crazy. If the coach yelled "Go left!"

McHale would go right just to get a rise out of Fitch. But the gangly Minnesotan was a potent weapon off the bench. He was an unstoppable turnaround jumper and a worthy successor to the role of Celtics sixth man. McHale never forgot his roots. His hero was his father, Paul, a taconite mine worker in the Iron Range for more than thirty years. "Paul's my main man," McHale would say. The center-forward was also loyal to his friends from Hibbing, Minnesota, and the university. It wasn't unusual to see a Winnebago with Minnesota license plates parked outside the Celtics hotel headquarters when the team played in Milwaukee. McHale was particularly fond of a friend he called "Big Joe," and Big Joe's presence at any game usually meant McHale had partied too long the night before. Bucks coach Don Nelson graciously offered to supply Big Joe with a suite whenever the Celtics visited the Mecca.

The addition of Parish and McHale was accompanied by the sudden subtraction of the starting center, Dave Cowens. On October 1 (the same day punching-bag Red Sox Manager Don Zimmer was fired), during the preseason, the six-foot-eight-inch redhead stunned his teammates when he announced that he was retiring and boarded a bus in Terre Haute, Indiana. He wrote a 1,500-word career obituary for the October 2 *Globe* that read, in part, "I can no longer play that caliber of basketball, and it is unbelievably frustrating to remain in a rugged occupation with waning skills. . . . I have enjoyed performing for you over the past 10 years while hopefully engraving myself into the history of the Celtic organization."

Ever humble, Cowens had nothing to worry about. His place in Celtics history is secure. He forever will be the man who brought the franchise back one year after Russell left. Havlicek bridged the gap in 1969–70, but the Celtics would not win again until they got the big man back in the middle. It is interesting that Cowens played one year with Bird, just as Havlicek played one year with Cousy. The passing of the torch somehow seems gentler when the carriers get to run side by side for a few miles.

Bird inherited the fire. His belly started burning after the fifth game of the Philadelphia series in the spring of 1980. He thought of himself as a winner, but when the play-offs were over he felt like a loser. It reminded him of the feeling he had after his Indiana State team was beaten by Magic and Company in the NCAA championship final in 1979. Bird was Rookie of the Year in the summer of 1980, but Magic Johnson and the Lakers had championship rings. This gave Bird the conviction he needed to prepare for the 1980–81 season. He was determined not to go home early.

The 1980–81 Celtics went 62–20, matching Philadelphia for the best regular season record. A victory over Philadelphia in the Garden on the last day of the regular season guaranteed the Celtics the home-court advantage throughout the play-offs. Boston beat Chicago in four straight games to advance to the conference finals versus Philadelphia, and, as happened so many times before, this proved to be the true championship series. At this hour, Andrew Toney was the scariest streak shooter in the game. Philadelphia won three of the first four games and led Game 5 by six with 1:40 to play. The Celtics came back to win Game 5, then went to Philly and recovered from a ten-point third-quarter deficit to win again. Game Six in the Spectrum is always remembered as the game in which Maxwell dove into the stands to save a loose ball and wound up getting into a fight with a combative Sixer fan. It was shades of the old Syracuse days. McHale blocked a Tony shot in the final minute to send the series back to Boston.

Game 7 was played in the Garden, and Bird still claims it was the most emotional game of his career. His mother flew in from Indiana for the occasion. The Sixers led by nine with five minutes to play. The Celtics tightened the screws on defense, and, luckily, officials Jake O'Donnell and Darrell Garreston elected to let the players play. With nothing being called, Boston held the Sixers to one point in their final ten possessions. Bird wrote, "Players were knocking each other down all over the court. We were all beating each other to death." An eighteen-foot banker (shades of Sam Jones now) by Bird provided the difference in Boston's 91–90 victory. The Celtics won the final three games by a total of five points. There was a sense of inevitability about Games 6 and 7 after the Boston comeback in Game 5. The Celtics were, dare we say, playing like a team of destiny. Philadelphia appeared to have more experience and weaponry, but there was something about the 1981 Celtics that would not allow defeat.

Carr remembers, "They [76ers] always knew we had the opportunity to come back, and one of the greatest motivating speeches a coach can give was when Red told us, 'Until they beat you one more time, they can't win a championship. They got to beat you. And if you don't let 'em beat you one more time, you win it.' So we never thought of it that way—'Gee, we're down 3–1'—Red said they got to beat you one more time. Don't let 'em do it tonight. You do that three times, you win it."

Philadelphia's Bobby Jones: "They played well. We were up, and I think we took things lightly. They . . . had that mental toughness. They kept at it and plugged away, and they made the breaks."

The finals were something of a letdown. Magic Johnson's Lakers were upended by Houston in the play-offs, and the Rockets carried a ridiculous 40–42 regular-season record into the championship series. Houston had one potent weapon: Moses Malone, a backboard-eating center. The Rockets managed to win two of the first four games of the series, including a game in Boston. Moses put some spice into the series by announcing that he could round up any four friends from his Virginia hometown and still beat Boston. Bird scored only eight points in each of the two games in Houston. Robert Reid was credited with shutting down Bird, and Bird bristled at the suggestion.

It took the Celtics six games to beat the Rockets. The 107-game season ended on May 14, 1981, when Bird scored twenty-seven points in a 102–91 victory at the Summit. Maxwell won

Most Valuable Player in the series, and Bird celebrated by putting one of Auerbach's stogies in his mouth and giving the V-for-Victory sign as flashbulbs popped. The Celtics partied at Stouffer's, their Houston hotel. The party stretched into the morning. Hours after winning the flag, Larry Bird tossed cheeseballs into the open mouth of Rick Robey, who had fallen asleep on a hotel couch.

Ford says, "They got us a room, and we sat around for hours and hours. I had one of Red's cigars and got sick as a dog. It was absolutely tremendous."

The festivities picked up two days later at a Celtics rally at City Hall Plaza. Bird stunned a live television audience when he spotted a MOSES EATS SHIT sign and said, "You're right. Moses does eat shit."

Auerbach went back to work. He'd landed Maxwell, Bird, and McHale in the previous four drafts, plus dealt for Parish. Faced with a series of low selections, he was going to have to be creative once again. And so it was that in the spring of 1981, with flag fourteen on order, Auerbach drafted Toronto Blue Jays infielder Danny Ainge with his second, second-round selection. Celtics tradition is nothing if not cyclical, and Auerbach had to persuade Ainge to give up baseball for Celtics green—just as he had done with Bill Sharman thirty years earlier. In parts of three major-league seasons (1979–81), Ainge played 211 games with the Toronto Blue Jays. He was a backcourt All American at Brigham Young during the off seasons. His lifetime big-league batting average was .211, and he hit two homers. The Jays had him signed to a long-term contract, and when Ainge asked to be excused, the Blue Jays balked. Toronto won the court dispute, and the Celtics had to pay for the privilege of getting Danny Ainge out of baseball. Ainge joined the team on December 9, 1981.

The defending-champion 1981–82 Celtics won sixty-three games, finishing five full games ahead of Philadelphia. Boston wiped out Washington in a five-game play-off set, then prepared to meet Philadelphia once again. Boston won Game 1 in the Garden, 121–81, outscoring the visitors, 31–11, in the third period. This game became known as the Mother's Day Massacre. The Sixers, of course, won Game 2 by six points. Philly took the next two in the Spectrum, and again the Celtics were down, 3–1, in a play-off series. Again, Boston came back to force a seventh game. The Celts forced the clincher by outscoring the Sixers, 14–2, in the final 4:28 of Game 6 at the Spectrum. The Celtics were doing a number on the Sixer psyche by this point, and there was plenty of talk about Garden ghosts haunting Game 7.

There was no mystique this time. Dr. J scored twenty-nine points and Toney poured in forty-three as the 1981–82 76ers did something no Philadephia team had ever done: they won a seventh game on the Garden floor. Celtics fans, in a rare spirit of generosity, chanted, "Beat L.A., Beat L.A.," to the stoic Sixers during the final seconds of the blowout. Great winners are not always gracious losers, but this was one instance when Boston's fandom could look in the mirror with pride.

Bobby Jones: "That was sort of a soul-searching thing for our team. It wasn't that the Celtics didn't respect us, it was almost like we didn't respect ourselves enough to do the job that needed to be done. We had to suck it up and do what we needed to do. The teams that are successful are the teams that are able to play through that stuff. As I look back at those teams, there were a lot of different talents, but they were fairly even the whole time. It was really the mental thing that pulled one team or the other."

McHale says, "I thought we were a much better team that year than we were in 1980–81, but Tiny dislocated his shoulder [playing] against Philly. That was the year we won eighteen straight. We were really on a roll. But Tiny got hurt, and that's when I realized how fragile everything was in the NBA. A guy goes down, and all of a sudden you're just not the team you were."

The Bird era of the 1980s had another pair of championships

in store, but they had to endure a season of landmines and a coaching switch before returning to the top. This was a surprise to Bird, who says, "After I won the first one, I thought I was gonna win five or six in a row. I thought we had a good enough team."

The 1982–83 Celtics won fifty-six games, hardly an embarrassment. They were unable to stay with the 65–17 Philadelphia 76ers, but it was still a strong NBA entry. They had Bird, McHale, Parish, Maxwell, and Robey up front and added former All Star forward Scott Wedman early in the season. Fitch rotated four guards: Archibald, Gerald Henderson, Ainge, and Quinn Buckner. Buckner was picked up when Cowens tried a comeback with the Milwaukee Bucks. Auerbach demanded compensation (just as he did when Cousy came out of mothballs in 1969) and got a solid starting guard, a former NCAA and Olympic champion. On the surface, the team was stronger than any of the teams of the Bird era (to that point), but something was missing. Chris Ford and Eric Fernsten were cut during camp, and the club missed their practice ethic and spirit.

There were problems with roles. Not one of the four guards thought he was getting enough playing time. Archibald, ever moody, sulked through the entire season. Maxwell tried to keep Tiny pumped up, but it was a losing battle. Up front, Robey and Carr had reduced roles, and there was some grumbling. Veterans Parish, Maxwell, McHale, and Carr were fed up with Fitch and his zealous overcoaching. Fitch force-fed videos constantly, and one of the season highlights came when the VCR crashed to the floor in the locker room in Atlanta. Maxwell and Carr could be seen whooping it up when the equipment went down.

Carr says, "Coaching the Celtics was a tremendous opportunity for Bill. Right off the bat he sort of set policy. We were young and we listened. I think he was great for that first team, perfect when we were young players. But eventually you grow up. It got to a point where guys wanted to police themselves. It was hard for Bill to relinquish that total control. He was one that liked to control every aspect of the team and what the players did and the whole thing. We'd become veteran players—if we did not police ourselves, *then* crack the whip. But don't crack the whip when the horses are running full speed. You don't have to beat 'em all the way around the track."

The 1982–83 Celtics went through the motions most of the season. They had enough talent to win a majority of games, but it was clear they were heading for a fall. Fitch was losing control, and there was little he could do about it. Bird always remained loyal, but other players were sniping at him or laughing at him behind his back.

"Bill was always suspicious of everything," says McHale. "I remember once in Houston we went to the Summit to practice, and Bill sees this guy sitting by himself in the top row of the arena. He sent poor Jimmy [then-assistant coach Jimmy Rodgers] up after the guy, and I'll never forget the sight of Jimmy running up all those steps. It was like watching *Rocky*. Finally, Jimmy gets to the top, and it turns out to be some janitor blowing dope on his lunch break."

Behind the scenes, Fitch was out of control. He ripped into Volk when a Patriots draft pick was introduced during a Celtics game in the Garden. Upset with unfavorable stories in a few newspapers, he ordered the public relations staff to move the seats of the offensive papers—to the upper deck. Angry with officials, he'd have Garden personnel make sure the refs didn't have hot water for their showers. Out-of-town writers couldn't attend Celtics practices. "You wouldn't want them to sneak in here and see us running those seven plays we've been using for forty years," joked McHale.

Boston got by Atlanta in a best-of-three series. The Celtics lost the one road game in that series, but the only memorable moment came when Tree Rollins bit Ainge's finger during a free-for-all. In years of retelling, the story has somehow turned around, and now wherever he goes, Ainge is taunted by poor historians who shout, "Danny, why don't you go bite some-body?"

The Celtics faced the Bucks in the conference semifinals, and for all practical purposes, the series ended when the Bucks won the opener, in Boston, 116–95. The Celts were thoroughly thrashed, and Fitch humiliated his veterans by making them go back in the game after it was lost in the fourth quarter. There was uncharacteristic booing at the Garden that night. Fitch said, "We had about four or five minutes out there where we just plain quit. It's hard to get that to roll off my tongue." Bird admitted, "Maybe there is something wrong with us." Two days later, Bird sat out with the flu, and the Celts were beaten again, 95–91. They knew it was over when they went to Milwaukee. Fitch kept calling meetings, but he had lost it. He told the players that the media had driven a wedge between himself and the team. It was too late. The Bucks won in straight sets, 107–99 and 107–93. It marked the first time in their history that the Celtics were swept in a play-off series. Auerbach had trouble being gracious. He was mad at comments made by Bucks coach Don Nelson (one of Red's vaunted alumni), comments that had provoked the Milwaukee crowd to boo Ainge every time he touched the ball. It was an old Red trick, thrown back in his face, but Auerbach didn't like it.

Nelson says, "I think he [Auerbach] was embarrassed as much as anything. The Ainge thing came up and that ticked him off, but it wasn't anything that he wouldn't have done. He called me a whore in the paper. I asked for forgiveness, but I'd say it took a couple of years. I wrote him some letters. I told him that I didn't mean anything by it and that I learned from him."

Bird was troubled, more than at any other time in his career. He'd come back to play the final two games in Milwaukee, leading Boston in scoring and rebounding in each game, but some of his teammates left their games at home. When McHale said, "I can still hold my head up high," and walked out of the locker room, Bird privately ripped his teammate. Bird has always said this was the low point of his basketball career.

The seeds for title number fifteen were planted in the loser's locker room at the Mecca in Milwaukee. Bird made a vow to himself that he would come back stronger than ever and never again subject himself to this kind of humiliation. "I'm going to punish myself all summer so this doesn't happen again next year," he said. This boot-camp pledge of Bird was the start of one of the most newsworthy off-seasons in Celtic history.

On May 24, twenty-two days after the Milwaukee massacre, Mangurian announced that he was selling the team. Three days later, Fitch tendered his Nixonian resignation. Fitch said it wouldn't be the same for him without Mangurian around. It is impossible to say what would have happened if Big Brother Bill had stayed, but his departure was just the kind of no-fault divorce the Celtics players needed. There was plenty of speculation about who would be the next coach, and on June 7, Auerbach went back to the huddle and tapped K. C. Jones's shoulder. The team was put back in family hands, and this would prove to be a good decision. Auerbach wasn't done. Archibald was waived.

On the day before the draft, Boston traded backup center Rick Robey to Phoenix for All Star guard Dennis Johnson. This stands as one of Auerbach's great transactions. "They were down on Dennis," he says. "And a lot of times people trade guys because they're down on them, and as a general manager you've got to avoid your coach being down on certain people. That's a very tough thing."

Paul Silas says, "It wasn't a physical thing, it was more of an attitude thing. I played with DJ, and he could be a tough customer. He could play, but what DJ needed was somebody like Larry to get him in line. He had nobody in Phoenix that way, so he just disrupted everything."

A month after the Robey-Johnson trade, Kevin McHale ended speculation that he was bound for the Knicks when he signed a four-year contract with the Celtics. In August, Mangurian officially sold the team to the trio of Don Gaston, Alan Cohen, and Paul Dupee. Larry Bird signed a seven-year contract in September, and the Celtics were ready to win a championship.

It was clear from the start that the veteran Celtics would play harder for Jones than they did for Fitch. K. C. was much closer to the players (Gerald Henderson still says, "If it wasn't for K. C., I don't know if I'd have made it. I got some consolation out of talking to K. C."), and many resented the way Fitch had treated Jones. Fitch never wanted Jones around, didn't include him in anything, and the two had engaged in a pushing match on draft day a few years earlier. Jones's supporters wanted to show they could do more with him in charge. It's a fact of life that many of today's professional athletes simply respond better to former players than they do to clipboard guys who never did it. But this was more than that. Jones's laid-back personality was exactly what the Celtics needed and wanted at this point. The goose step was out. It was time for a little soft shoe. Parish, Maxwell, McHale, Carr, Buckner, Ainge, and Henderson all played better without Fitch wearing them down physically and mentally. Bird, as always, was Bird. If Dan Quayle were named coach of the Celtics, Bird would be the same player.

Auerbach would never admit it, but he, too, was happy to see Fitch gone. The cigar-toting Red started showing up at practice again, talking with players. When reporters asked about some of Fitch's strict media-access rules during practices, Auerbach said, "There'll be no more of that chicken-shit stuff."

Meanwhile, Dennis Johnson immediately looked like the kind of clutch, experienced guard the Celtics needed. A defensive player cut from the cloth of his new coach, DJ was also the best big-game player the Celtics had. Bird has called him his finest teammate, and anyone who watched the Celtics from 1983 to 1988 will verify that Johnson ranks with Cousy, Sharman, and the Joneses as one of the better guards in franchise history. The fact that Auerbach was able to obtain a player of this caliber without giving up anything is evidence that Red lost nothing on his fastball in his later years. Robey was a terrific teammate and an affable sort, but he wasn't needed on a team that had Parish and McHale. After leaving Boston he played parts of three seasons with Phoenix. Robey was often hurt and never averaged more than 5.6 points for the Suns.

Robey's departure did wonders for Bird. Bird was a top NBA player from 1979 to 1983, but once Robey left, Bird became one of the greater players in the history of basketball, winning three straight Most Valuable Player Awards. There is some cause-and-effect here. We'll never know what might have happened if Robey stayed, but Bird is the first to admit that he started taking better care of himself once his favorite pal moved to Phoenix. Robey was a night owl. Nicknamed "Footer," Robey liked to party all night, and he liked to drink beer. These are not unusual characteristics for young profes- sional athletes, but Bird is the first to admit that he simply had too much fun when Robey was around. Like most Amer- ican males, Bird enjoys a beer now and then (although he won't drink anything out of a green bottle because of an episode in college when he accidentally swallowed some cigarette butts), and Robey was good company. When the Robey trade was made, Bird said, "It's like losing a brother," but his career was well served by the removal of his favorite running mate. In his autobiography, Bird wrote, "Rick says the best thing that ever happened to my career was him getting traded to Phoe- nix—and in many ways I've got to agree with him."

It was clear that this was going to be a memorable season when the defending-champion Sixers came to the Garden for an exhibition game and a fight broke out between Moses Ma- lone, who had been signed away from Houston, and Cedric Maxwell. Bird and Marc Iavaroni got into it and so did Sixers coach Billy Cunningham and Auerbach. Red saw the Sixers using one of his old tricks—waste one of your stiffs (Iavaroni) to get the other team's star (Bird) ejected. Nonunion referees (NBA officials were on strike) were calling the game, and Auerbach got out of his seat, crossed the floor—just like the old days when he'd slugged Ben Kerner in St. Louis—and entered into a heated discussion with Cunningham, then with Malone. Cunningham's jacket was ripped to shreds, and the tone was set. Red's message was clear: "Not in my building." The fire was back.

The 1983–84 Celtics lost their opener at Detroit, then ripped off nine in a row. The Sixers stayed in the race until mid-December, but Boston won the division by ten games, compiling a 62–20 record. After the summer of turmoil, the Celtics went through the entire season without a single roster move. They ascended into first place for good on December 30 and enjoyed three nine-game winning streaks.

They drew the Washington Bullets in the first round and beat Jeff Ruland and Company, 3–1. The series ended with two little Napoleons, Gerald Henderson and Frank Johnson, grappling on the floor on the Capital Center. K. C. Jones was particularly happy with the victory over the Bullets because Washington had fired him after the 1975–76 season.

The Knicks were next. This series started when Maxwell predicted that he would keep Knicks forward Bernard King under wraps. "He has scored his last forty points," said Maxwell. "We're going to stop the bitch. The Knicks are going to lose, there's no question about it."

"That was a confident, cocky team," says Carr. "Like when Max said Bernard wouldn't score forty, and I started imitating Bernard. We were just a cocky team. I remember the time one of the writers in Philly said we were like the L.A. Raiders in short pants—a bunch of thugs. But the bottom line was you just couldn't shake our confidence."

This was the kind of Wrestlemania boast that made this Celtics edition so controversial. Boston fans loved it. Celtics-haters found new inspiration.

The Celtics won the first two games, and McHale announced,

"They're in the grave right now. We've got to keep pouring dirt on 'em. We've got the shovel in our hands." The Knicks went home and won the next two, taking Game 4 when Bernard King scored forty-three points in Maxwell's face. Game 5, a Celtics win in the Garden, was highlighted by a Danny Ainge–Darrell Walker fight, but the Knicks won Game 6 by two points. Bernard King single-handedly forced this series to go the limit. In Game 7, Bird scored thirty-nine points with fifteen rebounds, ten assists, and three steals, and the Celtics won, 121–104. An exhausted Knicks coach Hubie Brown said, "Bird was the difference. You just saw one of the great performances."

The Celtics played Milwaukee in the conference finals. Things were going Boston's way. The Nets had eliminated the ever-dangerous Sixers, and the overachieving Bucks had wiped out New Jersey. With the Celtics facing the Bucks, it was widely assumed that there was a revenge factor working for Boston, but the Celtics were focused on a championship, not a petty dispute with Don Nelson's team. There were no hard feelings toward the Bucks after 1983 (except for Auerbach's). The Celtics and the Bucks were gracious and professional throughout, as the Celtics took the series in five easy games. It was the only 1984 Celtics play-off series without at least one fight.

The 1984 finals pitted the Celtics and the Lakers for the first time since 1969. The Celtics have won three NBA championships during the Larry Bird era, but this one stands alone because Boston beat Los Angeles in seven games. Beating the Houston Rockets doesn't compare. This marks the only time that a Larry Bird team beat a Magic Johnson team in a championship final.

It was the eighth Celtics-Lakers final, and Boston carried a 7–0 record into the series. Lakers fans had Frank Selvy flashbacks, and there were many nostalgic stories about Russell over Chamberlain and Jack Kent Cooke's balloons. It was Boston's sixteenth appearance in the finals and the Lakers' nineteenth. The Celtics and Lakers had combined to win 60 percent (twenty-three of thirty-eight counting 1984) of all NBA finals at this point. The Bird-Magic matchup gave CBS television the hook it needed to put the NBA back in the big league. Larry versus Magic was your classic "tastes great" versus "less filling" argument. The series came five years after the famous 1979 NCAA championship final. Bird or Johnson appeared in each of the first four, post-1979 NBA finals, but never simultaneously.

M. L. Carr predicted, "Get the convertible out, put the top down, and don't be coming here with any Polos and Pierre Cardins. Make sure you don't mind getting wet, 'cause the Garden's gonna be a sweatbox."

The Lakers took the opener in the Garden. Los Angeles had a lock in Game 2 in Boston, and that would have been it for this series. Late in Game 2, Kevin McHale missed two free throws, and Los Angeles had a two-point lead and the ball with ten seconds to play. Magic inbounded, and James Worthy lobbed a crosscourt pass, which was intercepted by Gerald Henderson. Henderson converted a game-tying lay-up as Celtics radio legend Johnny Most went into his dog-whistle voice, screeching, "Henderson stole the ball." John Havlicek watched from the stands. The Lakers had a chance for a last shot, but Magic dribbled out the clock and never got a shot off. Boston won in overtime, 124–121.

Henderson: "We were pretty down after Kevin missed those fuckin' free throws. M. L. and me had been coming in as a defensive tandem for a while, and we'd tell each other, 'Let's make somethin' happen. We gotta make it happen.' It wasn't hard to get pumped up with M. L. around. I think I had Byron Scott. Magic took the ball out. He passed it to Worthy, and I left my man anticipating because whoever went to double-team Worthy had left their man. You rotate and I rotated to the open man. I guess it was an instinctive thing. I was at full speed. After I got it Worthy came over. He wanted the ball back, but at that point, it's two."

If the Lakers were demoralized, they didn't show it. In Game 3, Los Angeles scored forty-seven points in the third quarter at the Forum and destroyed the Celtics, 137–104, in Game 3. "Today, the heart wasn't there, that's for sure," said Bird. "We played like sissies." Meanwhile, the *Los Angeles Herald Examiner* announced that Worthy deserved to be Most Valuable Player of the series.

Los Angeles should have been up 3–0. They had won Game 1 in Boston fairly easily, then taken Game 3 by thirty-three points. In Game 2, they'd held a two-point lead with the ball and ten seconds to play. Henderson's steal was the only thing between the Lakers and a commanding 3–0 lead.

The series turned around in Game 4 when McHale, playing like a man responding to Bird's "sissy" tag, clotheslined Lakers forward Kurt Rambis on a breakaway fast break. Both benches emptied, and there were a lot of hard feelings after the game. The Celtics trailed by six when McHale made his tackle. There were more incidents. Bird bumped Michael Cooper into the stands. Kareem Abdul-Jabbar elbowed Bird in the head and the superstars had to be separated. The Celtics trailed by five with a minute to play, but forced an overtime. In extra innings, Boston taunted Magic and Worthy at the foul line. Carr told Worthy he was going to miss. When Worthy missed, Maxwell chuckled, walked across the lane, and gave the choke sign. Magic missed a pair, Worthy missed one of two, and Boston won the game by three points.

In the days after Game 4, Maxwell smiled and said, "Before Kevin McHale hit Kurt Rambis, the Lakers were just running across the street whenever they wanted. Now, they stop at the corner, push the button, wait for the light, and look both ways."

McHale: "I didn't know what the hell was going on there. Sitting next to M. L. on the bench, he'd scream every time they got a lay-up: 'No more lay-ups! Grab 'em, grab 'em!' I heard this for the first six minutes of every game. So I got out there, and coming down on the break, they passed it one way, and they got it back to Kurt, and I just . . . turned. It looked like I horsecollared him. I was trying to grab him. His momentum carried my left arm so far away I couldn't lock 'em. He just went down really hard, and I went, 'Oooooh.' At that point, it was such a physical series, I wasn't going to help him up. I felt bad, and I hoped he wasn't hurt. Hey, if I was trying to hurt somebody I'd try to hurt Magic or somebody, not Kurt Rambis. It just happened. That kind of set the tone for our team, but I just wanted to grab the guy. I sure didn't want to get him like that."

Riley called the Celtics thugs. Little did he know what he was in for when the series returned to Boston.

The Lakers were frustrated. If not for a dumb pass in Game 2 and a blown five-point lead in the final minute of Game 4, they'd have earned a four-game sweep. They *knew* they were the better team. Everybody knew it. Licking their wounds, they had to fly three thousand miles back to Boston, and when they got there it was ninety-seven degrees and humid. Of course, there were no cabs to be had at Logan Airport. Boston was experiencing a vicious June heat wave, and the Garden, built in 1928, was without air-conditioning—without windows. The name of the Boston hotel where the Lakers were staying got into the papers, and players received calls at all hours of the night. There was a rash of fire alarms. Lakers coach Pat Riley was more alarmed than anybody. He could not believe this was happening to his team.

Bird: "That was a time when we had to fly after a game, all night, then practice the next day and play the next night. That's what basektball's all about, boy. I mean, that's rough. The fifth game is the most important game of any series you play. I guarantee you, whoever wins the fifth game is usually going to win the whole thing."

On Friday, June 9, on a night when a Bermuda air mass transformed the Causeway Street train station into a fountain of sweat and Lakers sorrow, Bird scored thirty-four, on fifteen of twenty shooting, and the Celtics vaporized the Lakers, 121–

103. It was like the Fourth of July on the Esplanade. Through the steamy heat and haze, the maestro worked his magic and a storied Boston institution thrilled the assembled masses with a traditional performance of harmony and brilliance. Bird was Mr. White Heat, but he had plenty of help—much of it from the steamy conditions. Referee Hugh Evans left at halftime due to dehydration, and Kareem (7–25) spent much of the night at the end of the Laker bench inhaling oxygen from a mask. Asked to explain what it felt like, Abdul-Jabbar said, "I suggest that you go to a local steam bath, do one hundred push-ups with all your clothes on, and then try to run back and forth for forty-eight minutes."

They flew back to Los Angeles, and the Lakers won Game 6 by eleven points. Debris flew after the game, and Carr was hit in the eyes by some unidentified flying liquid. He would have to wear goggles for Game 7. Maxwell told Johnson, "Let's kill them on Tuesday. Let's kill those freaks."

A half hour before Game 7 (the 113th game of an eight-and-a-half-month season) in Boston, Maxwell told his teammates, "Well boys, one more time. Just hop on my back, and I'll take you on in." He did too. Maxwell scored twenty-four with eight rebounds and eight assists in a 111–102 victory, which brought banner number fifteen to Boston. The date of the championship game was June 12, Flag Day.

Auerbach was buoyant and couldn't resist rubbing it in. Red has never been humble in moments of victory. "You guys [the media] were talking about a dynasty the Lakers had," he shouted. "But what dynasty? Here's the only dynasty right here. This team."

"Eighty-four was the best . . . period," remembers Carr, "because we beat the Lakers, and no one believed we could beat 'em. That was the most gratifying year that we had. We came together as a team and did things that we felt we were capable of doing. Even when we got beat by thirty-three on national TV in Game 3, our confidence still wasn't shaken. There was something we would do to win at any time. Top to bottom, we were so confident. The Lakers, athletically, were probably a stronger team. They had better athletes. But if I were a cardiologist, I'd think we had the better team. We had more heart than they did."

Years later, Cooper admitted to Scott Ostler and Steve Springer of the *Los Angeles Times*, "They don't talk so much anymore, but they did in 1984. And I'll tell you, they backed it up. They were the Muhammad Alis of basketball. That was something new to me that I kind of enjoyed about them, because that's what you do on the playgrounds—you do a little talking to see where the opponent's heart is, try to intimidate 'em."

The Celtics were invited to the White House by President Reagan and flew to Washington a few hours after their clinch party. Again, the tradition continued. Just as Satch Sanders got off a memorable line in the presence of John F. Kennedy twenty-two years earlier, Dennis Johnson did the trick in 1984. President Reagan received the champs on the Rose Garden lawn and gave a brief talk in stifling ninety-degree heat. Reagan said, "As the leaders of your organization changed, as one group of stars was replaced by another group, the Celtics not only survived, they maintained their championship form because the Celtics have been a team of champions, larger and greater than any one player, coach, or manager." DJ took the microphone and said, "Mr. President, how do you stand out here and don't sweat?"

The Celtics summer of 1984 was calm. Gerald Henderson and Cedric Maxwell were in search of new contracts, but there wasn't much other Celtics news. Henderson and Maxwell both held out at the start of camp. The Celtics signed Henderson first, but they felt they were paying too much, and, in typical Auerbach fashion, Henderson found himself en route to Seattle. An hour before an exhibition game in Houston, Henderson was informed that he'd been dealt to the Supersonics for Seattle's 1986 number-one draft choice. This was not strictly a revenge-motivated deal. Coach Jones and Company believed Danny Ainge was ready to start. It was obvious to all that the Celts had to improve their draft status if they were to remain strong into the late 1980s. Henderson was gone. Maxwell didn't sign until a few hours before the season opener at Detroit. He was out of shape and down with a knee problem for a good part of the season. When the Celts raised flag fifteen before their home opener, Bird made a few remarks and paid special tribute to Henderson. In Seattle, Henderson wore number 15, and his new teammates asked him if it was because of flag fifteen. Without Henderson's steal, there would have been no championship in 1984, but this was 1985 and Celtics management was thinking ahead.

There wasn't much of a letdown in 1984–85. There was evidence that the passion was still strong when Larry Bird and Julius Erving got into a fight during a Friday night Garden game in November. Bird had forty-two points, and the Celtics led by twenty late in the third quarter when Bird and Dr. J started grappling near midcourt. Boston won the game, and neither player commented about the fight.

The Celtics were 15–1 on December 2. McHale got some headlines on March 3 when he scored a franchise-record fifty-six points against the Pistons, but ten days later Bird hit for sixty against Atlanta in New Orleans. That same week, Bird was on the cover of *Time*. He was at the absolute top of his game. In thirty-three minutes in Utah, he hit for double figures in points, rebounds, and assists, plus had nine steals. Maxwell hurt his knee in a February loss to the Lakers, and McHale moved into the starting lineup. Maxwell had arthroscopic surgery and was never the same on the court. The Celtics finished 63–19 and won the division by five games, but some of their depth was missing. Gerald Henderson was gone, and the "Max factor" was gone. Quinn Buckner was on his way out. Ray Williams was acquired to beef up the backcourt.

The Celtics drew Cleveland in the first round, and Bird had to miss a game in Richfield due to bursitis in his shooting elbow. Cleveland fans chanted "We want Bird," at the end of the

Cavaliers' victory. Big mistake. Bird said, "They want me, they'll get me with both barrels."

This was a great time in Bird's life. He was in the middle of this three-season Most Valuable Player dominance and was able to back up any boast. He was also more comfortable with the media than at any time before, or since. Traveling on a team bus during the daytime in Portland in 1985, Bird sat near the front and kidded with the four beat writers who were covering the Celtics. Bird said something that struck a nerve in Mike Fine, a veteran reporter from the *Quincy Patroit Ledger*. Fine wheeled around, put a finger in Bird's face, and said, in a voice loud enough for the whole bus to hear, "Oh yeah? Well, how come every time I see you talking on these television commercials you sound so smart and smooth, but in person you sound like such a douchebag?"

Bird laughed and shot back, "Because those guys pay me to talk."

Given Bird's early sensitivity with the media, it was a fascinating exchange. The star was insulted by a writer in front of the entire team, but he didn't get mad.

After Bird's boast in Cleveland, he came back and torched the Cavaliers in front of a hostile crowd in a Game 4 clincher. The Cleveland fans booed Bird every time he touched the ball, and he loved it. The Celts eliminated the Pistons in six games, then met Philadelphia in the Eastern Conference finals. The Celtics won the first three games of the Sixer series, then dropped Game 4 in the Spectrum as Cedric Maxwell played like a brother from another planet. Sometime between Game 2 in Boston and Game 4 in Philadelphia, Bird further injured his already mangled right index finger. His shooting was subpar for the remainder of the play-offs, and this injury might have prevented the Celtics from winning three straight championships from 1984 to 1986.

The true story of Bird's injury has never come out. What is known is this: Two nights after winning Game 2 in Boston, Bird went to a downtown bar, Chelsea's, with Quinn Buckner and Bird's friend Nick Harris. Harris and Mike Harlow, a former Colgate football player, got into a fight, and Bird came to the defense of his friend. Bird has never commented on it, but agent Woolf admitted that Harlow received an out-of-court settlement from Bird. Bird shot 52 percent during the 1984–85 season, but his percentage dropped to 43 percent after the incident.

Bird wasn't the only Celtic hurting when the 1985 finals got underway. Maxwell's knee hadn't recovered, and he was sulking because McHale had taken his job in the starting lineup. Game 1 was in the Garden on Memorial Day, and the Celtics decimated the Lakers, 148–114. Scott Wedman made eleven of eleven floor shots, and Kareem Abdul-Jabbar looked like Willie Mays flopping around the field during the 1973 World Series. Boston fans knew better than to assume the series was over. The Memorial Day Massacre was similar to the Mother's Day Massacre of 1982, when the Celts beat the Sixers by forty points in Game 1, then lost the series. Kareem came back with thirty points, seventeen rebounds, and eight assists, as the Lakers won Game 2. The series moved to Los Angeles, and the Lakers took Game 3 by twenty-five points. The Celtics won Game 4 on a Dennis Johnson jumper at the buzzer, but Los Angeles won Game 5 in the Forum and came back to Boston needing only one win in two games to avenge 1984.

Before Game 6, Johnny Most got his evening off to a fine start by telling his listeners that Lakers forward Kurt Rambis had just crawled out of a sewer. The anthem was performed by Bo and Bill Winiker, a bugle and snare-drum combo that had played dozens of anthems at the Garden over the years. Los Angeles-based superstar performer Stevie Wonder offered his services for the anthem, but loyal Celtics Vice President Tod Rosensweig said, "There is superstition."

The Celtics were attempting to become the first NBA team since the 1968–69 Celtics to win back-to-back titles, but Los Angeles took Game 6, 111–100, and owner Jerry Buss, speaking for Fred Schaus, Jerry West, Jack Kent Cooke, Frank

Selvy, and two generations of Lakers fans, said, "This removes the most odious sentence in the English language. It can never again be said that the Lakers have never beaten the Boston Celtics." Lakers coach Pat Riley added, "Boston can never mock us as they did a year ago." Kareem Abdul-Jabbar invoked memories of the Brooklyn Dodgers.

Kevin McHale: "We had a better team than they did that year. Max got hurt and everything, but they came to the Garden not thinking they could beat us in that sixth game, no way. We had played like crap. We shot the ball poorly. If we had played well that sixth game, I'm not sure they'd have showed up for the seventh game. They were a great team and all, but they did not believe at that point that they could beat us. That was a turning point for them."

Unable to mock the Lakers, Auerbach went back to work. He was officially "retired," but he was in motion after the 1985 finals defeat and said, "Just because you lose in the play-offs, you don't panic and decimate your ball club. That's what separates the men from the boys. The boys panic."

It wasn't a panic, but the bench gang had to go. Jones used his starters in 430 of a possible 480 minutes in Games 5 and 6. Cedric Maxwell, Quinn Buckner, Ray Williams, Carlos Clark, and M. L. Carr never got off the pine in the final game of the season. All would be gone before opening night five months later.

Bill Walton called the Celtics in the spring of 1985. According to his contract with the Clippers, he was a free agent for sixty days after any season in which the Clips failed to make the play-offs. Walton was shopping, and the Celtics were interested in buying. After losing the finals, Bird stopped by Auerbach's office before heading home to French Lick, Indiana. Auerbach asked him what he thought of Walton, and Bird said, "Get him if you can."

Auerbach got Walton, but the price was Maxwell. It was a deal that had to be made. There was plenty of evidence that Maxwell had given all he could give to the Boston Celtics, but it was hard for teammates to say good-bye to the rubberband man. He was flakey and fun. He annoyed some fans with his habit of leaving the court to use the bathroom during the national anthem. In his final season in Boston, Maxwell annoyed Auerbach so much that Red had praise of Maxwell stricken from a book he was writing. But Max was an original. Only he could claim, "You know what I like to do in the off-season? I like to get in my big, fancy car, drive around to construction sites, and watch guys work. Then I roll down the window and say, 'Guess what, boys? I got nothing to do today.' " He was also a terrific post-up player, a primo defender, and, like DJ, a great big-game player. He played amid the ruins of the John Y. Brown regime. He was a play-off Most Valuable Player in 1981, and he carried the team on his back in a seventh game against the Lakers in 1984.

There was more subtraction. Quinn Buckner was dealt to Indiana for guard Jerry Sichting. M. L. Carr retired, Ray Williams signed with Atlanta, and Carlos Clark was cut. Few teams trim five players from a championship-final squad, but Auerbach and Volk knew this tuning was necessary to put the Celtics back on top.

The arrival of Walton put Celtics fans in hardwood heaven. Walton was *the* player of the mid-1970s, and basketball aficionados from coast to coast regarded him as the consummate team center. Due to a series of foot injuries, he had officially retired in 1981. Perhaps the greatest college player of all time, Walton longed to return to the big games. He'd won championships at UCLA and in Portland. He was a sports fan, and he loved the tradition of the Boston Celtics. He could pass from the high or low post, and he threw the fast-break outlet as well at any big man who ever played the game. The memory of his near-perfect game in the 1973 NCAA finals is part of basketball lore. His teammates loved him more than the fans. McHale loved to kid him about his senior status and his time on the disabled list. "I've been in the league for six years, and I've never seen him play a game," said McHale. "I saw some

film of him once, but it was on a black-and-white television."
Bird relished the moments of purity that Walton could bring
to practice and to games. Walton wore bell-bottoms, drove big
American cars, bought a home in Cambridge, and continued
to follow the Grateful Dead. He was happy and loquacious in
his first year in Boston. He would talk about anything other
than his rumored knowledge of the whereabouts of Patty
Hearst. He was demonstrative on the bench, exhorting his
teammates like a desperate, bespectacled high school team
manager who could never make varsity.

Opening night was a disaster. Playing in the shadows of the
giant Exxon signs off the New Jersey Turnpike, the Celtics
blew a nineteen-point lead and lost to the Nets in overtime.
Walton committed five fouls, turned the ball over seven times
in nineteen minutes, and said, "I was a disgrace to my team
and to the sport of basketball."

The first-night jitters did not carry over, and the 1985–86
Celtics won sixty-seven games, one less than the franchise
record. This might have been the finest front line in basketball
history. On a few occasions, Jones employed Parish, McHale,
and Walton simultaneously. McHale improved for the sixth
straight season, Parish again was an All Star, and Bird won
his third straight Most Valuable Player. When McHale went
down for eighteen games due to an Achilles problem, Scott
Wedman started and scored fifteen points per game. The Celtics went 15–3 without McHale. Walton was a major force off
the bench. The big redhead hadn't been able to carry the Clippers, but given the luxury of playing a backup role, he was a
weapon unlike any other. The low point of the season came on
Christmas Day in New York when the Celts blew a twenty-
five-point third-quarter lead and lost in double-overtime, but
they won seventeen of eighteen after that, including a 110–95
victory over the Lakers in the Garden. Walton scored eleven
points with eight rebounds, four assists, and seven blocks in
only sixteen minutes against Los Angeles. He was on his way
to the Sixth Man Award. Red Auerbach invented the sixth

man. Frank Ramsey, John Havlicek, and Kevin McHale filled the roll for three decades, but no one ever envisioned Bill Walton serving in this capacity.

They won twenty-nine straight games in the Garden and finished 40–1 at home. They were committed. Bird and McHale even swore off beer during the play-offs. The Celtics drew the Chicago Bulls in round one and swept three games despite a dazzling display by Michael Jordan. "Air" Jordan scored forty-nine points in Game 1, then poured in a play-off–record sixty-three points in Game 2. Despite this scoring binge, the Celtics won both games and took the clincher, 122–104, in Chicago. Atlanta was next, and it took the Green only five games to dismiss the Hawks. Game 5 will be remembered as the game in which the Celtics scored twenty-four consecutive points against the Hawks, taking the quarter, 36–6. "It was the best quarter I've ever played in," said Dennis Johnson. The Bucks came to Boston for the Eastern Conference finals, and coach Don Nelson admitted, "It's like—what is it? *Man of La Mancha.*" He was right. Boston won the conference finals in four straight games. "The Celtics don't come to split, they come to sweep," Bird said when he left the Mecca.

There was only one disappointment in the 1985–86 Celtics season, and that was the absence of the Los Angeles Lakers in the championship finals. The Celtics, Lakers, and all of America had come to think of the basketball World Series as June showcase for Boston and Los Angeles, for Bird and Magic. The 1984 and 1985 championship series brought interest in the league to a new high, and it was assumed that 1986 would feature the rubber match in this best-of-three.

Enter Houston, coached by none other than Bill Fitch. The Rockets were in a rebuilding program, led by Fitch and the Twin Towers of Akeem Olajuwon and Ralph Sampson. The up-start Rockets beat the Lakers, 4–1, in the Western Finals and came to the Garden intent on asserting themselves as the NBA Team of the Future. The Celtics won Game 1, 112–100, and members of Boston's starting lineup all scored between eighteen and twenty-one points. In Game 2 the count was Boston, 117–95. They went to Houston for three games (if necessary), and most of the Celtics figured they were through playing in the Garden for the year. Houston won two of the three, taking Game 5 after the seven-foot-four-inch Sampson got into a fight with six-foot-one-inch Jerry Sichting. Bird said, "I can't believe he picked a fight with Sichting. Heck, my girlfriend could beat him up." Dennis Johnson had a cut over his eye, and when Bird saw DJ's blood, he knew the series was only going one more game.

The Celtics were smoking when they got back to Boston. They were mad at themselves and at the Rockets, and coach K. C. Jones had to call off practice so none of his frothing players would get hurt. On game day, June 8, Bird scored twenty-nine points with eleven rebounds and twelve assists while Sampson shot 4–12 and never made it to the free-throw line in Boston's 114–97 victory. Bird changed his uniform at halftime, stuffing a souvenir jersey in his equipment bag. He wanted to have *two* championship shirts, and he knew this was the day it was going to end. It was 87–61 after three periods. Celtics starters were popping champagne corks while the scrubs finished off the Rockets on the parquet.

"I think it's one of the greatest, if not the greatest team that I've ever been associated with," said Auerbach.

Bird says, "Eighty-six was good because of Walton and everything that went on. I thought that was our best team. We had a great team, and it seemed like everybody did what they had to do to make us a great team. It was a fun year."

"We knew we were going win," says Rick Carlisle. "It was just a question of how we were going to embarrass the other team."

The Celtics were at the top for the sixteenth time. Sweet Sixteen. In many ways, this Celtics edition was more pleasing to the eye than any other. They had the full complement of weapons, and they passed and played defense as well as any champion entry. Bird is the best passing forward the game has seen, and no center ever passed better than Walton. It was like watching Edward R. Murrow and Walter Cronkite together behind the anchor desk. Bird has said it was his favorite team. It spawned a new generation of Celtics fans and gave them something in common with the two generations preceding them. Rooting for the Celtics became chic, and pockets of Green people suddenly started appearing in hotel lobbies and arenas across the land. It would be a while before the Celtics would win again, but after sixteen championships in thirty years, the Celtics had earned their status as an American institution.

10
Today's Green

THE World Champion Boston Celtics were getting a little long in the tooth. As banner number sixteen was being stitched, Boston's best players were growing dangerously old by NBA standards. Robert Parish was 33, Bill Walton 34, Larry Bird 29, Dennis Johnson 31, Scott Wedman 34, and Kevin McHale 28. New blood was needed, and it appeared that it was on the way because of Auerbach's bold move in the autumn of 1984. Gerald Henderson, a starting guard and the hero of the 1984 championship series with the Lakers, had been swapped for Seattle's number-one pick in the 1986 draft. Once again, Red had peeked into the future when no one else was looking. He could see that Seattle was on a downward spiral. The Supersonics were coming off a 42–40 season when Auerbach made the trade, but he figured in two years they'd be down and out. Seattle did exactly what Auerbach wanted. The Supersonics went 31–51 in 1984–85 and matched that woeful mark again in 1985–86. They were easily one of the seven worst teams in the NBA, which meant they qualified for the draft lottery.

The NBA's lottery did not yet exist when Auerbach made the trade. The lottery was established to eliminate the suspicion that nonplay-off teams were tanking in order to qualify for the first pick with the worst record. With the lottery in place, the seven nonplay-off teams all had an equal chance at number one, and in 1985 the Knicks won the lottery and the right to select Patrick Ewing as the first pick in the draft.

As Seattle staggered through the 1985–86 season, it was clear they'd be in the second lottery pool, and when Auerbach went to New York for the dramatic ceremony, he was delighted to come away with the number-two pick in the 1986 draft. Red knew who he wanted. Auerbach's good friend, Maryland coach Lefty Driesell, had a shooting forward who could touch the rafters, run the floor, and rebound with the big guys: Len Bias.

Bias was no stranger to the Celtics. He'd been a counselor at Auerbach's camp in the summer of 1985. He'd played in all the scrimmages with Celtics rookies and free agents and nightly emerged as the best player on the floor. People in Marshfield went home every night talking about the junior from Maryland. What if the Celtics could land a player like that? Bias was the type of player who could carry the Celtics into the 1990s.

There were other highly touted players in the 1986 draft, including North Carolina's Brad Daugherty, Memphis State's William Bedford, Kentucky's Kenny Walker, Auburn's Chuck Person, and Miami University of Ohio's Ron Harper. The Celtics had the number-two pick, and Auerbach was in love with both Daugherty and Bias. Just as he had done in 1956 (Russell) and 1978 (Bird), the Redhead put himself in position to land another franchise player. Boston was in a no-lose situation. With the draft coming on the heels of a flossy, championship season, the Celtics were once again the envy of the NBA. How did they keep doing it? How lucky could a team get?

Bias was six-foot-eight, weighed 220, and had the tools of a premier NBA forward. He had a body like New Jersey's Buck

Williams, but he could also stick the jumper from fifteen feet. He could handle the ball, block shots, run the break. He could do everything. Auerbach saw him play many games because Maryland was in Red's D.C. backyard. Bias averaged 23.2 points in his senior season and was a consensus first-team All American. He had dinner with Auerbach. He came to Boston to meet with Volk and the Celtics brass.

Volk: "Frankly, we brought him in for a physical more than we did anything else. We felt we had a handle on him right along that allowed us to make that type of judgment. . . . As I recall, he came in right around the time of the first or second game of the championship finals. He went to a game and maybe even a practice. The thing I recall so vividly was when he was sitting out in the front hall waiting for transportation to the airport and I passed through and said hello and wished him well. And he said, very, very emphatically, with a firm handshake and a square look in the eye, 'Please draft me.' "

The Celtics were happy to comply. Philadelphia had the first pick and took Daugherty, and there was no decision to be made. Boston drafted Bias, and Lenny Bias said, "Praise the Lord." He donned a green Celtics cap and posed for pictures. The Celtics told him he'd wear no. 30, M. L. Carr's number. Reebok signed him to a million-dollar sneaker deal. Bird told Auerbach he'd come to rookie camp to work with the kid—just as Cowens had worked with Bird and Havlicek had worked with Cowens. Bird said Bias would be the player to take his place.

On the morning of June 19, while partying with friends in his Washington Hall dormitory room, Len Bias died of cocaine intoxication. The drug interrupted the normal electrical control of Bias's heartbeat, resulting in the onset of seizures and cardiac arrest. An autopsy revealed that he had 6.5 milligrams of cocaine per liter of blood. At the time of his death, there were close to thirty known cases of sudden cardiac deaths associated with cocaine.

"Len Bias is gone because of one mistake," insisted Driesell. Two of Bias's teammates, Terry Long and David Gregg, testified that they snorted cocaine with Bias the morning that he died. A court case, *People* v. *Brian Tribble,* attempted to convict Tribble of supplying the cocaine. Tribble was acquitted, but the prosecution portrayed Bias as an experienced drug user.

There was evidence that he'd lost some of the discipline that made him everybody's All American. Bias was twenty-one credits short of graduating at the time of his death. He finished his academic career with two Fs and two incompletes. His party friends reported that Bias's last words were, "I'm a bad motherfucker."

Auerbach says, "That was one of the biggest disappointments of my career because in my honest opinion, he was not a druggie. He was a super kid. He celebrated. Three weeks before his death, he was examined by Golden State, the Knicks, and by us, and he was clean in all places. I had been to dinner with him and his folks. I used to see him at the games, I used to go to Maryland practices."

Bias passed drug tests issued by all three teams. The tests were conducted illegally, but they showed no traces of cocaine.

Volk: "Unknown at the time, the NBA's drug policy with the Players Association prevented testing him. But we did drug test him. Golden State did the same thing, and so did the Knicks. I did it in blissful ignorance of the rule. He passed all three tests. No one had any abnormalities. They all concurred that he was in exceptional shape. He was the best one they had, and they had seen a number of people. I got a call from Larry Fleisher [executive director of the Players Association] afterwards, criticizing us for having drug tested him. I said to Larry, 'Are you saying now that we had no reason to be concerned? It may be the rule, but it didn't hurt anybody, but it sure didn't help anybody. . . . ' It still is unclear exactly what happened. It makes you wonder if there was anything more we could have done. We try to find out as much as we reasonably can, trying to protect ourselves. If your normal inquiry doesn't suggest anything, then you don't go to that

next step. . . . Four years later, I'm persuaded that it wasn't
a one-time thing. This is what I believe—that he had some
involvement, early, that he had had some use, some familiar-
ity, but had made up his mind that his goal was to be an NBA
player and that he had been able to put [the drugs] aside in
order to achieve that goal. Feeling that he had reached the
pinnacle of success and had achieved his goal, I think he let
loose."

Gerald Henderson was stunned. He was the starting guard
dealt to Seattle months after winning the title in 1984. Compensation for Henderson was Seattle's first-round pick two
years later: Len Bias. Gerald Henderson-for-Len Bias turned
out to be a deal that helped no one. "I think everything happens
because of the Lord," says Henderson, ever wounded at being
traded days after signing a new contract with Boston. "Maybe
it just wasn't right from the very beginning. You never know.
Maybe it just wasn't right for everybody involved. At that
point, they didn't know who they were going to get. You know.
It just wasn't right."

The death of Bias got the 1986–87 season off to a rough
start. The tragedy kicked off a campaign lined with potholes
and landmines. Scott Wedman had heel surgery two weeks
after the 1986 finals and played in only six games in the new
season. Bill Walton broke the little finger of his left hand, then
hurt his right ankle while riding a stationary bike. He didn't
start playing until March and then played in only ten regular-
season games. K. C. Jones used eleven different starters in
this title defense. Stripped of their bench strength, the Celtics
started losing regularly on the road and in one sorry stretch
dropped nine of ten games away from home. They finished 39–
2 at home but 20–21 on the road. It was the first time during
the Bird era that the Green finished sub-.500 on the road. Greg
Kite moved up from twelfth man to sixth man and couldn't
handle the work load. K. C. Jones, operating the way Red
always did, pushed to win every game and wore down his
starters in the process. McHale had his best year, but his

ankles and feet couldn't take the pounding. He suffered a bone break when Larry Nance stepped on his foot late in the year. The Celtics managed to win fifty-nine games, but the Lakers won sixty-five, and Boston was far from full strength when the play-offs started. McHale's right ankle was a scrap heap, and at the start of the play-offs he was running the floor with a hairline fracture of his navicular bone. Parish turned his ankle in the play-offs. Bird had back problems.

Owners Don Gaston, Alan Cohen, and Paul DuPee had a nice year. They decided to put 40 percent of the team up for sale and collected forty million dollars in private stock. Everybody wanted to buy a piece of the Celtics, and certificates of ownership hang in dens and offices across the land. The Celtics were more popular than ever. The 1986–87 Celtics were certainly the whitest NBA team in many years; the team was made up of eight white players and only four blacks, and this reversal of color no doubt made the Celtics more attractive to white fans threatened by black dominance of the sport.

They wiped out the Bulls in three games, then survived a rugged seven-game set with the Milwaukee Bucks. Boston trailed the Bucks by nine points with six minutes to play in Game 7 at the Garden. The series took its toll. Detroit was next, and this turned out to be a conference final worthy of the Boston-Philadelphia clashes in the early 1980s.

The Celtics and Pistons loathed each other. Boston players detested Detroit center Bill Laimbeer. They hated the way he cried to the officials and flopped on the floor to draw offensive fouls. When the All Star team was announced each February, the first thing Bird checked was to see if Laimbeer would be his teammate. One year, after being told that Laimbeer did not make the All Star squad, Bird said, "Good, now I won't have to get on the bus game day and have him say, 'Hi Larry,' and then I have to say, 'Fuck you, Bill.' "

Parish didn't like Detroit strongman Rick Mahorn; the "Chief" considered Mahorn a dirty player and would not shake his hand before the center jump at the start of games. All of the Celtics were outraged by the hot dogging of rookie Dennis Rodman. The Pistons were young and hungry, and they believed they were better than the Celtics. Like so many other losers over the years, they felt Boston always got the benefit of the doubt from the media, the officials, and the networks.

The Celtics won the first two in Boston, then lost two blowouts in Pontiac. Bird and Laimbeer were ejected for fighting in Game 3. Game 5 provided the most memorable moments of the series. First, there was the frightening sight of Parish's seemingly unprovoked assault on Laimbeer. The Chief punched the Detroit center to the floor, and nothing was called. With seconds remaining, Detroit had a one-point lead and the ball at the Celtics end of the court. Piston coach Chuck Daly was signaling for a time-out, but no one could hear anything, and Bird intercepted Isiah Thomas's inbounds lob intended for Laimbeer. Instinctively, DJ cut for the basket, and Bird hit him in stride. Victory.

Parish was suspended for Game 6, and the Celtics went back to Pontiac and lost by eight. Game 7 was in Boston on May 30. While watching the Celtics on television, Lefty Driesell commented, "It would have been so different with Leonard [Bias], believe me. There wouldn't have been two seven-game series if Leonard had been around. The Celtics would have won much easier. Leonard was such a great outside shooter, he would have forced changes in the other teams. It would all have been so different. But that's speculation, I guess. We'll never know, will we?"

"I said at the time that we'd feel the effects of this for ten years," says Volk. "That 1986–87 team was championship caliber except for the injuries, and had Bias been involved in that I think we would have won the championship. He provided the type of ingredient that could have been utilized. . . . It's very easy to overdramatize and maybe glorify, but the way we viewed him was that he was Michael Jordan, three inches taller, didn't drive quite as well, but shot better from the outside. That's what we had. It's hard to recover from that loss."

In Game 7, the ghosts of championships past delivered once again. The Celtics got the break they needed when Detroit stars Vinnie Johnson and Adrian Dantley banged heads during the third quarter. Dantley wound up in the hospital with a concussion. It was the kind of break the Celtics always seemed to get.

Boston won by three. After the game, Dennis Rodman said Bird was overrated because he was white. Isiah echoed, "If he was black, he'd be just another good guy." There was considerable furor after those comments, and Thomas had to go to Los Angeles to meet the press and apologize on national television. Bird was very gracious and helped him smother the fire.

The Lakers were next. This presented the third matchup of Boston and Los Angeles—Bird versus Magic—in four seasons. Los Angeles was deep, Boston wasn't. This was the first of Magic Johnson's Most Valuable Player seasons, and the Lakers had a deeper bench thanks to the addition of Mychal Thompson. The Lakers won the first two in Los Angeles, then dropped Game 3 in Boston. The series turned when the Lakers won Game 4 in Boston. The Celts led it by sixteen points in the third period, but blew the lead and lost the game when Magic hit a running hook over three Celtics. The Celtics were faced with an impossible task. They were down, 3–1, and had to win three straight, playing the final two games (if necessary) in Los Angeles. Boston took Game 5, 123–108, then went to Los Angeles to die. In Game 6 on June 14, the 1987 Lakers overcame an early Celtics lead and took out Boston with an 18–2 run in the third quarter.

Boston has been to the NBA finals nineteen times, winning sixteen and losing only three. No one can safely predict how long it'll take to get back to the championship series. It looks like it's going to be a long time, but that's been said before about the Celtics. Since 1956, Boston fans have not gone more than five years without an NBA title.

By the start of the 1987–88 season, it was painfully obvious that there was a changing of the guard underway in the NBA.

Everybody was catching up with the Celtics and the Lakers. It became almost impossible for Boston's aging team to keep up with the speedy young legs of teams in Cleveland, Detroit, and Atlanta. Celtics fans came to expect losses whenever the team played on the road in the Central Division. Greg Kite was waived, Sam Vincent and Scott Wedman were traded, and Artis Gilmore was brought in as a backup. Like Pete Maravich and Dave Bing, Gilmore was an over-the-hill superstar coming to Boston for a taste of parquet before retirement. Peter May of the *Hartford Courant* nicknamed Gilmore "Rigor Artis." Jerry Sichting was traded for Jim Paxson. These were attempts to give the Celtics more depth, but they simply weren't enough. K. C. Jones came under fire for playing his starters too many minutes and letting young talents rot on the bench. Rookie Reggie Lewis was getting the same splinters San Vincent got a year earlier. McHale was recovering from foot surgery and didn't play the first part of the season. Jones's pedal-to-the-metal overdrive produced fifty-seven wins and Boston's eighth division championship in nine years of the Bird era, but even Celtics fans could feel it slipping away.

The Celtics beat the Knicks in a four-game first-round series. The highlight of the series came when Jones announced that this would be his final season on the bench, and that Jimmy Rodgers would coach the team in 1988–89. Auerbach worked this trick when he named Russell Coach-of-the-Future during the 1966 play-offs. There was some suspicion about the motivation behind Jones's resignation. It was widely rumored that he was pressured to step aside, and this impression was fortified when he accepted a job as an *assistant* coach in Seattle, one year after stepping down. Would the president of Bloomingdale's voluntarily resign, then take a job as a floor manager at JC Penney? In 1990, Jones became head coach of the Sonics.

The up-and-coming Hawks were Boston's second-round opponent, and the Celtics fell behind, 3–2, when Atlanta took Game 5 in the Boston Garden. When the Celtics arrived at the Omni for Game 6, they saw a sign that read, WELCOME TO

K. C.'S RETIREMENT PARTY. Not quite. Boston won Game 6, 102–100, then Bird guaranteed a Game 7 victory and backed up the boast, hitting nine of ten shots in a *mano-a-mano* Game 7 fourth-quarter duel with Dominique Wilkins. Dominique scored fifteen points in the final period. The two teams shot an aggregate fifty-nine percent from the floor and committed only fifteen turnovers in forty-eight minutes of fast-break basketball.

Detroit put an end to Boston's waning hopes in the spring of 1988. The Pistons took Game 1 in the Garden, 104–96, and that set the tone for the series. Game 2 was a double-overtime Celtics victory featuring a miracle three-point buzzer-beater by McHale, but it was only a matter of time before the Celtics caved in to the Detroit roadrunners. Bird shot 35 percent in the series, and Detroit won it in six games. He shot 4–17 in the final, a 95–90 loss in Pontiac. The torch was passed. The Pistons would finish the decade as the beast of the East.

The Boston Celtics fell to earth during the 1988–89 season. It wasn't as bad as 1969–70 or the dismal two seasons that preceded Bird's arrival, but the Celtics were a team in transition and half of the league flew past them. Coach Jimmy Rodgers was plagued from the start when Bird went on the shelf for good after playing only six games. Bird underwent Achilles tendon surgery on both heels—an event that inspired media coverage usually reserved for presidential elections and the World Series.

With Bird out and K. C. Jones upstairs, Reggie Lewis shook off the cobwebs and showed he could play. Rookie Brian Shaw got more playing time after the Celtics shipped Danny Ainge to Sacramento for Ed Pinckney and Joe Kleine. In its own way, the departure of Ainge symbolized the end of an era. With Bird, Parish, McHale, and Johnson, Ainge had been part of the best starting five in basketball for three full seasons. The core of the team was getting old, and the youngest member of the group was dealt to infuse some youth and depth. Ainge also had a spirit of competition that is rare in today's professional athlete. Danny Ainge loved to play ball, and he loved playing for the Celtics. Bird called him the best athlete on the team. There was not much Ainge couldn't do. He was one of the faster players in the league, played tight defense, made all of his free throws, hit the three-pointer regularly, and was constantly getting into scraps with other players. Ainge never learned the art of the intentional foul. He always looked like he was trying to hurt someone. He was also a constant whiner to the officials, and his face would take on the look of a spoiled child who didn't get dessert. Mix that with his talent, his high salary, and his breach of contract with the Toronto Blue Jays, and you had one hateable player. Ainge routinely topped the boo-meter everywhere the Celtics played, and this reaction was a source of great joy for his teammates, particularly McHale. Ainge's teammates genuinely liked him as a person and respected him as a ball player. "He's like your younger brother," Bird would say. "You love to beat up on him, but you won't let anybody else beat him up 'cause you really like him."

Ainge was missed and is still missed, but it was a move the Celtics felt they had to make. Despite this trade and several other transactions, nothing could reverse the aging process and nothing could make up for the loss of Bird. The Celtics failed to win two straight road games for the first time in forty years. They went 0–23 in road games against .500 teams. They finished 42–40 and dropped three straight play-off games to the eventual NBA champs, the Detroit Pistons. It was Boston's first opening-round play-off elimination since Russell came on board in 1956.

Knicks assistant coach Paul Silas notes, "The Bias thing set 'em back ten years. You can't recapture that. And now they're going to be just good enough that you can't get top draft picks anymore. And people aren't as dumb as they once were when Red could sit back and say, 'Well, you know I really don't like this guy.' "

Auerbach and Volk did not have a good summer in 1989. After the play-off wipeout, the Celts drafted Brigham Young's Michael Smith and Dino Radja of Yugoslavia. Smith didn't get many minutes, nor did he play as well as several players who were drafted after him. There was fear that he was a player of the 1950s, rather than the 1990s. The Celtics lost a legal battle with Radja's Yugoslavian team, and Dino returned to his homeland. There was even more international distress when Shaw signed a contract to play in Italy. This was a massive Boston blunder. Auerbach hates to overpay anybody, but Shaw had leverage in the international marketplace. Stripped of one of his young starting guards, Rodgers went into the season using a haywire rotation of fossils Dennis Johnson, John Bagley, and Jim Paxson, plus Kevin Gamble, Kelvin Upshaw, Charles Smith, and forward-guard Reggie Lewis.

Bird came back from his surgery and scored fifty points against the Hawks in November, but it was clear that he'd lost a step on defense, and he was unable to shoot with his old consistency. Invoking an old Auerbach tactic, Rodgers put McHale on the bench as sixth man and started Pinckney, but the team didn't jell early in the year. Bird took only six shots on a night when they were slaughtered in Detroit, then complained that he was a "point forward," just doing what he was told. Rodgers became increasingly tense, closed practices, and snapped at the media. There were suggestions that nice-guy Jimmy was in over his head. Despite this criticism, the Celtics were tied for first place on Larry Bird's thirty-third birthday (December 7). The Lakers made their annual visit two weeks later and beat the Celtics by nine points. It was clear that the rivalry was at least temporarily dead. Magic Johnson said, "We have a good mix of old and young. What hurt Boston the most was the fact that Bias was gone. That was the key there. You have a superstar like him, a number-one pick. If he's here, things would be different, a lot different."

There was a winter storm just before Christmas when the *New York Post* and then the *Boston Herald* ran stories quoting unnamed Celtics players saying bad things about Bird. A huge photograph of Bird ran on the back cover of the December 20, 1989, *Herald,* and the headline read, PROBLEM CHILD, BIRD'S

THE ROOT OF EVIL ON CELTICS. Bird was blamed for "tearing the team apart," according to one player in the *Post* story. Bird responded to the stories with a forty-point effort against Utah the day the *Herald* headline ran. Privately, he believed Paxson and McHale were the traitors, but he never named names publicly.

Bird's shooting form did not return until late in the year. He was getting older. "We used to go into these games, like [against] Minnesota," he said, "and I knew some guys might not be into the game, so I'd just take the game over. I'd get forty and fifteen rebounds, and I wouldn't have to worry about it, but now the roles have changed, and they don't want me to do that anymore. They don't want everybody standing around and watching me, so I just take what I get. Everything's different. But I guarantee I'd still rather have the ball in my hands at the end of a game than [in] anybody else's. I shot too many jump shots in my life. I've shot millions more than them other guys. I'd rather take my chances."

Things got better after the controversy. The Celts went west and took three straight before celebrating New Year's Eve at home. The team suffered a curious home malady in midwinter. Suddenly, they were unable to win Friday night home games. The Nuggets, Sixers, Lakers, Clippers, and Spurs came to Boston and won on Friday nights. Rodgers heard a lot of catcalls from the crowd, and Paxson became the fans' target on the court. There were a lot of stories about dissension in the Celtics, and Rodgers appeared worn by the task of holding things together.

"We should be a lot better than we are," said Bird. "There's been so much going on."

Bird praised former coach K. C. Jones, and everybody took it as a knock on Rodgers—even Rodgers.

"That was no stab at Jimmy," said Bird. "Next day, I went to practice and Jimmy walks up and says, 'Larry, we got to get this team going. We're up and down and all this stuff.'

Then he goes, 'Fuck all this shit in the papers about whether you like me or not.' You know how he gets, he gets real red. He says, 'That's all bullshit, and I don't care about that.' And I said to myself, 'Holy shit, I wonder what was in there,' so I read the article. That was not a stab at Jimmy at all, but what can I do about that?"

The Knicks spent much of the winter in first place, but they still couldn't beat the Celtics in the Garden. New York General Manager Al Bianchi, a veteran Celtics-hater, said, "I can't even sit in my seat at Boston Garden anymore. The ghosts come down, they aggravate me. When I was a player, somewhere in the back of your head you think something crazy is going to happen. When you have that thought process, that's not good."

Danny Ainge returned to the Garden on February 4 and made only one of seven shots in Sacramento's 121–89 loss to the Celtics. Ainge's return provoked much local longing for a return to the '"good old days," and the star guard admitted, "I didn't really feel that much until I was out shooting in warm-ups and saw Red walk in and sit in his seat. Red's a guy I've always idolized. To me, he's what the Celtics are."

The Celtics went west for an eight-game trip after the All Star break and went 4–4. March and April were good months for the Green Team. Bird regained his shooting touch and McHale returned to the starting lineup. They won nine of their last ten, eighteen of their final twenty-three, and finished 52–30, just one game behind the first-place Philadelphia 76ers.

Hopes were high going into the playoffs. Conventional wisdom around the NBA was that the Celts were playing their best ball of the season, peaking for the playoffs much like the equally old 1968–69 team. Because of their experience and dominant frontcourt, the Celtics were a team that nobody wanted to play in a five- or seven-game series.

Head coach Jimmy Rodgers, the tenth man to coach the Celtics, was finally looking good. He'd taken abuse for calling too many plays and employing irregular lineups. Players supposedly were confused about their roles and there was still a hint of friction between Bird and the head coach. Despite all of this, Rodgers had his team where he wanted it when the regular season ended. The Celtics were injury-free and well-rested. They were also set to play the New York Knicks, a team that had lost twenty-four consecutive games in the Boston Garden since 1984.

Bianchi said, "It's very hard up there. Somehow, they have those ghosts. They put in Joe Kleine and those ghosts tap the ref on the shoulder and say, 'See him? That's Dave Cowens.' They put in Reggie Lewis and it's, 'That's Sam Jones.' "

The Knicks were reeling. While the Celtics finished strong, New York went 13–21 down the stretch. The Knicks lost eight of their final nine road games.

The Knicks came to the Garden and predictably, dropped the first two games in the best-of-five set. Game 2 was a nationally televised, 157–128 Celtic blowout. New York's ragged team was embarrassed and former Knick standout Walt Frazier, working as a radio color commentator, said that Knick center Patrick Ewing had "quit" during the game.

The series moved to Madison Square Garden and Knick fans booed their own team during pregame ceremonies. The mood shifted as the Knicks battled to a late-game lead, and with 7.6 seconds to play, the Knicks led by three as the Celtics prepared to inbound. The Celtics got what they wanted, a Bird three-point shot. Bird was wide open, out top to the right of the key when he let it fly. It was a brick and the Knicks were winners.

"I couldn't believe it," said Bird. "I thought it was going to swish when I let it go, then it took off like a curveball. It was like when you're playing outside and you take a shot and the wind takes it off to the side. It was terrible."

Game 4 in New York was a Knick blowout. The New Yorkers danced to a 135–108 victory and McHale admitted, "We should have won it in three games."

The fifth and deciding game was Sunday, May 6, at the Boston Garden. Everything was going the Celtics' way. They'd

won twenty-six straight in their own building against New
York. They were 7-1 in winner-take-all games during the Bird
era. They hadn't lost a home play-off game to the Knicks since
1974. And only two teams in NBA history (1956 Fort Wayne
Pistons and 1987 Golden State Warriors) had won a five-game
series after losing the first two games.

Despite all of the above, Red Auerbach was worried. "How
can you not be worried after what they did to us Friday night?"
he asked.

"I really feel the pressure is on them," said Ewing.

Ewing was right. The Knicks were a confident group when
they walked into the Boston Garden for the final game. The
Celtics looked old.

The Garden crowd roared as Andy Jick bellowed the usual
introductions:

"in his 14th season from Pepperdine . . ."

"in his 14th season from Centenary . . ."

"in his 11th season from Minnesota . . ."

"in his 12th season from Indiana State . . ."

So there they were. Dennis Johnson, Robert Parish, Kevin
McHale, and Larry Bird teamed with youngster Reggie Lewis
to see if they could do it one more time. They could not. Ewing
scored 31 points and dished off 10 assists while Charles Oakley
added 26 points and 17 rebounds. Veteran guard Maurice
Cheeks played all 48 minutes and directed a 121-114 Knick
victory while the Garden crowd went silent. Late in the game,
Bird missed a reverse dunk that could have turned the tide;
instead, the parquet floor was put in storage for the summer.

"I'm in shock," said Bird. "This is about as low as it gets
since I've been here. When you're in the Garden, you should
win this kind of game. I'll wake up tomorrow and still be in
shock. This is unbelievable, really unbelievable."

"I'm as disappointed as I've been in my career here," added
McHale.

It was a sad day for the Green. It was like watching Arnold
Palmer play golf for the last time. It was like watching the

last "Ed Sullivan Show." There was a feeling that it was the
end of an era.

Don Nelson, a man who has his Celtics number 19 hanging
from the Garden rafters, says, "I've done a lot of thinking
about this. We're always talking about that Celtic pride and
all of that. There really was something. I don't know exactly
what it was. I don't know that pride is a good word. There
was something special. It helps that the teams were good and
winning and good guys and good athletes, but when I really
look back, it's Auerbach. He's the thing that made this mystic
kind of thing. And now as he's getting older and he's not as
dominant as he was, it's disappearing. When he goes, it *will*
disappear. . . . It's not the same. The values of the team aren't
the same. His philosophies aren't the same. Maybe they can't
be 'cause of all the changes. It's a little different now. But still,
the relationship was still there when Bird came in. Red was
dominant. And it was there for a while with Bird. But now
you can say that they are just another one of us."

More proof that the Celtics are just like other teams came
two days after the loss to the Knicks. Jimmy Rodgers was fired.
Assistant coach Lanny Van Eman was also dismissed. The
Celtics have never been quick to fire head coaches, but Rodgers
was axed after winning fifty-two regular season games.

There was not much glory to spread around. Volk was ripped
for letting Shaw get away. Auerbach was suspect for the drafting of Smith. The Ainge trade looked bad. But how much of
this was Rodgers's fault? The Celtics apparently decided that
while Rodgers may not have been the problem, neither was
he the solution. Owners Cohen and Gaston began a search for
a new head coach and assistant Chris Ford was the early favorite to land the job. Days after Rodgers was fired, it was
learned that the Celtics wanted Big East Commissioner Dave
Gavitt to come on board as a new director of basketball op-
erations. It was time for a change and Auerbach wanted to
bring in a man with a strong basketball background and proven
administrative skills.

On May 30, 1990, Gavitt was anointed senior executive vice president and chief operating officer of the Celtics. The press release stated that, "Gavitt will have full and complete authority and responsibility with respect to all phases of the Celtics basketball operation."

Immediately, there were questions about Auerbach's status. Red was secure with a lifetime contract and Gavitt was sufficiently reverent, likening himself to an apprentice painter, "having an opportunity to work with Michaelangelo."

It was a happy day all around and there was hope that the Celtics were back on track with a new leader.

It was one of the last calm days of the summer for the Celtics. One day after Gavitt was hired, word leaked that Gavitt was courting Duke coach Mike Krzyzewski. Gavitt and the rest of the Celtic front office denied that Coach K was actually offered the job, but Krzyzewski rejected Boston's interest/offer as Ford twisted in the wind. On June 12, Ford was named the eleventh head coach in Celtic history and there was every appearance that he was Boston's second choice. There were also rumors of a rift between Auerbach and Gavitt, rumors that were strongly denied by both executives. Things were calm for three days, then Brian Shaw attempted to get out of the $6.2 million Celtic contract he signed. Shaw said he wanted to stay in Italy, that he'd signed the new pact under duress. The Celtics and their fans were furious and the matter dragged through the courts for the rest of the summer. On draft day, the Celtics had the nineteenth pick and selected six-one speedster guard Dee Brown of Jacksonville. From Indiana, Larry Bird broke his month-long silence and said it would be crazy to trade Kevin McHale. Back in Boston, folks were wondering who would be in the Boston backcourt in 1990–91; Dennis Johnson was a free agent, Brown was unknown, and Shaw looked like he'd be in court more than on the court. The fall from the heights of 1986 was ongoing. Things hadn't been right since the death of Len Bias.

11
Green Voices

RAY Flynn was born in south Boston in 1939, the second oldest of four sons. Flynn never had much money. The family lived at 418 East Sixth Street. Ray Flynn's father was a longshoreman who was struck down by tuberculosis, and his mother scrubbed floors in office buildings downtown. Young Ray was thirteen when his dad became ill, and Ray helped out by shining shoes and selling newspapers at Fenway Park and Braves Field. He was a three-sport star at South Boston High, but basketball was his first love. He poured tar over the dirt in his backyard and shot jump shots for up to ten hours per day. He would hitchhike to Harlem to get a game on weekends. He was a Garden rat. He made it a practice to sneak into the Causeway Street Palace whenever the Celtics were playing. The kid befriended the work crews and would sit with electricians during games. He'd help clean up after games and sometimes get to dribble on the parquet floor and shoot at the same baskets that Bob Cousy shot at. Flynn graduated from high school in 1958, then starred in basketball at Providence, where he was Most Valuable Player of the National Invitational Tournament in 1963. At Providence he played with Johnny Egan and John Thompson. After a stint in the service, he tried out with the Celtics, and he was the last player cut from the Celtics in 1964. He gravitated toward politics and today is the forty-sixth mayor of Boston.

Ask Flynn what the Celtics mean to the city of Boston, and he says, "What does the Eiffel Tower mean to Paris? It's such an important feeling of spirit and pride that it brings to Boston. It's world known. I was in Ireland, visiting the president of Ireland at a luncheon. The star player of one of their teams came over to me and said, 'You're the mayor of Boston? You see the Celtics play basketball, don't you? Would it be too much for you to get an autograph of Larry Bird?' And with that, the president of Ireland joined in and said, 'If you could get two, I'd appreciate it.'

"We're lucky in Boston. We've had a number of stars that have really brought great interest to the sport. Boston became a very sophisticated pro basketball town. I always admired the people of New York City for their understanding of college basketball, but I think Boston professional basketball fans became very knowledgeable. And I think whoever coined the term 'pride,' it's true. You think about how unselfish they were as a team. They always gave it that extra pass or two that always made the shot a better percentage shot. That's what the Celtics were really all about—working as a unit, working as a team, working as a family. And that's something you can learn an awful lot [from]. Sacrificing for one another is what makes strong families and strong neighborhoods and a strong country. And that's why people look up to teams that do that. That's why they were one of the truly unique teams in sport that sacrificed the individual for the better of the team, and that's what people admired so much about the Celtics."

Climate and geography may have contributed to the Celtics' family atmosphere. Basketball is a winter game, played in heated gymnasiums. It is the only major sport invented in

America, and, in most parts of the United States, the game is played when it it very cold outside. Basketball is cozy, and its players are close. Even at the junior high level, there are usually only a dozen players on a team. Traveling to games through ice and snow and bitter cold tends to bring the players together; this is the blizzard/hurricane mentality at work. Think of the times when we are threatened by natural forces— when the electricity goes out and we gather around candles and listen to transistor radios. We are kinder to strangers and to our neighbors because they share our plight. We are pioneers, survivors against the elements. Once the threat is passed, the moments of darkness and uncertainty become special and memorable. This is the dynamic that makes basketball teams in cold climates so close knit. At the lower levels, players walk to practice, crossing patches of ice and pushing forward into the teeth of subzero wind chills. They travel on yellow school buses with plastic seats and no heat. The buses break down. There is always exposure to the outside, but a warm locker room and a toasty gym await. There is no better feeling than pulling on a big metal door and crossing from the frosty tundra into a gym sweet with steam and sweat. Boston basketball players know this feeling. It doesn't change at the professional level. Bill Russell and John Havlicek walked through blizzards to the Garden, and it's still a challenge to navigate the icy, curved roads that surround the Celtics practice site at Hellenic College in Brookline. Braving the elements is part of the job, and there is always something to talk about. Weather and traffic are two top common denominators, and the Boston basketball experience has an abundance of both. In some small way, this partially explains the closeness of Celtics players, past and present. They went through it all together.

M. L. Carr on the Celtic mystique: "I think it's experience that's been gained over the years, and it's living proof that no matter what adversity you confront, someway, somehow you can come together and make it happen. There's an effect on the players. Larry can score fifty points, and you look over in the stands and there's John Havlicek who's done it before. Robert Parish can go out and get twenty-five rebounds, and you look over there and there's Bill Russell who got forty. DJ can make the greatest pass in the world, and you look over there and there's Bob Cousy who's made that pass with both hands many times before. I can look over there and there's any alumnus of the Celtics that's waved a towel before me. Those banners up there are a symbol that men have come together and have won through all kinds of adversity. It's a never-think-quit type situation when you work for the Boston Celtics, and the fact of the matter is that the guy that or-chestrated it and carved it out is still over there. Will it have the same effect when you don't smell the cigar smoke? I still think it will because he put the system in place, and that system will work. It works whether you change players or not. That's why the system . . . which is big contracts, player egos, big television exposure, no-cut contracts, has withstood the test of time. Those banners will wave above you forever to remind you of that so it doesn't matter who fills the spot. There will always be someone who will try to carve out their piece. And the fact that those guys, the alumni, are over there, that have been a part of those championship teams—no matter what you do, you can only be a part of it. You cannot surpass any of that. The name Bill Sharman is mentioned. You have an im-mediate association. That means family. The name Bob Cousy is mentioned. That means family. Because those are people who went through situations and have been able to forsake personal egos for the sake of the whole. And because of that, you feel proud. If I'm introduced at a banquet or to a bunch of kids and they say 'M. L. Carr, formerly of the Boston Celt-ics,' that means something. That's major because these guys have won at every single level you can think of."

Red Auerbach says, "The Celtics are the Celtics. We're the target. When we go into a town, they are sold out. They are ready. And it just makes it that much tougher. . . . People got tired of giving every award to the Celtics, so when they talk about the best team, they talk about the 1967 Sixers and pull that kind of stuff."

Ex-Celtic Paul Silas, now an assistant coach with the Knicks, says, "The guys that I'm with now hate Boston. They cannot stand Boston. I don't think it was that we were so arrogant or whatever, but we were confident in our ability to play and play well and do exactly what we had to do to win, and we went about doing it in a very businesslike manner. Because we played one way—and that's hard, all out offensively and defensively—it always seemed as if we got the majority of the calls. And a lot of players resented that, and, even today, players that I know cannot stand the Celtics. They tease me a lot when we play Boston. They say that I still have green running through my veins. Nobody really realizes I won a championship in Seattle. Everybody identifies me with the Celtics and that sixth-man role."

Dave Bing grew up in Washington in the days when a rotund man with a cigar patrolled the D.C. playgrounds. Bing had a Hall of Fame career and played his last NBA season with the Celtics. Bing says, "You never had a problem getting up for the Celtics. They didn't care how good you were or how bad you were, they were coming after your blood. If you didn't want to get embarrassed and beat up, you had to go in there ready. That's been a trademark of the organization."

Chris Ford: "If you play for the Celtics, people think of you as a Celtic forever. People don't remember that I played for the Pistons, even though I spent six years and started a seventh year there. One of the amazing things when you travel with this team is to see the wave of green out there—at the hotels, the airports, the arena. I can only liken it to maybe Notre Dame and the Yankees as far as having fans around you, universally. Even in Spain last year. I grew up in Sixer country, but I was a Celtic fan."

Gerald Henderson broke into the NBA with the Celtics when they won twenty-nine games in 1979–80. He was there when

Bird and Fitch turned it around a year later and Henderson won a pair of rings before he was dealt to Seattle in 1984. After leaving Boston, he became a card-carrying NBA journeyman, playing in Seattle, New York, Philadelphia, Milwaukee, and Detroit. "Playing with the Celtics was the most fun," he says. "I had better years, individually, in Seattle, but you have fun when you're winning, especially when you're with a bunch of guys who care about each other. You experience a lot of tough times together, and you're able to overcome things. The impossible happens. They were some good times. When they traded me it was sort of shocking because that was the only thing I knew. It was almost like it was the end. I felt it was the end of my career, almost because at that point the only thing I knew was green and white. As far as pro basketball was concerned, that was the only blood I had, green blood."

Dave Cowens looks at it with less emotion and says, "I think they think they have the same kind of magic out there in Los Angeles. And in their own way it's the same in places like Denver and Milwaukee and Philadelphia. They all got a good tradition. Boston just happened to win eleven out of thirteen, and nobody else is gonna be able to do that. And then you build on that. Red was the guy that made it happen and kept it going. We all know it's hard to keep it going. They can all win one, but to do it every time is different. Being on the Celtics, there's always more people at the games when you go away. It was good. I think all the players liked that. You want to beat them when they really want to beat you."

Chuck Daly has been around the NBA for almost twenty years. He coached at Boston College before coming to the NBA and saw the Celtics up close for a couple of seasons. He was head coach of the Detroit Pistons during the 1980s when Detroit's young team started to challenge Boston. The Celtics and Pistons had vicious play-off series against each other in 1985, 1987, 1988, and 1989. Daly saw his team displace Boston as the power of the Eastern Conference and the most despised team in the league.

Daly: "Obviously, Red was way ahead of his time with his projections on what it took to win in this league and the kind of people it took to win in this league. Then he developed such a roster that he was able to make decisions about specific players—[from] projecting to filling roles on his club. There never was any question that in the management portion of it they were way ahead of their time. As I recall, there was basically respect because they did it with no flair, no showmanship. They did it with solid basketball, unselfish on the defensive end. If anything, there was envy more than anything else. You wanted to be as good as the Celtics. They were so good, they were intimidating with their talent, and they had coaches that utilized the talents. They didn't overcoach. I used to go to their practices when Tommy [Heinsohn] first began to coach. They were even smart enough to get rid of their franchise when it wasn't any good and get a new one. When I came to Detroit, for us to play the Celtics was the ultimate challenge. It was the biggest game of the year every night we played 'em. We learned and kept learning from them. I think everyone in the league has learned. By their demeanor, by their style, and by their abilities, they showed other people how to progress and get to the point where you might be able to win. You're always thinking, 'What do we have to do to beat the Celtics?' I don't think they were arrogant. I like the word 'confident.' I think inside they knew they were better than anyone else in the league. I know people talk about the Garden mystique. I just think it's the way it's constructed, the way the people are involved, the closeness and the talent— the combination of all this culminated in a mystique."

Walt Frazier, star guard with the Knicks championship teams in the 1970s, says, "You first come to Boston and you're awestruck by all the banners hanging there. Everyone's heard of the Boston Celtics. They dominated the game so long. And there is a certain mystique about this place. When you came here, you didn't have the feeling that you could win, you had the feeling that you could win for forty-five minutes, and then

they would always someway pull something out. Once the
1970s came around and their players started to age, I felt we
were on a par with the Celtics. My first trip in was 1967. They
were aging, but they were winning with their savvy like this
team is winning now. I grew up in Atlanta and I hated them
because I liked the underdog; I didn't like the team that always
won. But I respected them and what they always did. They
were admired and respected because of their dominance."

Gary St. Jean is an assistant coach under Don Nelson with
the Milwaukee Bucks. St. Jean also served as a coach under
Nelson in Milwaukee. He grew up in Chicopee, Massachusetts,
when the Celtics were winning the NBA title eight consecutive
seasons. He has experienced both sides of the Celtic mystique.
He says, "I'm a guy who grew up in western Massachusetts
and was a Celtic fan for the first twenty-eight years of my life.
I ate, slept, and drank Celtics. When I then went with the
Bucks, it was a different color green. You'd get in a traffic jam
coming through the tunnel and you'd hear the veterans say,
'Red's here again.' Then you'd get to the Parker House. The
rooms wouldn't be ready and they'd say, 'Red's here again.'
Then you'd go to the shootaround. Maybe the floor was down
and maybe the balls were there. But you'd come to the game
at night, and maybe there'd be no heat in the locker room or
maybe it'd be a hundred and five degrees. A lot of interesting
things happen when you come here. But of course, I pushed
'em all aside because I thought, what the hell, you couldn't
knock the Cs. It was like a dream for me to come play in the
Garden. I played in the high school tournament there in 1967.
For me to sit there on the bench and have family and friends
come down, it was the thrill of a lifetime. And occasionally to
beat 'em and become a pretty good rival. . . . There's been a
lot of neat things happen—getting married and having children, but that might come after that. You just go back. I grew
up during the days of the Russell era when they won all the
titles. When I first played in the Garden, I just wanted to
touch the rim that Bill Russell touched. Of course, you'd get

bummed out because you have to dress in the back locker room where they had the elephants who were in the week before. It stunk and you would come to find out there was only one shower and no hot water. It was still a thrill."

Don Nelson broke into the NBA with Chicago and played with the Lakers when they lost to the Celtics in the 1965 finals. He joined the Celtics in the autumn of 1965 and retired from pro ball after winning five championship rings. He has since served as coach of the Milwaukee Bucks and Golden State Warriors and has seen the best and worst of the Celtics from both sides.

Nelson: "In the old days when I was here, and even before when I was with the players, the stuff Red did aggravated the coaches more than the players. We just kind of put up with it and laughed at it. But then as I became a coach . . . life is hard enough on the road anyway, but then to have to put up with these trivial things makes it more difficult. It's no big thing, but we would like to show courtesy to the teams when they come into our place and treat 'em well and expect the same on the road, but when you come here it's different. It's just not the same. He believes in the 'us against them' mentality, and I can't say that he's wrong about it. I think the league has changed a little bit where there's more respect for the hard jobs we all have to do. Every city's the same really. We all strive to do the same things. And why complicate it with a bunch of silly, pain-in-the-ass maneuvers? So what does it do when we're not treated well here? There's only one thing you can do, and so we have to treat them poorly when they come into our place, and I don't like to do that. . . . Underneath everything, the Celtics were always kind of America's team. You either hated 'em or you loved 'em, but you respected 'em and you followed 'em, and when they were on, everybody wanted to watch because they knew it was good basketball."

Rick Carlisle was drafted from the University of Virginia in 1984 and spent three seasons at the end of the Celtics bench. After playing in Boston he went to New York and then New

Jersey before he became assistant coach of the Nets in 1989.

Carlisle: "I started in Boston first and that's why I gained a great appreciation for it later on. I didn't notice it until the first time I went back in there to play those guys. You're sittin' there, and your team is introduced, and then their team is introduced. You can be riding high when your team is introduced, but once they're out there, they'll come out one by one, and then you see Larry come out there. From the other end of the court, he looks like the terminator. He has a certain presence about him that's really unusual. When you're with the Celtics, you always had a sense of security. You always felt like there was something pulling everything together. There was just something there. Going to lesser teams, you got to see things a different way. A lot of guys I played with after I left liked playing there and had good games there, but they never won there. I could always sense a greater building tension with [coach Rick] Pitino. Pitino really wanted to win there, and there were close games we should have had, but we always seemed to lose. When you played the Celtics in your own building, you noticed how much of your crowd they got. In New Jersey, it seemed like two thirds of the crowd was with the Celtics."

Bailey Howell played eight NBA seasons with Detroit, Baltimore, and Philadelphia. Today he lives in Mississippi, and people who remember his game remember only his four seasons with the Celtics. "It's because of the success of the Celtics and because of the fact that the Celtics were on TV a lot," he says. "I still keep up with 'em and pull for 'em. I think Red's been the glue all of these years, the one element that's endured and been consistent from success to success."

Kevin McHale grew up in Hibbing, Minnesota, hometown of Bob Dylan. McHale spent a lot of time on skates during his youth because hockey was the game everybody played on the iron range. He grew up a Lakers fan. The Lakers originated in Minneapolis, and there was still some loyalty when McHale was growing up in the 1960s. "I followed the Lakers," he says.

"I always followed Wilt, and when he had to go against Russ, I always felt so bad. My real introduction to Red didn't come until I actually signed. I had gone to Italy, and I was really going to play there. I came back, and I was all bleary-eyed from the flight. I signed the contract at the Garden, and Red drove me over to Hellenic College going one hundred miles an hour. He was all over the place, and there was cigar smoke, and he was looking over at me and talking while he was driving. And I was thinking I was going to die on my first day in Boston. That was my first experience with Red. I was aware of his legend. Being in Minnesota you knew of him, but you didn't know that he was an institution like he is. When I got back home I started to realize how many people in Minnesota actually were Celtics fans. Then I started to have an appreciation for what it was like to be going there. You enjoy all that stuff, but you realize that as a player that doesn't mean anything. Bob Cousy's not going to win any games for us now. I wish he could. I wish Bill Russell could play a game for us. It's a good thing for the media to write about, but as a player you realize that none of that means anything. I think the Celtic mystique is that they've been able to assemble the type of players that will complement each other and get along and play well together. I think that's the Celtic mystique. You've just got to get the right players, like a Don Nelson who no one wanted. Paul Silas. Go right down the line. Bill Walton, Scotty Wedman, Jerry Sichting, M. L. Carr, Maxwell. People that fit in and can do it. That's the Celtic mystique."

K. C. Jones: "It's the Celtics logo. I was in Orlando on the Fourth of July to make an appearance signing autographs at a car dealership. There were lines around the building. Just being coach of the Celtics. Corpus Christi. Same thing. Lines all over the place and television cameras. When we were in Madrid, they all knew Larry. On the road, fans would wear green jackets to support us, and that worked against us because the other team was totally inspired seeing people wearing green jackets in their place. . . . It's the personnel and

Red. The players are the reason we had success, and the reason for the mystique was the players, not the building. It was the players and how we dealt with each other. That's it right there. Personnel. When you keep in contact throughout the year. Frank Ramsey calls. He'll have a little Jack Daniels and a phone and call everybody. Cousy, Heinie, Sam Jones, Russell. It's comaraderie, and that's hard to beat."

Johnny Most: "It's special to me because it's become part of my life. I've seen them put long pants on. When I came here they had short pants on. They were struggling. It used to be that if we would get three thousand people in here we would cheer. That was a wonderful crowd. On a Sunday afternoon, that was a marvelous crowd. Now, of course, you've got to have cable TV to see a home game. I've watched so many phases of this ball club. The frustrations. Red Auerbach used to throw a hat into a shower in complete disgust after we'd be eliminated from the play-offs. Walter Brown came down a couple of times, and he got angry at the players after being eliminated from the play-offs. He never meant it because the players were like his family. I've seen all that, I've lived through all that. The frustration and the exaltation of being a winner eight years in a row. That ten-year period of the dynasty team where they won nine championships—I'll never forget that. I've been around for the recovery periods. Being knocked down in 1969–70 to being the division winners when they won fifty-six games in 1972, and they won sixty-eight games by 1973. That was a glorious time. It was very, very exciting just to have that experience, being part of it. And after they lost that edge, they came back again under Fitch and K. C. Jones. So that's three generations of Celtics that I've lived with. They've all had their ups and downs, but they've all been equal to it. They get knocked down, but they don't quit. That's the big thing about the Celtic organization— they don't quit. If things don't go well, they'll try something else, they'll try another way. They're going to keep on whacking away at it, and they won't quit. I don't think that this group is ever going to think in terms of quitting. I don't. If I can continue to work when I'm eighty—if I get to be eighty—I'll work."

Henry Finkel was the symbol of the collapse of the Celtics dynasty in 1969–70, but lived to laugh about it. He became a fan favorite when the Celts turned it around in the early 1970s and earned a championship ring with the 1973–74 team. He played nine-and-a-half years in the NBA, six-and-a-half with the Celtics. He says, "I still go to New York three or four times a year, and I'll walk the streets and people come up to me and ask if I'm Hank Finkel who used to play with the Celtics. They don't remember anything you did prior to the Celtics. The exposure that the Celtics get is unbelievable. They say New York is the media capital, but as far as the sports capital, I wouldn't think there's a better city than Boston. There's definitely a family atmosphere when you're on this team. There were guys intermingling all the time. It was hard for me to leave. Red called me over in practice during mid-season and told me they'd decided to put me on waivers. That was it. I knew my career was over. When you can't play for Boston anymore, you can't play for anyone. They appreciated the things I did. I only averaged two or three points a game, but they appreciated my contributions. They appreciated the intangibles, and no other team would go for that. I was very grateful to play here. . . . I love the comaraderie. And if I could tonight, I'd still suit up and play. That's how much I loved it. Everything else is secondary to me. I never made a lot of money at it. I just loved playing ball, and I loved the Celtics."

Finkel now works in sales in the Boston area, and he has a green shamrock on his business card. "Not a day goes by when someone doesn't mention my affiliation with the Celtics. It opens a lot of doors, it really does. . . . People want to talk about the Celtics and the pride. It really has a big meaning. There's only a few great teams in all of sports history—the Yankees are one, Green Bay's another, and the Celtics are another. So we're one of a rare breed, and if you played for the Celtics, then people still want to talk about it. I've been retired fourteen years already, and sometimes I'll make a call and people will [act as if] I was playing with the Celtics last year."

What is a Celtic-type player?

Auerbach: "It differs today. Years ago, you had so few teams, you could pick out and know more about the character of the players than you do today. Today it's hard because there's so many good players, it's hard to learn about the character of a player. If I wanted to know about Havlicek, I'd call up his coach and I'd call up a couple of rival coaches and ask what kind of a kid he was. Was he a real competitor? And they were all friends of mine. I was the only pro coach that used to go around and lecture at college clinics. So I got to know all these college coaches throughout the country. So I would call 'em up and get this information. And then you have your alumni scattered all around. Because I started so early, I had bird dogs all around the country. I believed in roles after your first five or your first six, then you go to roles. But your first five got to be all-around basketball players."

Frank Ramsey was the first famous "sixth man." Auerbach invented the sixth man role, and Ramsey paved the path for John Havlicek, Paul Silas, Kevin McHale, and Bill Walton. Today the NBA hands out a Sixth Man Award. The award should be named after Ramsey, a man who made the NBA Hall of Fame without ever being a regular starter.

Ramsey: "I wasn't good enough to start. I was playing behind two All Star guards, Cousy and Sharman. I have a picture on my wall and there's nine Hall of Famers from one team, 1961: K. C., Cooz, Red, Walter Brown, Sharman, me, Sam, Russell, and Heinsohn. We had a bunch of guys that just refused to give up. It's a great feeling. I guess it gets more meaningful the older you get because of the things we accomplished and really we were not aware we were accomplishing 'em at the time. It's great. There's no way you can experience it. You can't buy it, you have to earn it. What's special about the Celtics is being part of a group of caring players. Red and Walter and Howie McHugh practically ran the whole thing. After practice we'd all go to the Horse down there and get franks and beans. We were just together all the time, and we liked one another. The wives liked the other wives, and when one would get sick they'd be there to take care of the kids and everything. And we're still friends. I talk to 'em all the time."

Larry Bird: "Red's been there from almost the beginning until now, and I think that's the biggest thing. And of course, the championships mean a lot. But the biggest thing is, when you talk to Bill Russell and you talk to K. C. Jones and you talk to these guys, it's their whole life. The Celtics were their life not only then, but it seems like *now*. You see Bill Russell and you start talking and all of a sudden he's saying 'we used to do this and we used to do that.' That's impressed me more than anything."

Eddie Andelman says, "There's definitely Celtic pride. Celtics players were always known as players who put the team first. When you compared them to the Red Sox, they were so different. The Red Sox really had the following, and the Celtics were hardly covered. But the Red Sox had all this selfishness and outrageousness in the clubhouse. With the Celtics, you never got that. You went to look at the stats, and there was never any Celtic in the top five of anything except Russell in rebounding. If you looked at the scoring, the Celtics dominated the spots around eight through fourteen. It would all be Celtics. That was really the difference, and people came to appreciate this team play, this idea that the team has to win. And the Celtics, generally speaking, really jump out of the gate and have these great home records. It showed you how hard their training camps were. And then there were the revolutionary things that got everybody's attention: the sixth-man concept, the fact that the Celtics lived together on the road. Frank Ramsey lived with a black guy. That was a revolutionary idea. The result of all this is that they have been treated like sacred cows in the media. I find it very hard to be critical of them when I have been present for about eleven or twelve of the championships. There's never been a question in my mind that they are trying their hardest to win. And unlike any of the other teams, you can trace who is responsible for the decisions. If you try to find out today who thinks of something on the Red Sox, you don't know if it's Lou Gorman or Haywood Sullivan or John Harrington or Mrs. [Jean] Yawkey. How does it all work? There was never any question with the Celtics."

Why are the Celtics more popular today than they were when they dominated basketball in the 1960s?

Paul Silas, who played in Boston during the transition years of 1972–76, says, "A lot of it has to do with basketball itself and its popularity. It's gone crazy all over the country. I think people here were spoiled. Even when they had their down years after Russell left, they came back and started winning right away. After I left they had some really troubled years here with Wicks and Rowe, and it was very distasteful. When Bird came, they really started to appreciate what they had. You know, they have McHale and Bird, and I think those are players that everybody can really identify with."

Tom Sanders says it's marketing. John Havlicek says it's because Boston fans appreciated titles more after the 1969–74 drought. K. C. Jones says it's because white fans identify with Larry Bird.

Volk says, "I think, as with other things, as you become accustomed to them and you take them for granted, there's less of an appreciation for them. However, suddenly having lost what was taken for granted, there is not only maybe the appropriate appreciation, maybe there's a disproportionate appreciation. And we've gone through this twice. There was the Russell transition, then the so-called Havlicek transition, and we ended up with the team we have now, which has been not only a very successful team but also a very exciting team. I think added to that there's a maturity of the game. The game has become a mature game in the minds of many people who have grown up playing it rather than coming into it later in

life. There's a base of young people who [were] not . . .
Russell-era fans."

Earl Strom, an NBA official who worked for four decades
before retiring in 1990, says, "The Celtics mean tradition at
its finest. I think the Celtics have set the standards for all
professional sports for winning tradition. It was fun going in
there every night knowing you had to perform, for many reasons, the most obvious being that Red was sitting in the stands
and knew the game so well. It meant you had to work every
night at your optimum best. I love Red Auerbach. I think Red
made me a better referee. You had to work every night. When
he was coaching, you worked, and you worked hard. And you
knew the rules because Red knew the rules as well as any
referee. And he was instrumental in putting a lot of the rules
in. Red was great for the game. He would come down hard
on us if his team wasn't playing well. He might come up with
a technical foul when the team was playing poorly or even get
thrown out to get the team to play better, and invariably they
did. They'd be behind and Red would get thrown out and lo
and behold they'd come back and win the ball game. I tossed
Red a few times."

Are the Celtics global?

Auerbach: "The Celtics are the best-known sports team in
the world. You could go to Australia, you could go any damn
place, they'll know the Celtics. They don't know baseball, they
don't know football. What the hell do they know about that?
I made trips around the world. I made trips with Cousy, I
made trips with Havlicek, I made trips with Nelson. I got
Russell to go on a trip. I got K. C. to go on a trip."

National Basketball Association Commissioner David Stern
grew up in New York City when the Celtics were dominant.
He says, "I think that the league has the most famous sports
franchise in the world. You can think about the Cleveland
Browns and say something about the New York Yankees or
even the Montreal Canadiens. But when you say the Celtics,
you knew that the most famous, most successful sports team

in the world was being described. I think that gave the league probably its single identification in difficult times. And I think that Red Auerbach was the most famous coach on a global basis because of the importance of basketball globally. In this country someone could say Paul Brown or Casey Stengel or Walter Alston, but on a global basis, the Celtics and Red Auerbach were the number-one sports team."

Volk: "The team of Yugoslavia is the Boston Celtics. There is no question about it. That's what everybody's interested in. They follow what we do very carefully, very closely. There's a definite recognition factor that goes way beyond what people here in Boston would expect. When we were in Madrid last year, our players were recognized in the street."

Celtics radio broadcaster Glenn Ordway was in London, vacationing with his family, when the Il Messaggero Roma team was negotiating with Celtic guard Brian Shaw. Ordway reported, "I was reading the reports every day in the *International Herald Tribune*. The stories were coming out of Rome, and all they were talking about was how they were going to get a starting guard from the most prestigious basketball team in the world. I never read any quotes about Brian. They never talked about what kind of a player he is or what he can do. They just talked about him being a Celtic."

The Golden State Warriors in 1989 signed the NBA's first Soviet Union player, Sarunas Marciulionis. When Marciulionis made his Boston Garden debut, he said, "The first time I ever heard of the Celtics was when they were playing the Lakers for the championship. Larry Bird was my favorite player. I got tapes of their games, but I never dreamed in a few years I'd be playing against him."

Lew Shuman was producer-director of telecasts for the Celtic ex-flagship station WLIV-TV, and said, "The green people were there in every building we went into. We'd be down on the court doing our preparation, and as soon as the doors opened, they'd be there—the green shirts, the green jackets, the green faces . . . everywhere. A lot of people came up and told us that they used to live in New England, but many hadn't ever been to Boston. Every time we went to Atlanta, there were two women who'd drive eight to ten hours from Alabama, either by themselves or with their kids. They'd leave their husbands at home and drive to see the Celtics. They'd be at the bus entrance and say hi to the guys. I don't think they'd ever been north of the Mason-Dixon line. And I saw this everywhere. Everywhere we went. It was amazing in Cleveland for years. There were as many Celtic fans as Cav fans at those games. We interviewed [former Washington Bullet] Jeff Ruland once on the halftime show, and he said it's hard to get up in your own building when they're cheering for the visiting team. You especially noticed it in the cities we went to one time a year. Seattle, Golden State, Phoenix. And at the hotels, they'd be waiting. And these weren't just the autograph seekers. These were people who were true Celtic fans. Even overseas when we were in Spain. Bird was scheduled to sign autographs, and fifteen hundred people stood in line before the store even opened. The big thing in the States now is the satellite dishes, and I have gotten mail from all fifty states asking for satellite information."

In November 1989, Red Auerbach opened a letter from Carolyn Boyd. The letter read, "Dear Celtics, I am a fourth grade teacher in Baton Rouge, Louisiana. I submitted this story to *Reader's Digest*, and thought you might enjoy it as well. Recently, my students were learning the states and capitals of the northeast region of the United States. One astute youngster had just identified the state of Massachusetts. 'That's great,' I said, 'Do you remember the capital?' After several seconds of thoughtful silence, he proudly exclaimed, 'Celtics!' "

Source List

Auerbach, Red, and Joe Fitzgerald. *On & Off the Court.* New York: Macmillan, 1985.

Auerbach, Arnold "Red," and Joe Fitzgerald. *Red Auerbach an Autobiography.* New York: G. P. Putnam's Sons, 1977.

Auerbach, Arnold "Red," and Paul Sain. *Red Auerbach: Winning the Hard Way.* Boston: Little, Brown, 1966.

Bird, Larry. *Drive.* New York: Doubleday, 1989.

Cousy, Bob. *Basketball Is My Life.* Englewood Cliffs, New Jersey: Prentice Hall, 1957.

Cousy, Bob, and Bob Ryan. *Cousy on the Celtic Mystique.* New York: McGraw-Hill, 1988.

Fitzgerald, Ray. *Champions Remembered.* Brattleboro/Lexington, Massachusetts: The Stephen Greene Press, 1982.

Halberstam, David. *The Breaks of the Game.* New York: Alfred A. Knopf, 1981.

Havlicek, John, and Bob Ryan. *Hondo.* Englewood Cliffs, New Jersey: Prentice Hall, 1977.

Heinsohn, Tommy, and Joe Fitzgerald. *Give 'Em the Hook.* New York: Prentice Hall, 1988.

Libby, Bill. *Goliath.* New York: Dodd, Mead, 1977.

Ostler, Scott, and Steve Springer. *Winnin' Times.* New York: Macmillan, 1986.

Powers, John. *The Short Season.* New York: Harper & Row, 1979.

Russell, Bill. *Go Up for Glory.* New York: Medallion Books, 1966.

Russell, Bill, and Taylor Branch. *Second Wind.* New York: Random House, 1979.

Russell, John. *Honey Russell: Between Games Between Halves.* Takoma Park, Maryland: Dryad Press, 1986.

Ryan, Bob. *The Boston Celtics.* Reading, Massachusetts: Addison-Wesley, 1989.

Ryan, Bob, and Terry Pluto. *48 Minutes.* New York: Collier Books, 1987.

Schron, Bob, and Kevin Stephens. *The Bird Era.* Boston: Quinlan Press, 1988.

Sullivan, George. *The Picture History of the Boston Celtics.* Indianapolis/New York: The Bobbs-Merrill Company, 1981.

Index